Fumihiko Maki, Maki and Associates 2015
Time, Figure, Space
—Toward the Construction of Place

槇文彦＋槇総合計画事務所 2015
時・姿・空間―場所の構築を目指して

Weaving: Thread and Strand

Space, City, Order, Making— these are recurrent themes that have engaged the thinking and the pencil of Fumihiko throughout his career. Space has been continually addressed as the matter of architecture, the city as architecture's central responsibility, order as that which gives form, and making as that which materializes the intentions. These we can view as threads continuously present in Maki's mind. With these threads he creates a woven strand, the cross section of which becomes a piece of architecture at each particular time. It is an open-ended strategy whereby he carefully selects and unifies elements that have been accumulated throughout the years of his practice. Depending on the site, the brief, and the intellectual and technological stages of the date of the project, various threads will assume greater importance over others, and may adopt different characteristics which will identify the work as being of a new era.

This ability to weave past discoveries, accumulated during years of exploration, with new eventualities has allowed Maki to retain his position as one of the major creative figures in international architecture. Since the 1960's, he has kept modern architecture alive, and has continually regenerated and extended it with a fresh spirit suited to the moods and demands of shifting times. Strangely, at any point in time, he has emerged as one of the most consistent architects world-wide, yet one of the most innovative. To modern architecture he has brought an unmatched touch of delicacy, elegance and sophistication.

Jennifer Taylor. *The Architecture of Fumihiko Maki*. Birkhäuser 2004.

Foreword

Fumihiko Maki Translation: Hiroshi Watanabe

Maki and Associates, the office of which I am the principal, celebrates its 50th anniversary this year. To commemorate this event, we have planned an exhibit entitled "Fumihiko Maki, Maki and Associates 2015— Time, Figure, Space: Toward the Construction of Place" at Hillside Terrace, Tokyo, that opens in October this year. This book, published concurrently with the exhibit, is a record of the broader context of our half-century of design activity, namely our priorities and interests, and the social character that the works reflecting those priorities and interests have subsequently achieved.

◎ Is Architecture Art?

Architecture may possess artistic value, but it is not itself art. Whether it turns out to be rubbish that is quickly discarded or something highly marketable and worthy of display in a museum, a work of art is a world complete in itself to the extent that artists are responsible to themselves. That is not the case with architecture, because, as history shows, architects are responsible through the works they create to clients and to society including the places where the works are constructed.

Vitruvius once wrote that the three basic qualities architecture must possess are utility, solidity and, depending on one's interpretation of *venustas*, beauty or delight. When Kaze-no-Oka Crematorium, which I designed, was completed in Nakatsu City, many local residents were pleased by it and told me they could now die in peace. I remember vividly even now how happy I was, as an architect, to have discovered, and been able to make possible the fulfillment of, a subconscious desire of humankind.

◎ The Construction of Place

Why the construction of place? Unlike art, which, with the exception of installations, is movable, architecture is fated to remain fixed in the place it was constructed, in some cases for centuries. At times, a place inspires the architect's imagination, and at other times, architecture may determine the character of not only a place but the larger environment. Such is the power of place to affect the success or failure of architecture.

On the other hand, I have had the good fortune to realize the design of collective forms since the early years of my practice. I have learned a great deal from the Rissho University Kumagaya Campus completed in 1969 and Hillside Terrace which took a quarter-century starting in 1969 to complete. Collective forms number more than ten if those I have participated in designing (for example, the New World Trade Center Buildings, of which 4 World Trade Center is a part, and Roppongi Hills complex, which includes TV Asahi) are included. A collective form is, to put it succinctly, a microcosm.

On the other hand, diverse constraints are imposed in cities, particularly Japanese metropolises. For example, there is SPIRAL, where architectural expression on the exterior was limited to a single elevation, and Rolex Nakatsu Building in Osaka, where an adjacent raised expressway left little room for expression on three sides of the structure.

For the sake of convenience, individual buildings included in this exhibition and catalog are divided into three categories— city, countryside and the special environment that is a university campus— and the special characteristics of the design approach that was adopted have been compiled.

◎ Time and Architecture

I have accumulated a wealth of memories and experiences over a half-century of time. In my youth, I was fortunate to have countless unforgettable encounters on two "voyages to the West" in 1959 and 1960. That was also the period when my association with many other architects began, for example, the fellow members of Metabolism and the members of Team X. As for memorable places I visited then, there was for example Hydra, one of the Greek islands— a world of humans and donkeys rather than automobiles, with spatial and formal order established through the assemblage of units. Insight gained through such experiences led to a proposal for group form included in the Metabolist declaration at the World Design Conference in 1960 in Tokyo and to *Investigations in Collective Form*, published by Washington University in 1964.

I also discovered the underlying humanism of villages and cities in Asia, the Middle East and Europe. My suggestion in "Modernism on the Open Sea," published in 2013[*1], that a "humanism of empathy" or "Another Utopia" may be a world-wide trend today is perhaps connected on some deep level to what I learned on those youthful voyages.

A building may also come into being as an *hommage* to a work encountered by chance many years ago. A mezzanine space I experienced as a child was recreated in the first phase of Hillside Terrace. My memory of the time I first saw the then just-completed World Trade Center across the Hudson River no doubt shaped in part the image I developed for 4 World Trade Center. Time is also a mediator between architecture and the city. Hillside Terrace took six phases and 25 years to complete. Tokyo, which continued to undergo a transformation in that time, taught me many things about what sorts of facilities the project should have and what sorts of residential units were in demand.

Buildings, like human beings, experience birth and death. At times, they undergo major surgery, regain their health and are able to lead productive new lives. Technology was able to restore the exposed concrete finish in the Toyoda Memorial Hall Renovation project for Nagoya University. In another project, the former Yokohama Specie Bank Annex (built in 1929) was moved and subsequently amalgamated with Yokohama I-Land Tower (2003), enabling it to restart life as a community facility for Yokohama City. Like a parent with respect to an offspring, an architect may not only have an emotional attachment to a building he or she has designed but interest in how that building develops afterwards. *The 50-Year History of Maki and Associates* which will be published separately on this occasion is a record of the life and the death or present condition of practically every building the office has designed up to now.

◎ Figure and Space

In 1978, the architectural critic Alan Colquhoun published an intriguing analysis of figure and form in *Oppositions*∗2. According to him, form has no intrinsic significance; figure is form that has been invested with cultural meaning. The cultural meaning of classical architecture can be understood as rhetorical allusions to a style. Today, however, modernism as a style is undergoing dissolution and dispersal, and cultural meaning is inevitably diverse and ambiguous.

For someone who practices architectural design, figure today cannot help but seem diverse for that reason. In my case, a figure often emerges from the conflict between the way the desirable space suggested by the given place— admittedly a matter of subjective judgment— appears from without and the way sightlines are structured between various elements contained by the space. I call the space in this first stage of design a "nebulous whole." I have explained in detail this intellectual process in a 1994 issue of *The Japan Architect*∗3.

What I would like to emphasize here is the importance of constructing sightlines from within space. For example, when sightlines from within a space to the outside world are restricted, they naturally become inner-directed. For example, the courtyards of a townhouse in ancient Greece, Kaze-no-Oka Crematorium and Aga Khan Museum are different in size and character, but in each case the space serves to integrate behavior produced by sightlines.

On the other hand, in the Shenzhen Sea World Cultural Arts Center, the figure reflects sightlines toward the ocean, mountains, urban park and sky suggested by the distinctive place. Severe restrictions on sightlines, as in the abovementioned SPIRAL or the Rolex Nakatsu Building in Osaka, conversely give the architect an opportunity to create from scratch. In "Modernism on the Open Sea," I cite the Amsterdam Orphanage by Aldo van Eyck as a superb example of a building organized by internal sightlines.

Why sightlines? Seeing causes a person to sense something, which in turn gives rise to thought or action. In animals, herding together, fleeing, and attacking are basic patterns of behavior.

I have explained that a collective form is a world in miniature. That is especially so when the collective form is a theme park or an isolated university campus set in the countryside. A collective form introduced into a city naturally comes into contact in diverse ways with things on its outer boundary. How then is the identity of a collective form created? Two organizational principles— the characteristics of each constituent building and the characteristics of the outdoor space or spaces connecting buildings— are used to distinguish different modes of collective form. "Another Utopia" is what I call a further development of this approach— a collective form of open spaces rather than buildings.

However, the organization of sightlines naturally reflects the historical and cultural characteristics of the given region. The Japanese have little affinity for grand perspectives in the Baroque manner. Instead, various unique techniques have been developed in Japan to bend, layer and connect elements within a limited space. *Oku*, *kehai* (meaning a sign or indication of the presence of something that is not immediately visible), and *ma* are concepts distinctive to Japan.

The presence or the character of a figure is determined in many cases by the material and materiality of that figure. Moreover, demand for a sightline to the outside world from within an interior space will determine the way an opening is arranged or the use of a screen-like membrane. This is oftentimes where the ability of an architect to design details is tested. Here, the examples recorded include the glass used in 4 World Trade Center and the stone and treatment of metal surfaces in the Aga Khan Museum.

◎ The Social Character of Architecture— Scenes

How the client, users and society in general evaluate a building once it has been completed, that is, once it is out of the architect's hands, is an important indicator for the architect of the social character of that building. We at Maki and Associates always canvass the views of all parties concerned with regard to a building. The history of this office is in fact a compendium of information gleaned from such sources.

Emphasis is placed in this exhibition on scenes inasmuch as they represent cross sections revealing the social character of projects. Through scenes, especially shots that show the various ways people conduct themselves in indoor and outdoor public spaces, we have attempted to identify the social character of buildings. A phrase by Friedrich Nietzsche of which I am fond and which seems to me to describe one kind of social character is "solitude is my dearest home."

People enjoying solitude in various public spaces. A small group of people in earnest conversation. The way in which a festival, encountered by chance, is unfolding. The action of people reveals not just the given function of a space or building but its social character.

◎ Maintaining the Quality of Buildings

As this book shows, Maki and Associates is currently undertaking projects of various types and sizes not only in Japan but throughout the world. The social responsibility of an architect, discussed at the outset, must be assumed whatever the location. In a practice of more than half a century, I have seen many cases, both in Japan and overseas, of offices that started as ateliers losing their identities with growth in size and of architects who lose sight of the marvelous things they did and said in youth, or conversely, cling too much to the past— in what I call Burn-Out Syndrome. I will not deny that I too feel the pressure of advancing age. However, I feel that the community of architects with which I work— my atelier office of what I consider suitable size— has, up to now, fulfilled its social responsibility toward the projects it has undertaken. Although projects may be allocated to different groups within that community, a spirit of community is always maintained by seeing and talking together and sharing information in the same space and time. The best proposal is arrived at through an exchange of views within each group. That is a principle that I learned from my time in the Tange Laboratory.

I hope this book attests to the stance that I have adopted in half a century of design activity; that is, my desire and resolve to never let the design of architecture become stale.

Time and Architecture
1. Time is a treasure house of memory and experience.
2. Time is a mediator of the city and architecture.
3. Time is the final judge of architecture.

Space and Architecture
1. In space there is no difference between inside and outside.
2. Space contains and stimulates function.
3. Space brings people joy.

*1. Fumihiko Maki, *Tadayou Modanizumu* (*Modernism on the Open Sea*), 2013, Sayusha.
*2. Alan Colquhoun, "*Form and Figure*," *Oppositions* 12, Spring 1978, The MIT Press.
*3. Fumihiko Maki, *The Japan Architect*, April 1994, Shinkenchiku-sha.

序文

槇 文彦

私の主宰する槇総合計画事務所は、今年2015年には創立50周年を迎える。それを記念して10月中旬から代官山ヒルサイドテラスにおいて、'Maki Fumihiko, Maki and Associates 2015' 副題として '時・姿・空間—場所の構築を目指して' というタイトルのもとで展覧会が開催される。展覧会と同時に出版されるこの作品集は、半世紀にわたる我々の設計活動の背後にあって、何を重要視し、何に関心をもってつくってきたか、その結果生まれた数々の作品群の成果だけでなく、その後、どのような社会性を獲得してきたかの記録である。

◎ 建築は芸術か

建築は当然芸術的価値をもつものでありたい。しかし芸術作品（アート）ではない。アートはそれがゴミになって捨てられるものであっても、あるいは高価な市場性をもって美術館に展示されるものであっても、アーティストの自己責任の世界としてそこで完結している。建築はそうではない。古代から石や木を扱ってきた工匠の歴史が示すように、建築家はつくられたものを通して依頼者を、そして構築された場所も含めたより広い社会に対して責任をもたなければならないからである。かつてヴィトルヴィウスは建築が保持すべき三つの基本的価値として用・強・そして美あるいは歓び（ラテン語でvenustasという）を挙げている。

我々が設計した中津市の風の丘葬斎場が1997年に完成した時、多くの市民達は「これで私達は安心して死ねます」と喜んでくれた。人々の潜在的欲望を発見し、実現できたことを建築家として大変嬉しく思ったことを今でもよく覚えている。

◎ 場所の構築

何故場所の構築なのか。建築はインスタレーションを除き移動可能なアートと異なって、与えられた場所に定着させられる運命をもっている。時に何世紀にもわたって。場所は時に建築家の想像力を触発する。あるいは逆に建築がその場所を含めたより広範囲の環境の性格を決定することもある。それほど場所は建築の成否を左右する重要性をもっている。

一方、私は設計活動の初期から集合体の設計を実現する幸運に恵まれてきた。1968年に完成した立正大学熊谷キャンパス、69年から四半世紀にわたってつくられたヒルサイドテラス、これらから様々なことを学んできた。さらに集合体への参加（4 ワールド・トレード・センター、テレビ朝日等）を加えればその数は十指を超える。集合体とはひと言でいうならば一つの小世界の構築なのだ。一方都市、特に日本の大都市では様々な制約条件に直面することが多い。たとえば建物の一面しか表現が許されなかったスパイラル、高速道路際で残り三方も多くの自由度が与えられなかったロレックス中津ビル。

この作品集では、便宜上、単体の建築は都市、田園、そして特殊な環境でもある大学キャンパスに分けて、設計アプローチの特性を集録している。

◎ 時と建築

時、特に半世紀という時は私にとって豊かな記憶と経験の宝庫であった。蒼生の頃、1959年と60年の2回にわたる〈西方への旅〉は一生忘れられない数々の出会いに恵まれた。またこの時期は多くの建築家達との交流の始まりでもあった。メタボリズムの仲間達、あるいはTEAM Xのメンバー。そして場所としてはギリシャ群島の一つHydra。車はなくロバと人間がつくり出す世界。そして個の集合からつくり出される空間と形態の秩序。それらは1960年東京の世界デザイン会議におけるメタボリズム宣言の中の群造形の提案、そして1964年にセントルイス・ワシントン大学から発刊された"Investigations in Collective Form"へとつながる。またアジア、中近東、ヨーロッパの集落、都市の基底に存在する私なりに発見したヒューマニズム。それらは2013年に発表した『漂うモダニズム』*1の中で指摘している世界的なうねりの一つとして〈共感のヒューマニズム〉あるいは〈オープン・スペースの集合体〉の提言へと、その底流を分ち合う。

また時を介して偶然の建築との出会いから後年そのオマージュとしての建築が生まれる。子供の頃経験したメザニン空間のヒルサイドテラス第1期計画での実現。建立間もなかったワールド・トレード・センターとのハドソン河を介しての対面。その残像と4 ワールド・トレード・センターのイメージの交錯等・・・。

時はまた建築と都市の間のよき調停者でもある。ヒルサイドテラスは6期、25年間にわたるプロジェクトであったために、その間変貌を続ける東京から、どのような施設をもつことが好ましいか、どのような住居ユニットが求められているか、多くの教示を受け、それを実現している。

建築は人間の生命と似て、生もあれば死もある。そして時に大手術が行われ、再生、新生の生活を迎えることもできる。名古屋大学豊田講堂で行われたコンクリート打放しの再生技術、あるいは1929年に建てられた旧横浜銀行別館の移動と、その後横浜アイランドタワーとの合築（2003年）によって、銀行から横浜市のコミュニティー施設として新生を迎えた例等、今も記憶に新しい。こうして建築家はつくられた建築に対し、単に親から子に対してもつ感情だけでなく、それがどのように育っているかの関心を抱くようになる。今回別に出版する『槇総合計画事務所の50年の歴史』は、これまで建てられてきたほとんどすべての建築の生死、そして現状の記録である。

◎ 姿と空間あるいは空間体

1978年の"OPPOSITIONS"*2で建築評論家、Alan Colquhounが姿と形態について興味ある分析を行っている。彼によれば形態は本質的に意味をもたないが、姿は形態に文化的な意味が付与されたものだとする。古典の建築における文化的意味とはある様式に対する修辞的引用として理解しやすいが、現今のモダニズムが様式として溶解、拡散しつつある時代の文化的意味は当然多様となり、明快ではない。

現在、建築設計を行うものの観点にたてば、姿もまた従って多様とならざるを得ない。私の場合、その場所が暗示する好ましき―当然そこに主観が存在するが―空間体の外からの見え方と、空間体が内包する様々な要素間の視線構造のせめぎ合いの中から一つの姿が誕生するケース

が多い。この初期の段階の空間体を私は〈nebulous whole〉と名付けている。この一連の思考の詳細は『The Japan Architect』の1994年*3に詳述されている。

私がここで強調したいのは空間体の内部からの視線の構築の重要性である。たとえばその空間体の外部に対する視線が制限されている時、当然視線の多くは内に向かう。たとえば古代ギリシャの都市住居、風の丘葬斎場、あるいはアガ・カーン ミュージアムの中庭はそれぞれの規模、性格こそ異なれ、視線がつくり出す振る舞いの統合的空間としての役割を果たしている。

一方、深圳海上世界文化芸術中心では、その特異な場所が示唆する海、山、都市公園、そして空への視線の展開がその姿に反映されている。すでにふれたスパイラルあるいはロレックス中津ビルにあるように極めて限定された視線の制約は、逆に建築家に新しい創造の機会を与えてくれるのだ。私は『漂うモダニズム』の中で、視線から構築された建築の優れた例としてアルド・ファン・アイクのアムステルダムの孤児院を挙げている。

何故視線なのか。人間は視ることによって何かを感じ、その次に時に思考へ、あるいは振る舞いへと行動を起こしていく。動物の場合群れる、逃げるあるいは襲うと、その行動はより単純化されている。

集合体は一つの完結した小世界であると述べた。それはテーマパークあるいは田園の中に隔離された大学キャンパスについては的確な表現である。しかし都市の中に挿入された集合体は当然周縁境界面と多様な接触を展開する。しかし一つの集合体のアイデンティティーはどのようにつくられているか、集合体を構成する建築のあり方とそれをつなげる外部空間のあり方、この二つを軸にして、その様態を記録している。その発展形として、円集合、あるいはオープン・スペースの集合体を最後に紹介している。

しかし視線の構成は当然、与えられた地域の歴史的、文化的特性を反映している。日本の文化では広大なバロック的視線構成を好まない。むしろ限られた空間の中での屈折性、重層性、あるいは隣接性に対する様々な独特な手法を展開してきた。奥、気配あるいは間と称される概念。

姿の存在、その性格の多くは姿を構成する素材と素材感によって決定される。そして内部空間体から外への視線展開の要請によって、その開口のあり方、あるいはスクリーンのような被膜が採用される。多くの場合、建築家のディテールの能力が問われるところでもある。今回のここでは4ワールド・トレード・センターにおけるガラス、アガ・カーン ミュージアムの石、その他金属系の表層の取扱い等を例として記録している。

◎建築の社会性―情景
建築が実現した後、即ち建築家の手を離れた時から、その建築が依頼者、利用者、そして建築を取り巻くより広い社会からどのように評価されているかを知ることは、その建築の社会性を示すものとして我々は重要視し、その観察を、あるいは当事者の意見を聞くことを怠らない。当事務所の自己史はその集約である。

今回の展覧会では社会性の一つの断面としての情景に重点をおいている。情景を通して、特に内外のパブリックスペースにおける人々の様々な振る舞いを写し出すことによって、その建築の社会性を描き出そうとしている。たとえばフレデリック・ニーチェの〈孤独は私の故郷である〉という私の好きな言葉がある。

様々なパブリックの空間での人々が孤独を楽しむ姿。少人数の人々の語り合うひと時。あるところで偶然展開する祝祭の模様。与えられた機能を超えたこれらの人々の行動から、その空間、建築の社会性が現れる。

◎建築のクオリティーの維持
この作品集が示すように、槇総合計画事務所では日本のみならず海外各地で様々なタイプ、規模の建築設計が進行中である。そこでも冒頭に述べた建築家の社会的責任の存在が変わることはない。そして半世紀を超えるプラクティスの中で、私は国内外で、アトリエ事務所として出発しながら規模拡大とともに、そのアイデンティティーを失っていくもの、若い時の華やかな活動、言動がいつしか消滅し、あるいはそれに固執し過ぎたり、―私はそれを燃え尽き症候群と称しているが―を多く目撃してきた。当然私にも加齢の圧力が心身にあることは否定できない。しかし私と仕事をともにする適正な規模のアトリエ事務所は一種の設計共同体として与えられたプロジェクトに対して社会的責任を今日まで果たしてきたと思う。勿論複数のプロジェクトが共同体の中でグループ別に進行していても、同じ空間・時間の中で見たり、話したり、情報交換によって共同体のスピリットは常に維持されている。そしてグループ内の意見交換の中から最善のものを取り出していく。それはかつて私が丹下研の中から学んだ原則でもある。

この作品集はそうした半世紀の設計活動の中で、つくる建築の新鮮さを失わない、あるいは失いたくないとする姿勢の証言であるとみて戴きたいと思う。

時と建築
1. 時とは　　記憶と経験の宝庫である
2. 時は　　　都市と建築の調停者である
3. 時が　　　建築の最終審判者である

空間と建築
1. 空間には　外部と内部の差は存在しない
2. 空間は　　機能を包容し、且つ刺激する
3. 空間が　　人間に歓びを与える

*1　槇 文彦『漂うモダニズム』 2013年　左右社
*2　アラン・コフォーン「形と姿」, "Oppositions" 12, 1978年春刊
　　The MIT Press
*3　槇 文彦　季刊『The Japan Architect』 1994年4月　新建築社

Contents

- **Foreword** — 4
  Fumihiko Maki
  Translation: Hiroshi Watanabe

- **A Brightness Emerging in the Landscape** — 12
  —The Human Reality of a Half-Century of Architecture by Fumihiko Maki
  Yuzuru Tominaga
  Translation: Hiroshi Watanabe

- **Sightlines and Stance:** — 19
  Maki and Associates at Fifty
  David B. Stewart
  Translation: Kenichi Nakamura

- **Maki sketches** — 25

1 Journey to the West 1959–1960 — 50

2 Memory, Reincarnation, Rebirth — 54

- University of Tokyo Thesis Project
- Projects at Harvard University Graduate School of Design
- Nagoya University Toyoda Memorial Hall
- Washington University in St. Louis Steinberg Hall
- Katoh Gakuen Elementary School
- Brasilia Japan Embassy
- Iwasaki Museum
- Rissho University Kumagaya Campus
- National Aquarium, Okinawa
- Austrian Embassy in Japan
- Toyota Kuragaike Memorial Hall
- Isar Büropark
- United Nations Consolidation Building
- 4 World Trade Center
- Hillside Terrace
- Square 3, Novartis Campus
- Chiba University Inohana Memorial Hall
- Yokohama I-Land Tower
- PREVI Low-Cost Housing in Lima, Peru
- Floating Pavilion

3 Spatial Entity, Figure, Sightlines — 78

◎ Toward Cities — 82
- SPIRAL
- National Museum of Modern Art, Kyoto
- Tokyo Metropolitan Gymnasium
- Yerba Buena Center for the Arts
- Tokyo Church of Christ
- Jewish Community of Japan
- Rolex Toyocho Building
- Rolex Nakatsu Building
- Skyline Orchard Boulevard
- Nagano City Hall and Nagano Performing Arts Center
- Singapore Mediacorp
- Shenzhen Sea World Cultural Arts Center

◎ Toward Countryside — 126
- YKK Guest House
- Fujisawa Municipal Gymnasium
- Kirishima International Concert Hall
- Kaze-no-Oka Crematorium
- TRIAD
- Mihara Performing Arts Center
- Shimane Museum of Ancient Izumo
- Haus der Hoffnung
- Aga Khan Museum
- The Japanese Sword Museum

◎ Toward Campus — 172
- Keio University Mita Campus
- Washington University in St. Louis Sam Fox School of Design & Visual Arts
- University of Pennsylvania Annenberg Public Policy Center
- Massachusetts Institute of Technology The Media Lab Complex
- Tsuda College Sendagaya Campus

◎ Toward Ocean — 190
- Zeebrugge Ferry Terminal Competition
- Palazzo del Cinema Competition
- Vuosaari Tower Competition
- Hong Kong Ocean Terminal Extension

4 Group Form & Collective Form — 194

◎ Collective Form — 198
- Hillside Terrace
- Keio University Shonan Fujisawa Campus
- Miraisozojuku
- Frankfurt am Main Center Competition
- Isar Büropark
- Republic Polytechnic Campus
- Republic Polytechnic Expansion & Singapore Institute of Technology
- Tokyo Denki University Tokyo Senju Campus
- International College for Post-Graduate Buddhist Studies
- The Bihar Museum
- Passive Town Kurobe
- Cusco Samana Hotel & Residences

◎ Form & Counter Form — 238
- Makuhari Messe & North Hall
- Taipei Main Station Area Redevelopment

◎ Participation with Collective Forms — 246
- TV Asahi
- Square 3, Novartis Campus
- 4 World Trade Center

◎ Circular Collective Form — 264
- Nalanda University Competition

5 Scenery — 266

6 Collective Form of Open Spaces — 280

Fumihiko Maki Curriculum Vitae — 282
Project Chronology
Project Data
Maki and Associates Staff List
Exhibition Information

目次

- 序文 　　　　　　　　　　　　　　　　　　　　　7
  槇 文彦
  英訳：渡辺 洋

- 風景に現れ出る輝き 　　　　　　　　　　　　　16
  ──槇 文彦建築の50年、その〈人間の事実〉について
  富永 譲
  英訳：渡辺 洋

- 視線と姿勢：槇総合計画事務所の50年 　　　　 22
  デイヴィッド・B.スチュワート
  和訳：中村研一

- 槇によるスケッチ 　　　　　　　　　　　　　　25

1 西方への旅 1959-1960 　　　　　　　　　　　50
2 回想・再生・新生 　　　　　　　　　　　　　54
　◉ 東京大学卒業設計
　◉ ハーバード大学GSD時代の作品
　◉ 名古屋大学豊田講堂
　◉ セントルイス・ワシントン大学　スタインバーグ・ホール
　◉ 加藤学園初等学校
　◉ 在ブラジリア日本大使館
　◉ 岩崎美術館
　◉ 立正大学　熊谷キャンパス
　◉ 沖縄国際海洋博　水族館
　◉ 在日オーストリア大使館
　◉ トヨタ鞍ヶ池記念館
　◉ イザール・ビューロパーク
　◉ 新国連ビル
　◉ 4 ワールド・トレード・センター
　◉ ヒルサイドテラス
　◉ スクエア 3　ノバルティス　キャンパス
　◉ 千葉大学ゐのはな記念講堂
　◉ 横浜アイランドタワー
　◉ ペルー低層集合住宅
　◉ 浮かぶ劇場

3 空間体・姿・視線 　　　　　　　　　　　　　78
　◎ 都市へ 　　　　　　　　　　　　　　　　　82
　　◉ スパイラル
　　◉ 京都国立近代美術館
　　◉ 東京体育館
　　◉ イエルバ・ブエナ芸術センター
　　◉ 東京キリストの教会
　　◉ 日本ユダヤ教団
　　◉ ロレックス 東陽町ビル
　　◉ ロレックス 中津ビル
　　◉ スカイライン・オーチャード・ブールバード
　　◉ 長野市第一庁舎・長野市芸術館
　　◉ シンガポール・メディアコープ
　　◉ 深圳海上世界文化芸術中心
　◎ 田園へ 　　　　　　　　　　　　　　　　 126
　　◉ 前沢ガーデンハウス
　　◉ 藤沢市秋葉台文化体育館
　　◉ 霧島国際音楽ホール
　　◉ 風の丘葬斎場
　　◉ TRIAD
　　◉ 三原市芸術文化センター
　　◉ 島根県古代出雲歴史博物館
　　◉ 希望の家　名取市文化会館多目的ホール
　　◉ アガ・カーン ミュージアム
　　◉ 新刀剣博物館

　◎ キャンパスへ 　　　　　　　　　　　　　 172
　　◉ 慶應義塾図書館・新館
　　◉ セントルイス・ワシントン大学
　　　サム・フォックス視覚芸術学部
　　◉ ペンシルバニア大学
　　　アネンバーグ・パブリックポリシーセンター
　　◉ マサチューセッツ工科大学　メディア研究所
　　◉ 津田塾大学千駄ヶ谷キャンパス
　◎ 海へ 　　　　　　　　　　　　　　　　　 190
　　◉ ゼーブルージェ・フェリーターミナル　コンペ案
　　◉ シネマパレス　コンペ案
　　◉ ヴォサーリ・ニュータウン高層住居　コンペ案
　　◉ 香港オーシャンターミナル

4 群造形 & 集合体 　　　　　　　　　　　　 194
　◎ 集合体 　　　　　　　　　　　　　　　　 198
　　◉ ヒルサイドテラス
　　◉ 慶應義塾湘南藤沢キャンパス
　　◉ 未来創造塾
　　◉ フランクフルト・マイン・センター　コンペ案
　　◉ イザール・ビューロパーク
　　◉ シンガポール理工系専門学校キャンパス
　　◉ シンガポール理工系専門学校拡張工事&
　　　シンガポール工科大学キャンパス
　　◉ 東京電機大学　東京千住キャンパス
　　◉ 国際仏教学大学院大学
　　◉ ビハール博物館
　　◉ パッシブタウン黒部モデル
　　◉ クスコ・サマナ・ホテル&レジデンス
　◎ フォーム & カウンターフォーム 　　　　 238
　　◉ 幕張メッセ & 北ホール
　　◉ 台北駅再開発計画
　◎ 集合体への参加 　　　　　　　　　　　　 246
　　◉ テレビ朝日
　　◉ スクエア 3 ノバルティス　キャンパス
　　◉ 4 ワールド・トレード・センター
　◎ 円の集合体 　　　　　　　　　　　　　　 264
　　◉ ナランダ大学　コンペ案

5 情景 　　　　　　　　　　　　　　　　　　 266
6 オープン・スペースの集合体 　　　　　　　 280

槇 文彦プロフィール 　　　　　　　　　　　　 283
プロジェクト年表
プロジェクトデータ
槇総合計画事務所所員リスト
展覧会情報

A Brightness Emerging in the Landscape
—The Human Reality of a Half-Century of Architecture by Fumihiko Maki

Yuzuru Tominaga Translation: Hiroshi Watanabe

Can architecture today also be "human reality"? Today, when advanced capitalism and its invisible power have thoroughly infiltrated the system by which architecture is realized and gradually begun to render pallid everything human, is it possible to create human reality— a contemporary architecture that is designed down to its smallest details with the utmost care, cultivates the human spirit, evokes history and gives new meaning to life?

The evolution that the works of Fumihiko Maki and Maki and Associates have undergone over a half century is not only the history of an architect and the group of which he is the leader but a unique attempt to answer the above, enormous question. It is a journey of exploration of the domain of possibility by an architect who has met head-on the issues of modernity and can be said to be the very history of modern architectural thought.

Modern architecture came into existence a century ago. This book deals with the second half of that century, the fifty years that have passed since Maki began his practice. That half-century was also the period in which modernism was accepted by society and became firmly established in Japan, so much so that it now shapes the immediate environment in which we live.

At the beginning of the twentieth century, architects envisioned a world of life in a new industrial age and attempted to conceive through architecture a new man-made environment. The geometrical guise of modern architecture was at first a sign of soaring ambition to undertake the reformation of the old world. Architecture then was still human reality, bright and full of hope.

However, industrialization and standardization, two goals pursued by modern architecture, made it inordinately fecund. Today, modern architecture has permeated every corner of our immediate environment, and its spatial schema informs the entire world. A system of construction was activated and proliferated automatically all over the world as an integral part of economic activity. The brightness unique to each place dimmed and died, and our lives began to be surrounded by a tiresome sameness of place. Traveling in Japan and the rest of the world, one is struck by the fact that, though the natural landscape and the mountains in the distance continue to be subtle and diverse, an untidy collection of insipid, modern architecture-like objects serving the needs of contemporary society stands in that setting everywhere one turns. The situation has changed decisively in a century.

The fact that humans are trying to destroy the global environment through construction— even though this planet called earth on which we live is a tiny, finite thing— has led a philosopher, on the basis of new scientific evidence, to write as follows regarding the sense of foreboding that pervades the first half of this century.

> This is the intellectual condition we find ourselves in as we stand on the threshold of the twenty-first century: if "the death of God" was the Far North of thought at the start of the previous century, then its equivalent for this century can be said to be "the death of humans" or "the death of humankind." There is a premonition of death or the end of all things surrounding humans, or of humankind itself.*1

Let us suppose that the intense ambition of modern architects at the start of the twentieth century to construct a mathematical, abstract world that cut all ties to nature in an effort to reform the old world was fueled by a presentiment of "the death of God." After all, in the West, architecture has been a thing created entirely by humans— the field that suggests above all else human power and capability— as opposed to things in nature which have frequently been likened since ancient times to works of God.

From ancient times, architecture has been called the most complex structure, one that is involved in all aspects of human existence and life; it has been winnowed by time and become closely tied to humans. Modern architecture as originally conceived was, perhaps inevitably, unable to anticipate or to accommodate the complex situations it would be called upon to adapt to in human life. At the outset, even matter-of-course functions such as the capacity to withstand the rigors of climate and the passing of time and the capacity to adapt to customs lay outside the field of vision of modern architects; who then could have imagined, when modern architecture first came into being, the subsequent rapidity of change in use spurred by developments in industry and mass society, and the sudden conversion of architecture into forms of capital and information? Modern architecture began to be transformed when human tasks that architecture is expected to perform and uncontrollable urban phenomena were pushed to the forefront of society's consciousness.

However, modernism as a style, which developed in the first half of the twentieth century, became widely accepted by society in the second half of the century as a building technology and came to be produced by a mechanical process.

This was precisely the point at which Maki began his career as an architect. Looking at the results of a half century of design activities aimed at "the construction of place," we are amazed once more by the diversity of sizes, locations— from Japan to every part of the world— and figures revealed by the projects. These figures, each distinctive to a place, have been shaped based on a usage Maki has adapted from modern architecture. Because they are all based on the same, modern architectural usage, a succession of photographs that focuses on their surfaces may seem to the casual observer to be a record of things lacking distinctiveness or originality that are repeated over and over again. However, when one actually goes to the places where those buildings stand and experiences them, one realizes that each building, standing quietly in a natural landscape or asserting its presence amid urban clamor, has been produced through criticism of place and new interpretation of function. Each building is an application of the usage of modern architecture. It can be at first glance commonplace, and at times it can be unexpectedly unique in its geometry. However, it becomes obvious that the relationship between the body of the person experiencing the building and the place itself is the product of repeated studies undertaken from many different points of view.

Concerning the architectural images that are produced by Maki at early stages of the design process and reproduced in this book, I have previously written as follows:

> The architect is undoubtedly trying to discover in the blankness of the page the diverse situations that need to be checked as the building becomes reality, things such as "dialog with the mountain range," "weight and brightness of materials," "building type," "order of proportions," "unfolding of scenes with movement" and "space of light," as well as "client demands" and "laws and regulations." That is because he must ultimately discover a *kūkantai* that provides a solution to these situations which are on entirely different planes.*2

He first attempts to fix on paper, by means of intertwining and overlapping lines, a place of a certain extent expressed as spatial flow or density. Maki is not concerned with the application of an architectural schema that is easily understood from without or the demonstration of originality of style. He is intent instead on finding invention and originality in the application of skills necessary for the generation of architecture— that extraordinarily complex structure— skills such as the ability to project the body, respond to actual building tasks and place or inquire into function.

Maki often uses the term *kūkantai* (literally "space-body"). A frame is used to create a place in an environment, and a membrane defines an inside and makes form manifest. That is Maki's "architectural frame." At the end of his foreword,

Maki states that "in space there is no difference between inside and outside." We should take note of this insight Maki has arrived at based on 50 years of experience. The conversion of architecture into images and media seeks to select a specified place from an infinitely extended space, frame it by means of an "architectural frame," and exclude and ignore all other spaces as if they did not exist. This is something that statism and commercialism have been misusing and abusing since the twentieth century. That is a dangerous aspect of modern architecture, and through such conversion into media, modern architecture has gained global currency and appealed to mass society. One is apt to believe that the lens of a camera is acting as proxy for the eyes of the observer, but in contemporary society, that is not so. The conversion of architecture into media has brought about the death of the capacity to see architecture, the death of the capacity to sense architecture as something distinctive and the death of the irreplaceability of experience— that is, the estrangement of architecture from human reality.

When we experience architecture, we see various details or events, not as separate things but as a continuous whole, indeed as a *kūkantai*. Le Corbusier referred to this as an "architectural promenade." The human sightline is ever moving. We glide lightly over the surface of the *kūkantai* and see things without any awareness we are doing so. We live in this world, maintaining continuity by such glances, minutiae of everyday behavior and diversity of gratuitous glances. This is precisely where freedom of architecture, liberation of the body, discovery and joy of sensation reside. In that moment, what the prevailing media offers— the privileged camera lens that will not permit gratuitous glances and attempts to offer brief summaries instead, the forced consumption of dramatized images, and advertisement-like statements— is nothing less than the restriction of architecture, the death of the capacity to see architecture, the death of the experience of architecture. The statements in Maki's foreword, "space contains and stimulates function" and "space brings people joy" are surely expressions of hope that architecture will remain a medium that can only be discovered by experiencing it rather than what it has too often become in modern times, a medium that is "shown" to a passive, consumption-oriented society. He is hoping that architecture will return to playing what has been its "natural" role since ancient times, that it will exist in the outside world and in the city and provide people with support. He is trying to discover something fresh in contemporary life and the place where such an architecture comes into being.

Maki states that the conceived architecture changes and comes into being in the relationship between the human body and place. He maintains that, though a *kūkantai* is ephemeral, the extraordinarily complex structure that is the realized work of architecture continues to stimulate everyday life and give joy. Moreover, the thing that is examined particularly closely in this catalog is the immutable truth that architecture, even after it has been built, continues to change and come into being— the fact that architecture is a temporal medium. A building has life.

A building as material object is always subject to destructive forces both natural and human and to changes in function. When an architect has a half-century of experience, his thoughts inevitably turn to the time a building has to live. He tries to take the measure of a building's toughness, not only its physical strength but the degree to which it will tolerate as yet unknown modes of human behavior in the future. From the adoption of building type and form of layout to the assessment of details, he tries to read into drawings the effects of time, just as a player of Japanese chess sees in his mind's eye the endgame tens of moves into the future. As an architect ages, he realizes once more that an architectural frame, no matter how large, is dependent on the small physical frame of a human being. The theory of group form that Maki presented 50 years ago was the antithesis to Tange's approach. "The system is inherent in the element. Therefore, the element is more self-sufficient and individualistic; a stable element exists for an extremely long time. However, elements in the future must possess tentacles that enable them to exist as a group." This was the lesson drawn from his research into collective form in 1958-60 concerning the relationship between the parts and the whole as well as from history in his "journey to the West." Moreover, through the workings of time, architecture acquires a social character.

"Buildings, like human beings, experience birth and death. At times, they undergo major surgery, regain their health and are able to lead productive new lives." And "like a parent with respect to an offspring, an architect may not only have an emotional attachment to a building he or she has designed but interest in how that building develops afterwards." With 50 years of experience, having known the births and deaths and rebirths of many buildings in the present social system and having considered the contemporary era, he ends his foreword with the following gnomic statements.

   Time and Architecture
     1. Time is a treasure house of memory and experience.
     2. Time is a mediator of the city and architecture.
     3. Time is the final judge of architecture.

Time— the passage of time— is a question that must be asked, but, as everyone understands, it is a question that cannot be answered. The first statement can be said to express Maki's vision of architecture. The second expresses his vision of the city. The third is both an expression of the determination of an architect to ensure the continued existence of his work and an admission of the mortality of human beings.

Maki's usage, adapted from modern architecture, has produced buildings of different sizes, uses and locations included in this book; it is revealed in the consistency of the "figures" in which the rhythms of living forms are imprinted. He shapes each part distinctly and gives it character. Instead of blending those parts smoothly into an overall form, he seems to be trying to endow materials and details with a fragmentary brightness. It is as if, even inside a composition, "elements ought to be individualistic and self-sufficient."

At first glance he may appear to be eliciting a refined, romantic lyricism from the style of modern architecture, but even more than that, his is a magnificent, isolated world of autonomous objects created by relationships between the parts and the whole assembled by a fine sensibility and logic. It is the product of a kind of perfectionism; it may be lyricism but not what one generally refers to as romanticism. This is indeed "a prosody expressing the body at play in midair," but the extraordinarily complex structure responds to the diverse new building tasks demanded by contemporary society and generates brightness in place. Architecture is architecture. It is not a style. In pursuit of consistency of "figure," Maki attempts to express the individuality of the self within the universality of form called modern architecture on which our lives are already premised.

> All the actions of an artist, designing, writing and speaking, converge on the perceptual presence of individuality that one might call "figure." Ultimately art can be said to be the artist's pursuit of his own figure.*3

The number of design terms in the dictionary of modern architecture is limited, and the meanings assigned to those terms, after 100 years of repeated use, have become routine, worn-out clichés that are too rigid to adequately express the feeling of being alive in the here and now. That is where new expressions come into being.

Today, each architect adopts his or her own stance, trying to achieve a balance between modernism and his or her individuality. This is what Maki pointed out in his essay, "Modernism on the Open Sea." The sense of mission and the ideology of modernism have been lost, and modernism survives only in form. There are two ways of responding to such a situation. The first is to create a new language. Society longs for what is novel. New icons are converted into media and used for political or commercial purposes. However, just as a new linguistic system cannot in principle be discovered by an individual, an architecture that has been based up to now on a shared technology and empathy would become highly inconvenient if such new discoveries were incorporated into it; it would not achieve universality. A process of selection over time is needed. The other method is, in solving difficult tasks, to change the way much-used stereotypical expressions are employed, add new points of view, and endow those expressions with fresh meanings. Maki's response to the old usage of modern architecture has been to try to avoid expressions that have been used carelessly and to convey the "true character of architecture."

Indeed, from the start Maki may have seen stereotypes as precisely the foundation upon to build richer meaning, one offering greater potential for the language of architecture than individual originality. His approach represents a rejection of originality of appearance. His strategy is to disturb a neutral, uniform place and thereby affect people. Architecture, the expression of architecture, instead of being a media that unilaterally "shows" itself to those experiencing it, ought to be something that offers the possibility of being "discovered" or "reexamined." The final chapter of "Modernism on the Open Sea" dealing with the nature of life in an IT-oriented society in this century ends with a section on "a humanism of empathy," which is surely an expression of hope that a new humanity may emerge within the transformation of stereotypes and attain social character.

The hard, dignified "figure" or appearance of Maki's architecture is not something that replaces the universality of prevailing forms, that is, something that "shows" itself. Instead it is something that is "discovered" by people. It summons the gazes of people living everyday lives, small, everyday actions, and diverse gratuitous glances; it endows a corner of a vast, diffuse world filled with information with brightness, frames it with light, refreshing, solid materials, invites people into "a world within a world" that can only be discovered through experience, and presents architecture as human reality.

(Architect, Hosei University Professor Emeritus)

*1. Seiichi Takeuchi, *Onozukara to Mizukara— Nihon shisō no kisō* ('Onozukara' and 'Mizukara'— The Basic Layer of Japanese Thought), 2004, Shunjūsha.
*2. Yuzuru Tominaga, "Kenchiku— kūchū ni asobu shintai wo hyōmeisuru hitotsu no shihō" (Architecture— a Prosody Expressing the Body at Play in Midair), *Fumihiko Maki, A Presence Called Architecture— Report from the Site*, 1996, TOTO Publishing.
*3. Fumihiko Maki, *Kioku no keishō* (The Shape of Memory), 1992, Chikuma shobō, afterword.

風景に現れ出る輝き──槇 文彦建築の50年、その〈人間の事実〉について

富永 譲

現代において、〈建築〉はなおかつ〈人間の事実〉でありうるか。高度な資本主義とその見えない権力が建築を成立させるシステムの隅々にまで深く浸透し、何かしら人間的なものを次第に漂白させ始めている現在、人間の精神を耕し、歴史を覚醒させ、生活に新たな意味を呼び戻す、細部まで丹精された現代建築──〈人間の事実〉をつくることができるか。

槇文彦および槇総合計画事務所の辿った半世紀の仕事の変遷は、一人の建築家とその集団の歴史でありながら、近代建築様式（モダニズム）全体に向けられたそうした巨大な問いへの固有な挑戦であり、近代の問題を正面から引き受け続けてきた建築家が切り開くその可能な領域への探索の旅であり、近代建築が成立して1世紀を経過し現在へと至る、近代建築思潮が辿る歴史そのものとも見える。

槇文彦が活動を始めたこの作品集が扱う、その半分、50年の歳月は、社会が、様式全体を受け入れ、本格的に日本の大地に定着し始めた時期と重なって、今や私たちの身の周りの生活世界を形づくっている。

20世紀の初頭、100年前建築家達は、新しい産業時代の来るべき生活世界を夢見て、〈建築〉によって新しい人工世界を構想しようとしたのだった。当初、近代建築の幾何学的な容姿は、旧世界を変革する人間側の精神的な意欲へ示す指標であり、希望に満たされ、前方に白く輝く、〈人間の事実〉であり続けていたのだ。

しかし、近代建築が一面で追ってきた、工業化、画一化は過剰な生産力として、それ以後、今や私たちの生活世界の隅々まで浸透し、その空間図式はくまなく地球上を占領した。ある建設方式が作動し、経済活動の一環として、自動的に世界各地に増殖した。それぞれが独特でもあった、〈ここにしかない〉場所の輝きは次第に失われ、〈どこにでもある〉場所の退屈が生活を包囲するようになった。近年、日本や世界各地を旅して思うことは、自然の山並み、風光が相変わらず多彩、微妙であるにもかかわらず、その土地に現代社会の必要がつむぎだす、とどまるところを知らない近代建築的なものが、いかに無味乾燥で、雑多に乱立するものかということである。1世紀を経て状況は決定的に変わったのだ。

我々の住むこの地球という天体が、ほんのちっぽけな有限でしかなかったにもかかわらず、人間自らが建設によって進んでこの地球環境を破壊しようとしているという事実を新たな科学的知見をも踏まえて、ある哲学者は今、この世紀前半を覆う時代の不吉な予感を次のようにいう。

> 21世紀のとば口に立つわれわれをとりまく思想状況は、前世期初頭の思想の極北が見ていたものが「神の死」ということであるとすれば、今世紀のそれは、「人間の死」「人類の死」ということであるともいわれる。何かしら人間にまつわるもの、あるいは人間そのものの死が、終わりが予感されているということである。*1

20世紀初頭近代建築の、旧世界を変革しようとするキッパリと自然と手を切った数学的、抽象的世界の構築、激しいその意欲は底辺で「神の死」という時代の予感のうちに醸成されてきたのかもしれないと想像してみる。西欧において、古来しばしば神の作品に擬せられてきた自然物に対し、建築は徹頭徹尾人間によってつくられた物であり、何よりも人間的な力、人間の能力を示す領域（フィールド）であったからである。

また、建築は古くから人間の生存・生活のすべての面に関わり、時の淘汰を経て生き残り人間自体に密着していて、一番複雑な構成物だといわれてきた。当初の建築家達の脳内空間の中に構想された近代建築が、そんな人間の生活に対して果たさなくてはならない複雑な局面について、予知し得なかった、含み得ていなかったということは当然でもあっただろう。成立当初、視野に収め得なかった、風土、慣習、時間の経過の中での堅牢さといった地道な、当たり前ともいえる役割やその後の産業と大衆社会の繰り広げる予想だにしなかった用途の変化のスピード、建築の資本化、情報化への急激な展開を誰が思い描いただろうか。建築にとっては当たり前の人間的課題や制御不可能な都市現象が社会の前面に押し出されてきた時、近代建築は変貌していくのである。

しかし20世紀前半に成立した近代建築のスタイルは、世紀の後半ではすでに、世界の各地で、社会の中に一般化した建築技術として定着し、機械的手順によって生み出されるようになった。

槇文彦の建築家としての経歴が出発するのもまさにその時点である。〈新しい場所の構築を目指して〉という槇文彦のこの半世紀にわたる設計活動の軌跡を見る時、それが、様々な規模の、その都度、様々な社会活動に応じて、様々な土地の、それも日本から世界各地に至って、かくも多く、遍在し、多彩な姿で広汎に展開していることに改めて驚くのである。それらは、いずれも〈ここにしかない〉場所の固有の姿が、近代建築から選びとった槇の語法に基づいて形どられている。同じく近代建築の語法に基づいているから、通りすぎる目から見ると、その表面を定着している写真の連続は、一見特徴のつかまえ難い、独創のない、安定した繰り返しであるように見えてしまうかもしれない。しかし、建築のある場所に実際赴き、経験してみると、それぞれが、自然の風景にひっそりと佇む建築も、都市の喧騒の中で主張しようとする建築も、場所への批評、新たな機能への解釈から生み出されていることを知るのである。いずれも近代建築の語法の適用であり、一見平凡でもあり、また時に意外でユニークな幾何学の形体の構成物であるそれが、経験する人間の身体と場所との関わりについて、繰り返し多くの側面からスタディーされた結果であるという痕跡は浮かび上がってくるのである。

この本にも載っている槇の初期段階の建築のイメージスケッチについて、以前こんな風に書いた。

> 建築家の眼差しは、余白に満ちた佇まいのなかに、これから現実に成り立ってゆくうえでチェックされるべき多彩な局面を誰よりも発見しているにちがいない。〈山並みとの対話〉、〈材料の重量や輝き〉、〈建築の定型〉（ビルディング タイプ）、〈比例の秩序〉、〈移動に伴う場面の展開〉（シーン）、〈光の空間〉、そして〈依頼主の要求〉や〈法的な規制〉といったことまで。結

局はそれら全く異なったレベルのそれぞれの局面に解決を与えてゆくような〈空間体〉が見出されなければならないからだ。*2

線はもつれあい、重なり交錯しあいながらある広がりをもった場所を空気の流れや密度としてまず紙面に定着しようとしている。槇の建築思考の関心するところは、外側からわかりやすい建築図式を適用したり、建築家のスタイルの独創を提示したりするのではなく、身体を投入し、現実の建築課題（ビルディングタスク）やそれぞれの場所に応答し、機能を吟味し、建築—この〈途方もなく複雑な構成物〉を生成してゆくその一連の洗練された手際の最中に工夫や独創を見ようとするのだ。

〈空間体〉という言葉を、槇はよく使うが、そうした環境の中に場をつくる〈身体の枠組（フレーム）〉は、骨組みによって場を支持し、一応、被膜によって内部を切り取り形を現象させる。それが槇の〈建築の枠組〉だ。今回の序文の最後に、「1. 空間には、外部と内部の差は存在しない」とはっきり書かれてあるのも、50年経て、到達した槇の建築への認識であり、注意すべきであろう。限りなく広がる世界の空間から、特定された、一つの場所を選び、〈建築の枠組〉によってそれを切り取り、それ以外の空間は存在しないかのように排除し、無視することを求める建築の映像化、メディア化は、20世紀から今世紀にかけて、国家権力やコマーシャリズムが濫用し、悪用してきたものである。それは近代建築の危険な一面であり、またそうしたメディア化によって、グローバルに流布し、大衆社会に訴えかけもしてきた。カメラのレンズは人間の目の機能の代替を果たしていると思われがちであるが、現代社会において、むしろ事実はきびしく相反する関係にある。メディア化がもたらしたものは建築を見ることの死、建築を固有なものとして感覚することの死、経験のかけがえのなさの死ではなかっただろうか。〈建築〉を〈人間の事実〉から隔てるもの、深い断絶ではなかっただろうか。

私達の目が建築を経験する時、すでにそこにある現実の領域のうえで、様々な細部や出来事を切り出して個別に見ているのではなく、それらが連続する総体、まさしく〈空間体〉として見ているのである。ル・コルビュジエはそれを〈建築的散策〉といったが、人間の視線は、一瞬たりとも運動を止めることはない。人間の生きた眼差しは、〈空間体〉の表面を軽やかに滑り、普段、何も意識せずにものを見ている。そうした生活者の眼差し、細々とした日常の仕草、無償の眼差しの様々に支えられて、連続を保ちながら、この世界を生きつつあるのである。そこにこそ建築の自由があり、身体の解放があり、発見があり、感覚の喜びもある。その時、流布されたメディアが提示する無償の眼差しを許そうとしない手短に要約しようとする特権化されたカメラのレンズ、ドラマタイズ化した映像の強制、広告的な言説は建築の不自由、建築を見ることの死、経験することの死にほかならない。序文にある、「2. 空間は機能を包容し、且つ刺激する」「3. 空間が人間に歓びを与える」という言は、近代において顕著な現象となった、建築が経験されることなく消費社会の中で流通してゆく〈見せる〉メディアとしてでなく、経験されることによってのみ〈見出される〉メディアであらんとすることへの希望であろう。古くから、外側の世界や都市とともにあり、人間の背中を支えあげてきた当たり前ともいえる建築の役割への帰還であり、現代生活において、その生成される場所に新鮮な何かを見出そうとするのである。

槇は構想される建築が人間の身体と場所の関わりの中で変容し、生成するといいながら、完成した「途方もなく複雑な構成物」である当の建築作品は、〈空間体〉として刹那的でありながら、日常生活を刺激し、歓びを与え続けるという。しかも今回の作品集の中で50年を振り返って特にクローズアップすることは、建築が成立した後においてさえ、生成し、変容し続ける、それが時間のメディアであるという不変の事実についてである。「建築の生命」が初めて語られている。

物体—建築は、絶えず自然のまたは人為の破壊作用にさらされ、また人間側の機能の変化にも当面するから、半世紀の経験を積んでみると、建築がこれから生きてゆく時間についての思考が浮かび上がってくる。建築のタフネス、その物理的な強さだけでなく来るべき未知の人間の行為の様態に対する許容の度合いの広さまで測りとろうとする。建築類型（ビルディングタイプ）、平面の形式の採用から、細部のディテールの判断に至るまで、時の作用を、〈今・ここ〉の図面の中に深く読み込もうとする。将棋指しが、数十手先の終盤の局面を、現に戦っている盤上に思い描くように・・・。年齢を重ねるにつれて、どんなに大きな〈建築の枠組（フレーム）〉もこの人間を巡る小さなもの、〈身体の枠組（フレーム）〉の中に成り立っていることに改めて気付くようになる。50年前この建築家が丹下理論に対するアンチテーゼとして提出した、群造形（グループフォーム）の理論、「システムはエレメントに内在する。したがってエレメントはより自己充足的であり、個性あるものであり、安定したエレメントはきわめて長期的に存在する。ただし今後の時代のエレメントは群として存在しうる触手を持たなければならない」ことがそこで再確認される。部分と全体に関する1958-60年の集合体の研究、〈西方の旅〉が告げる歴史の教訓でもある。小さなものの中に宿る光を見出してゆかなくてはならないのだ。そして時の作用を介して、長い営みの中で建築は社会性を獲得してゆくのだという。

「建築は人間の生命と似て、生もあれば、死もある。そして大手術が行われ、再生、新生の生活を迎えることもできる」そして「建築家はつくられた建築に対し、単に親から子に対してもつ感情だけでなく、それがどのように育っているかの関心を抱くようになる」とも、槇は50年の経験を経て、現在の社会制度の中で誕生してきた幾多の建築の生死、再生を味わいながら、現代という時を考察し、「時間」を巡って、序文の最後に要約するようにポツリと述べている。

時と建築

1. 時とは　記憶と経験の宝庫である
2. 時は　　都市と建築の調停者である
3. 時が　　建築の最終審判者である

「時」、過ぎゆく時間、それは問われなければ、誰もがわかるが、問われたら、答えられないような問いだ。時を巡って、1.2.3.にそれぞれ「とは」、「は」、「が」という異なった繋辞が用いられていることが注意を惹く。さしずめ、

1.が槇の建築論であり、2.が槇の都市論であり、3.は〈人間の事実〉としての建築に永遠なるものを託す想いであり、それは物理的体そのものの持続を目指す建築家の心意気と死にゆく人間の宿命についてであろう。

近代建築から選び取った槇の語法、それはこの作品集に示されている、規模も、用途も、場所も異なった、それぞれの建築の中に潜んで、生きた形のリズムを刻むその〈姿〉の一貫性の中にある。くっきりと部分の形の一つ、一つを造形し、性格づける。それを全体の形のモチーフの中に滑らかに溶け込ませるというより、素材や、ディテールを粒立った輝きとして、強引にひっぱりあげようとしているかに見える。構成の内部にあっても〈部分(エレメント)は個性あるものであって、自己充足的であらんとする〉かのようだ。

一見、近代建築様式から、洗練された、ロマンティックな叙情をひき出しているかに見えるが、それ以上に、繊細な感性と論理によって組み上げられた部分と全体の関係がつくる、自立的な物達の華麗で孤独な世界を感じる。一種の完璧主義(パーフェクショニズム)、それはリリシズムであるかもしれないが、もはや一般にロマンティシズムとは呼べないだろう。硬質な物達がささやきを交わしあう肌理の細かい空気の流れがつくり出され、〈空中に遊ぶ身体を表現する一つの詩法〉であるが、それを〈空間体〉と呼べば、しかし、それはすでに100年を経て現代社会が要求する様々な新しい建築課題(ビルディングタスク)に応答し、場所に輝きを生み出す、一個の〈途方もなく複雑な構成物〉としてである。建築は建築である。様式ではない。〈見せる〉ものでなく人間によって〈見出される〉ものだ。そこで槇は〈姿〉の一貫性を追い求めることを通して、自己の個人性を近代建築という私達の生活がすでに前提としている形式の普遍性の中で、交換しようとするのだ。

　　　1人の作家の作る、書く、語るすべての行動はどこかで〈姿〉ともいうべき一つの個性の視覚的な存在に収斂してゆく。芸術とは、究極には彼が彼自身の姿を追い求める作業であるといってよいだろう。*3

近代建築を形づくる用語の辞書に登録されている造形言語の数は有限であり、それに宛われた意味は100年繰り返し使われ続け、続けているうちに、画一化(ルーティーン)され、擦り切れ、新味なく、この時代のヴィヴィッドな気分を適確に語り出そうとする時、硬直しているし、不十分を感じる。そこから新たな表現も生まれてくる。

現在、建築家の表現は、近代建築様式(モダニズム)と、その個人性を巡って、人間的な何かを求めてそれぞれのスタンスで取引をしている。槇が〈漂うモダニズム〉と指摘するところだ。モダニズムを支えた使命感、思想は失われて、モダニズム建築の形式だけが生き残った。事態に対して普通二つの方法がある。一つは新語を生み出すこと。社会の目新しさへの希求であり、新しいアイコンとしてメディア化され、国家やコマーシャリズムが利用するものでもある。しかし新しい言語体系を個人が発明することが原理的にできないように、社会が共有する技術と共感のうちに成立してきた建築は、その発明によって同時に大いなる別の不自由を抱え込み、決して普遍的なものに到達しないだろう。時の淘汰が必要なのだ。もう一つは、使い古し、ステレオタイプ化した辞書に登録されている言語の使用法を、難しい課題を解いてゆく中で、変形し、新しい視点を加え、新鮮な意味をそこに附与してゆくことである。だらしなくなった平常表現をいかに避けて〈建築の本性〉を表出させるか、それが槇の近代建築の古い辞書への返答の仕方だった。

むしろ、槇は、個人の独創でなく、ステレオタイプ化しているその事実にこそ、そこに豊かな意味を刻み込む基盤、建築という言語の可能性があると一段と深く読み込んでいたのではないか。見えがかりの独創に対する拒否。均質(ニュートラル)な場所を揺さぶり、人間に働きかけようとする戦略。建築、その表現が、経験するものに、一方通行的に〈見せる〉メディアとしてではなく、〈見出される〉あるいは〈見返される〉可能性を含んだものであらんとすること。『漂うモダニズム』の終章が今世紀のIT社会での生活のあり方を見透し、〈共感としてのヒューマニズム〉として、締めくくられているのも、新たな人間性のあり方をステレオタイプの変容の中に、社会性が獲得されてゆくことへの希望であろう。

硬質で、凛とした、槇の建築の〈姿〉―佇まいは、自らをそうした流布する形式の普遍性と交換することによって初めて生活者の眼差しや、細々とした日常の仕草、無償の眼差しの様々を呼び寄せ、情報が飛び交うこの茫漠と拡散してしまった世界の一隅の場所に輝きを与え、軽やかで、清々しく堅牢な物質で縁取り、経験されることによってのみ見出される〈世界の中の世界〉へと誘い出し、〈建築〉を〈人間の事実〉として提示したのである。
　　　　　　　　　　　　　　　（とみなが・ゆずる/建築家、法政大学名誉教授）

＊1　竹内整一『「おのずから」と「みずから」―日本思想の基層』2004年　春秋社
＊2　富永 譲『建築―空中に遊ぶ身体を表明する一つの詩法 槇文彦・建築という現在―現場からのリポート』1996年　TOTO出版
＊3　槇 文彦『記憶の形象』あとがき1992年　筑摩書房

Sightlines and Stance: Maki and Associates at Fifty

David B. Stewart

Hands down the doyen of Japanese architecture, Fumihiko Maki has never been a practitioner to mince words. A triad of terms takes pride of place in his exhibition title: 'time', 'figure', and 'space' with the middle term 'figure', I think, as pivotal. Yet a major surprise in Maki's Foreword is the following: "Architecture may possess artistic value, but it is not itself art." It isn't, in other words, "a world complete in itself," such as an artwork may be sensed to be. The decree, which is not without century-old historical precedent in Japanese architectural theory, sets the tone for Maki's "construction of place." For he continues, "architects are responsible through the works they create to clients and society, including the places where the works are constructed."

Here, then, is a stalwart profession of faith even if the dichotomy proposed may be more complex. For example, what Renaissance devotional masterpiece or later official history painting is not held similarly responsible to society and within a more circumscribed community the client? But no doubt what Maki is saying is that the pendulum of Romanticism has swung too far from art's origins and that unhappily architecture has tried to imitate its trajectory. In any case, Maki is far from unwilling to concede Vitruvian 'delight', as he does pointedly in his next paragraph.

Equally refreshing is the assertion that this book is meant as a record of "[the firm's] priorities and interests," thus of the "social character" of the work produced over the past half century since 1965. (Note: a few early works do predate the establishment of the office at Maki's return from abroad to Japan). Particularly, given the fact that in Japan a number of smaller firms are characterized as *ateliers*— or as being atelier-style, consciously reinforcing the notion of architecture-as-art— Maki's is a straightforward and unromantic approach.

Or, looked at another way, Maki's anti-art directive may best be understood as indicating an innovative and ever evolving vernacular, learnt like Le Corbusier in the architect's youthful world travels, and also in Maki's case at the feet of his acknowledged master the Catalan architect, Josep-Luís Sert. The latter's compass point of reference was the Mediterranean, to which Sert's own master, none other than Le Corbusier, was himself perennially drawn. Yet nicely to complicate matters, Le Corbusier regarded himself first as a painter and only secondly as an architect, while Sert was an art collector. Be all that as it may, the lineage is a clear one, from which Maki has never deviated. Sert easily became the defining influence at Harvard's Graduate School of Design, where Maki both trained and later taught, in addition to his brief period of employment with Sert Jackson and Associate's in New York City and Cambridge, Massachusetts.

While I've not yet had the chance to visit Maki and Associate's partially completed 4 World Trade Center tower in New York or the recent Delegation Building and museum for His Highness the Aga Khan, located respectively at Ottawa and Toronto, we in Japan are well versed in Maki's work. Its showpiece is the celebrated Hillside Terrace in Tokyo's Daikanyama— an ongoing project realized in six successive phases over a of a quarter-of-a-century span. A nationally recognized milestone in Maki's pursuit of collective or "group" form, Hillside Terrace provides the poster child for Fumihiko Maki's deeply held principle of responsibility to client, user, and place. Therefore, this midscale, diversified residential and commercial complex has been selected intentionally as a multiform venue for the present exhibition, since it embodies both construction of place and the role of time with regard to Maki's notion of collectivity— that he himself calls simply the creation of a microcosm.

If I look forward to seeing the new North American works in the flesh (especially after reading universally admiring accounts from at least three competing newspapers from across the U.S., plus the *Architectural Record*) it is really no surprise that the *Los Angeles Times* critic refers to 4 World Trade Center as "deft, thoughtful, and well-made." Virtually all buildings by Maki and Associates are that. I am less sure I agree with the part of the very positive evaluation by the *Chicago Tribune*, which cites the building's "minimalist geometry and sensitive, city-embracing urbanism." Superficially not inaccurate, I think the critic's description misses the active "construction of place"— replete with all the constraints that cities normally impose, as Fumihiko Maki would be the very first to acknowledge.

Hence, the unambiguous— if hardly minimalistic— employ of sightlines, whether it be at Ground Zero, where Time in the guise of memory resists a Form attempting to assume the role of Figure. As explained in Maki's Foreword, the latter pervades Maki's oeuvre. At Ground Zero, for nearly a decade, the overall master scheme by Daniel Libeskind tenuously clung to what Maki would call a "nebulous whole" but was also a cultural and professional minefield. I am convinced in this respect that 4WTC, the first of the sites to be realized, has in no small way helped to lead the entire scheme out of the wilderness.

A sightline by definition is neither more nor less than "a hypothetical line from someone's eye to what is seen." However, at Ground Zero what is to be seen? There is nothing beyond the eye of the observer. The newly redesigned transportation hub, which serendipity renders arguably the most important part of the undertaking, is largely below ground.

Meanwhile, the slowly evolving but now broadly popular National 9-11 Memorial Park comprises two water features staking out the footprints of the North and South WTC Towers, surrounded as they are by swamp oaks and other greenery and with a shard-shaped museum at one side. Thus, the polished and reflective 47-foot high east wall of the Office Lobby at 4WTC is aligned in parallel with the park's South Reflecting Pool with three outsized and unembellished Asplund-like portals guiding the user to the elevator halls occupying the remainder of its ground floor. This context is objectified and highlighted by means of a vast titanium filigree sculptural arc, 100-foot in diameter, entitled *Sky Memory*.

Other sightlines are more mainstream oriented. They accommodate but do not really "embrace" the tapering Lower Manhattan grid, which at this latitude diverges from the purely orthogonal in such way that the vast park consists on plan of four former city blocks now configuring a great slightly skewed lozenge, with the adjacent 4WTC site a near scalene trapezoid. The building then is perceived as a moderately complex volume, highly reflective depending on weather conditions and time of day, and at times appearing less a volume than a confection of planar surfaces. Only the north facade still presents a slight hodgepodge seeming to reflect the upper Church streetscape from which it is mainly now visible, since the westward extension of Cortland Street from which the facade rises will be pedestrianized and tree-lined between the 3WTC and 4WTC sites.

For possibly the first time, 4WTC presents a Makian collective form that is distinctly vertical in its emphasis, where sightlines intersect with skylines— the latter being yet another important design device that Maki has exploited in different ways over a number of years, as in the firm's half-submerged Tokyo Metropolitan Gymnasium. Moreover, given the reflectivity of the feldspar particles naturally embedded within the granite of the powerful east wall of the Office Lobby at 4WTC, much is made of what is virtually perceived. This extends to the building's various facade planes with deployment of reflective glass walling.

The 4WTC tower is governed by a rhomboid lower floor plan between the fourth to the fifty-sixth floors, including upper and lower floors masking mechanical services, and a trapezoidal upper floor plan from the fifty-seventh to the seventy-second floor, once again topped off by concealed mechanical services. The outlines of the two volumes thus generated are congruent except on the tower's principal west facade— where a substantial setback dictated by the western leg of the trapezoid induces a disjunctive reflectivity. This provides the major interest of the building's front facing the park. A three-dimensional reading is cleverly imposed by means of notching the southwest vertex of the rhomboid base, continued seamlessly upward along the matching vertex of the surmounting trapezoidal tier and is duplicated from tip to toe of the tower at its northeast corner. The effect is optimal when only a single wall of the notch is revealed, and less ethereal when the notch is perceived head-on. But the head-on view is mostly obscured from downtown and likewise will be mitigated once the adjacent 3WTC to the north reaches its fully projected height, thus blocking out more than a fractional view of 4WTC's least accessible north facade.

The strength of 4WTC almost seems to me to derive from medieval Japanese gardening art, where ground lines and contours are often allowed to persist and confront one another within a controlled whole. The latter tends to neutralize conflict, or absorb it, without trying to conceal or obviate component inconsistencies. There is a native realism here deriving from what is given, and although the gardening style frequently achieves "high style", its impulse is better described as vernacular. This particular Japanese form of awareness, or Japan-ness as it is sometimes referred to, is I think a unique attribute brought by Maki to the practice of "urban design". Hence, it can still be seen to diverge from the European, or Mediterranean, roots of that remedy for the dire postwar flight from U.S. downtowns as articulated somewhat differently in Josep-Luís Sert's teaching at Harvard and by Louis I. Kahn and others at Penn.

To return for an instant to those distant times, it was no accident that the Tokyo World Design Conference in 1960 was organized by Kenzo Tange, in emulation of the ongoing international discussions at Harvard's GSD where Sert was the leading catalyst. Metabolism, in which Maki participated as a young but nonetheless key figure, was the manifesto brought by Japan as host country to that table. So I would like to conclude this brief discussion of Maki and Associates' first half century by revisiting Maki's first building in Japan, namely the Toyoda Memorial Hall of Nagoya University. It was completed in the spring of 1960, at a time when Maki took leave from his teaching at Washington University in St. Louis (1956-1958) in order to take up a two-year Graham Foundation travelling fellowship and thus well before returning definitively to pursue a full-time design career in Japan.

Indicative of the proactive stance of the firm in lavishing care on completed works, Toyoda Memorial Hall has recently undergone extensive renovation, including the provision of a new atrium, under the auspices of Maki and Associates, and was reopened for use at the beginning of 2008. Interventions comprised HVAC updating, renewal of acoustical and lighting systems, asbestos removal, expansion of the stage and improvement of seating within the auditorium, repaving and landscape maintenance within the extensive forecourt area, selective structural reinforcement, and overall resurfacing of the form-faced concrete. In all of this work the original supervising contractor was retained.

The preservation-and-conservation outcome stands as impeccable and in 2011 Toyoda Hall was registered as a National Tangible Cultural Property. In the new atrium created by roofing over the open space between the hall and an adjacent structure, we find more than a touch of the firm's up-to-date twenty-first century panache. Most tellingly of all, 30 mm of concrete were removed from the weathered form-faced exterior and replaced by a 55 mm layer of mesh and new concrete impressed with form-markings; while on the interior of the building exposed concrete surfaces have been discreetly highlighted by a faux form-facing effect à la Georges Braques, whose father and grandfather had been specialists in false wood-graining, itself in early twentieth-century France a respectable and widespread division of the building trade.

Maki's building adheres to a postwar auditorium typology utilizing the contour of an existing slope. It is related to our smaller, and very different in materials and appearance, Seventieth Anniversary Hall (1958) at Tokyo Tech designed by Yoshiro Taniguchi (1904-1979), now also registered as a National Tangible Cultural Property. But, what is particular about Maki's version is that the rear of the auditorium space with its modest fly tower is construed as the main facade, centered upon a slight projection formed by the green room at the back of its stage.

The roof slab is supported visually by means of a composite system comprising engaged anti-seismic U-shaped pillars, flanked by three and five slim quadrangular-sectioned piloti, set respectively to left and right of center, the pairs of lateral pillars endowed with a flying profile in a way that Maki remarks Le Corbusier found puzzling. The whole is surmounted by a jutting rectangular concrete clock tower. This conveys urban status to the covered area of the South Plaza formed of ascending stairs that express the pitch of the interior seating. Above this area three meeting rooms are suspended in signature Metabolist fashion. Meanwhile, the frontispiece flanked by vertical pillar strokes recalls the Chinese character for 'gate'.

Here is Fumihiko Maki's earliest iteration of collective form evincing a social responsibility to which the main institutional client and its corporate patron, the Toyota Motor Corporation, have responded in kind with their unstinting restoration of his premier work in Japan. Just as at Maki's slightly later nucleus for Rissho University's suburban Kumagaya Campus in Saitama prefecture outside Tokyo, the hall was to be the key to a classic campus design manifesting both Western and Japanese design strategies, where fifty years ago principles of urban design were applied ex nihilo in an unstructured, not to say rural environment. With hindsight, it is surely also such early successes that furnished Maki and Associates with the grit and confidence to build anew at Ground Zero.

(Specially Appointed Professor, Tokyo Institute of Technology)

視線と姿勢：槇総合計画事務所の50年

デイヴィッド・B・スチュワート　訳：中村研一

誰もが認める日本の建築界の第一人者として、槇文彦はいつでも的確な言葉で建築を語ってきた。三つの言葉、すなわち「時・姿・空間」が今回の展覧会のタイトルとなっているのだが、2番目の「姿」が槇にとってもっとも重要な言葉ではないかと思える。それにしても、槇の序文の中でもっとも驚いたのは「建築は当然芸術的価値をもつものでありたい。しかし芸術作品（アート）ではない。」という言葉だ。言い換えると、建築は芸術作品とは異なり〈それ自身で完結した世界〉ではない。日本の建築理論において100年近くにわたる暗黙の了解事項が、槇の〈場所の構築〉という考え方の基調をつくっている。なぜなら、彼は続けて「建築家はつくられたものを通して依頼者へ、そして構築された場所も含めたより広い社会に対して責任をもたなければならない。」と語っているからだ。

この言葉には建築家の職能に対する強い信念が表明されているのだが、建築と芸術作品の区分はより複雑な問題だろう。たとえばルネサンスの宗教画や後世の歴史に残るような絵画のうち、いったいどのような作品が社会、そしてより閉じられたコミュニティーである依頼者に対して責任を取っていないといえるのだろうか？　もちろん槇がいいたいのは、ロマン主義の振り子が芸術の本来あるべき姿から振れすぎてしまったこと、そして建築は不幸にも同じ足跡を辿ってしまったという現状認識である。いずれにせよ、そうした風潮への辛辣な批判として、槇は続くパラグラフでヴィトルヴィウス的な〈歓び〉について語っている。

同様に、この作品集が「（槇総合計画事務所が）何を重要視し、何に関心をもってつくってきたか」を記録するために、すなわち槇総合計画事務所が1965年以降の半世紀の間に生み出してきた作品の〈社会性〉の記録のために作成されているという槇の言葉は、とても新鮮に感じられる（注：いくつかの初期の作品は槇が日本へ帰国して事務所を設立する前に設計されている）。特に日本では小規模な設計事務所の多くがアトリエと称し、アトリエ風作品として建築の芸術性を強調しようとしているのに対して、槇の建築へのアプローチは直截的で非ロマン主義的である。

あるいは別の見方をすると、槇の反芸術的アプローチは、槇自身が若い頃ル・コルビュジエのように世界中を旅したことで学んだ、その土地固有の事物を常に探し続け進化させようとする設計姿勢だと考えると理解しやすいのかもしれない。槇の場合は、ホセ・ルイ・セルトというカタロニアの巨匠の薫陶を受けたことも影響しているだろう。セルトの師匠、すなわちル・コルビュジエが生涯を通じて地中海に魅せられていたように、セルト自身の参照指針も常に地中海を向いていた。ル・コルビュジエは自分のことをまず画家だと考え建築家は2番目だったのに対し、セルトは美術の収集家だったというさらに複雑な事情があったのだが、いずれにせよル・コルビュジエから槇へと連なる血筋はきわめて明白で、槇はその血筋から決して外れることはなかった。セルトが決定的な影響を与えたハーバードの大学GSDで槇は学び、教え、それに加えて短い期間ではあったがニューヨークとマサチューセッツ州ケンブリッジにあったセルト・ジャクソン設計事務所で所員として働いた経験をもつ。

その一部が開業したニューヨークの4 ワールド・トレード・センター、そしてアガ・カーン氏のために設計したオタワのイズマイリ・イママット記念館とトロントのアガ・カーン ミュージアムを私はまだ見ていないのだが、日本にいるわれわれはそれらの槇の作品がどのようなものであるかを容易に想像することができる。東京の代官山で6期、25年間にわたって建設され、現在も進行中のヒルサイドテラスは槇の作品の中でももっともよく知られた作品であり、傑作といってよいだろう。ヒルサイドテラスは槇が追及してきた群造形、あるいは〈グループ・フォーム〉の集大成であり、槇が深く心に刻んだ設計姿勢、すなわち依頼者・利用者・場所への責任感をもっとも明確に示す代表作である。だからこそ、この住居と商業施設が多様に複合したそれほど規模の大きくない建物がこの展覧会の会場として選ばれたのだ。槇自身が小世界の創造と呼ぶ集合体として、ヒルサイドテラスは〈場所の構築〉と〈時の役割〉の両方を体現している。

北米に完成した槇の新作を実際に訪れることを私は楽しみにしているので（特に世界的に評価の高い三つの競合するアメリカの新聞とアーキテクチュラル・レコード誌できわめて高い評価の記事を読んだ後では）、ロサンゼルス・タイムズ紙の批評家が4 ワールド・トレード・センターを「巧妙で、思慮深く、完成度が高い」と評したことは驚くべきことではない。実際、槇総合計画事務所による作品はすべてそうなのだから。シカゴ・トリビューン紙がこの建物のことを「ミニマリスト的な幾何学による、繊細な、都市に対する深い愛情を感じさせるアーバニズム」と高く評価していることに対してはもちろん同感なのだが、物足りなさも残る。この評価を不正確とまではいえないが、槇が真っ先に取り組もうとする、都市の中のさまざまな制約の中でいかに〈場所を構築〉するかという概念をこの批評家は見落としているのだ。

これゆえ、ミニマリスト的とまではいえないとしても、ある特定の視線を設計のテーマとして掲げることは、それが記憶というかたちで〈時〉が示されるグラウンド・ゼロへ向けたものであったとしても、〈形〉が〈姿〉になろうとしていることを邪魔しているかのようだ。槇が序文で説明し語っているように、槇の作品全体が〈姿〉を目指していることとは矛盾するように見える。グラウンド・ゼロは文化的にも建築的にも、何を提案しても批判されてしまうようないわば地雷原なのであり、10年近くにわたってダニエル・リベスキンドによるマスタープランは、槇ならば〈曖昧な全体〉とでも呼ぶような曖昧性の中で揺れ動いてきた。こうした観点から見ると、この敷地で最初に完成した槇の4WTCは、荒地の中から計画全体をかなりの影響力をもって導くことができる建物であると私は信じている。

言葉の定義によれば〈視線〉は〈人の目と見る対象を結ぶ仮想の線〉であり、それ以上でも以下でもない。しかし、グラウンド・ゼロでは何が見られるべきなのか。そこに佇む人々の視線の先には何もない。新しくデザインされた交通のハブはこの計画全体の中でもっとも評判の高い計画になりつつあるが、そのほとんどが地下にあるのだ。

一方ゆっくりと完成へと向かい次第に評価が高まってきた911メモリアルパークは、WTCの南北二つのタワーが建っていた場所を水辺で表現し、その周辺をトキワギョリュウなどの樹木で囲み、その一画にはあたかも砕け

た破片のようなミュージアムが置かれている。4WTCのオフィス・ロビーにある高さ14mの、風景を反射するように磨かれた壁面は、公園の南の池と平行に配置され、まるでアスプルンドのような三つの大きな飾り気のない門を通して訪れた人々を1階の残りの部分を占めているエレベーターホールへと導く。こうした都市への接続は、スカイ・メモリーと題されたまるで透かし細工のような直径30mのチタンの彫刻によって物質化され、さらに強調されている。

その他の視線は街区全体の構成に向けられている。街区の直交グリッドは敷地のあるロウアー・マンハッタンまで下りてくると次第に先細りとなって不整形となり、以前の四つの街区を一つにまとめて計画された広大な公園は少し歪んだ菱形で計画されており、隣接する4WTCの敷地形状は不等辺の台形となっている。視線はこうした状況をそのまま受け止めるというよりは、より穏やかに対応している。したがって建物はやや複雑なシルエットをもつことになり、その日の天候や時間帯による変化を敏感に写し出し、時にその存在感はまるで四角い砂糖菓子のようにきわめて希薄になる。北側のファサードは、コートランド・ストリートが西側へ延長されて3WTCと4WTCの間の土地が歩道化され並木道となるためにチャーチストリート北側からよく見えるのだが、この北側ファサードだけは、チャーチストリートのさまざまな建築スタイルが混在した乱雑な景観をまるで反映させたかのように、建築的要素があまり整理されていないように見える。

4WTCはおそらく槇的な群造形を垂直に展開させおそらく初めての作品であり、視線がスカイラインと交差する。スカイラインは、そのヴォリュームの多くを地下化させた東京体育館にも見られるように、槇が長年さまざまな方法で探究してきたもう一つのデザイン手法である。さらに、4WTCのオフィス・ロビーのきわめて存在感のある東壁面に用いられた、花崗岩の中に含まれる長石の粒子がもたらす反射性を考えると、そこでは実際に目に見える以上のものが実現されている。こうした手法は、建物のさまざまなファサード面において反射性のガラス・カーテンウォールを用いることにつながっている。

4WTCタワーの4階から56階までは菱形平面によって構成され、その上階と下階に置かれた機械室は基準階と同様のカーテンウォールで仕上げて一体化されている。そして57階から72階までは台形で構成され、屋上階は同様に機械室をファサードの背後に隠している。このようにつくられた二つの異なる外形は一体化されているのだが、タワーの主要なファサードである西面においては、平面形が菱形から台形へ縮小される際に西面がセットバックすることによって、反射性には不連続が生じている。この操作が公園に面した建物のファサードにおいて、もっとも興味深い効果を生み出している。3次元的に形態を読み取るように巧みに誘導しているのだ。菱形状の基壇の南西の頂点にあたる部分には切り込みがあり、その上部にある台形の頂部に向けてシームレスにつながりながら、同時に北東コーナーでは足元から頂部までは同じ形がずっと続いている。この切り込みの一方の面だけが見える時にはその効果は最大限に発揮されるのだが、切り込みを正面から見ると、その効果はやや優雅さを欠くことになる。しかし、北側に隣接する3WTCが計画通りの高さまで工事が進む

と、4WTCへのアクセスにはほとんど用いられていない北側ファサードの断片化したような面を隠すことになるので、そうした切り込みを正面から見る視点はなくなり、気にならなくなるだろう。

4WTCのデザイン的な強さは、敷地にもともとある地形に敬意を払い、全体をコントロールしながらも部分の対比を強調する、中世の日本庭園から影響を受けているのだと思う。日本の伝統的庭園は、庭を構成する要素の不統一を隠したり取り繕ったりすることなしに、対立を和らげ、時には無化させる。ここには日本固有の与条件から導かれたリアリズムがある。造園様式はそれぞれの時代の〈流行のファッション〉をつくりだすのだが、そうした庭を生み出す原動力はどちらかというとその土地固有の自然条件なのだといったほうがよい。この優れた日本的な認識方法、あるいは時に〈日本的なもの〉といわれる特質は、槇がアーバンデザインの分野にもちこんだきわめてユニークな資質だと私には思える。だからこそ、そうした槇の手法は、戦後のアメリカのダウンタウンの悲惨な状況に適用された、ヨーロッパや地中海にルーツをもつデザイン手法から生まれたものでありながら、ハーバードで教えていたホセ・ルイ・セルトやペンシルバニアで教えていたルイス・I.カーンや他の建築家とは異なる形態を生み出すことができたのだ。

近況から遠い過去へと話を戻すと、セルトが中心的役割を果たしていたハーバードのGSDにおいて進行していた国際的な議論に対抗する形で、丹下健三の主催により世界デザイン会議が1960年に東京で開かれたのは偶然ではない。まだ若かった槇が中心人物の一人として参加したメタボリズムは、ホスト国として日本が議題に挙げたマニフェストであった。したがって私は槇事務所の最初の半世紀を語るにあたって、槇の日本での最初の作品、すなわち名古屋大学豊田講堂について語ることで締めくくりたい。豊田講堂が完成したのは1960年の春である。槇がグラハム財団奨学金を得て2年間の旅に出るためにセントルイスのワシントン大学での教職（1956-1958）を辞し、その後日本に帰国して本格的な設計活動を始めるしばらく前のことだった。

竣工した作品のその後の評価や使われ方に積極的に関わるという事務所の方針を示す好例として、豊田講堂は槇事務所の設計監理のもとに近年大規模な改修がなされ、新たなアトリウムとともに2008年初頭に再オープンした。改修項目は空調、音響照明システムの更新、アスベスト除去、オーディトリアムの舞台拡幅と客席の機能改善、前庭の領域を広げた再舗装と外構整備、部分的な構造補強、そして建物全体の打放しコンクリートの改修である。これらすべての施工は、最初にこの建物を施工した建設会社が請け負うことになった。

この保存に関わる改修工事は高く評価され、豊田講堂は2011年に国の登録有形文化財に登録された。講堂と隣接する建物との間のオープンスペースに屋根を架けることにより新しくつくられたアトリウムは、21世紀の最新の槇事務所らしさを強く印象付ける。特筆すべきは風化したコンクリート打放し外壁の補修で、表層の30mmを除去した上にメッシュ筋をかぶせて55mmの新たなコンクリートを増し打ちすることで打放しの表情

を再現している。内部においては、ジョルジュ・ブラック風にコンクリートの表面に型枠の痕跡を新たに加えることで、打放しの表現を微妙に強調している。ブラックの父と祖父はともに木目をフェイクで描く専門家で、そうした仕事は20世紀初頭のフランスにおいては建設業の中で広く行われた尊敬すべき仕事だった。

槇の建物は、既存の傾斜した地形を利用しながら戦後につくられた講堂というタイポロジーを踏襲している。規模は小さく、また材料や外観も異なるのだが、やはり国の登録有形文化財に登録された谷口吉郎（1904-1979）設計による東京工業大学の70周年記念館（1958）と比較することもできるだろう。しかし槇のデザインで注目すべきは、オーディトリアム空間の背面にある比較的小規模なフライタワーが、そのステージ裏にある少し突き出したグリーン・ルームを中心にメイン・ファサードとして設計されていることだ。

屋根スラブは、耐震構造のためのU型の柱のペア、その左側に3本、右側に5本を配置した矩形断面の細い柱、そして槇自身の回想によるとル・コルビュジエを戸惑わせた側面の斜めに傾斜したシルエットをもつペアになった柱、これらを複合させたシステムによって支持されているように見える。コンクリートの時計塔が全体のシルエットから突き出し、南側の屋根スラブの下の広場に都市的な性格を与えている。エントランスへ向かって上る階段が講堂内部の客席の勾配を思わせる。この上部に屋根スラブから吊られた三つの会議室がメタボリスト的な建築言語によってデザインされている。一方、垂直の柱にはさまれた正面は漢字の「門」を思わせる。

豊田講堂は群造形を社会的な責任として最初に示した作品であり、だからこそ依頼者である名古屋大学と後援者であるトヨタ自動車が槇の日本での最初の作品を修復することに惜しみない援助を与えたのである。少し後に埼玉郊外に設計された立正大学熊谷キャンパスと同様に、豊田講堂は西洋と日本のデザイン戦略を融合させたキャンパスデザインの古典ともいうべき質を備えていた。50年も前に、田舎とまではいかなくてもまだ開発が進んでいなかったこの土地に、アーバンデザインの計画原理が無から適用されたのである。今から思えば、このような最初の成功があったからこそ、槇事務所はグラウンド・ゼロに新たな超高層を設計するという仕事に恵まれたのだ。

（デイヴィッド・B.スチュワート／東京工業大学特任教授）

Numerous journeys to the West have provided a fertile ground for personal memories and experiences.
西方への旅 数々のPlacesの想い出

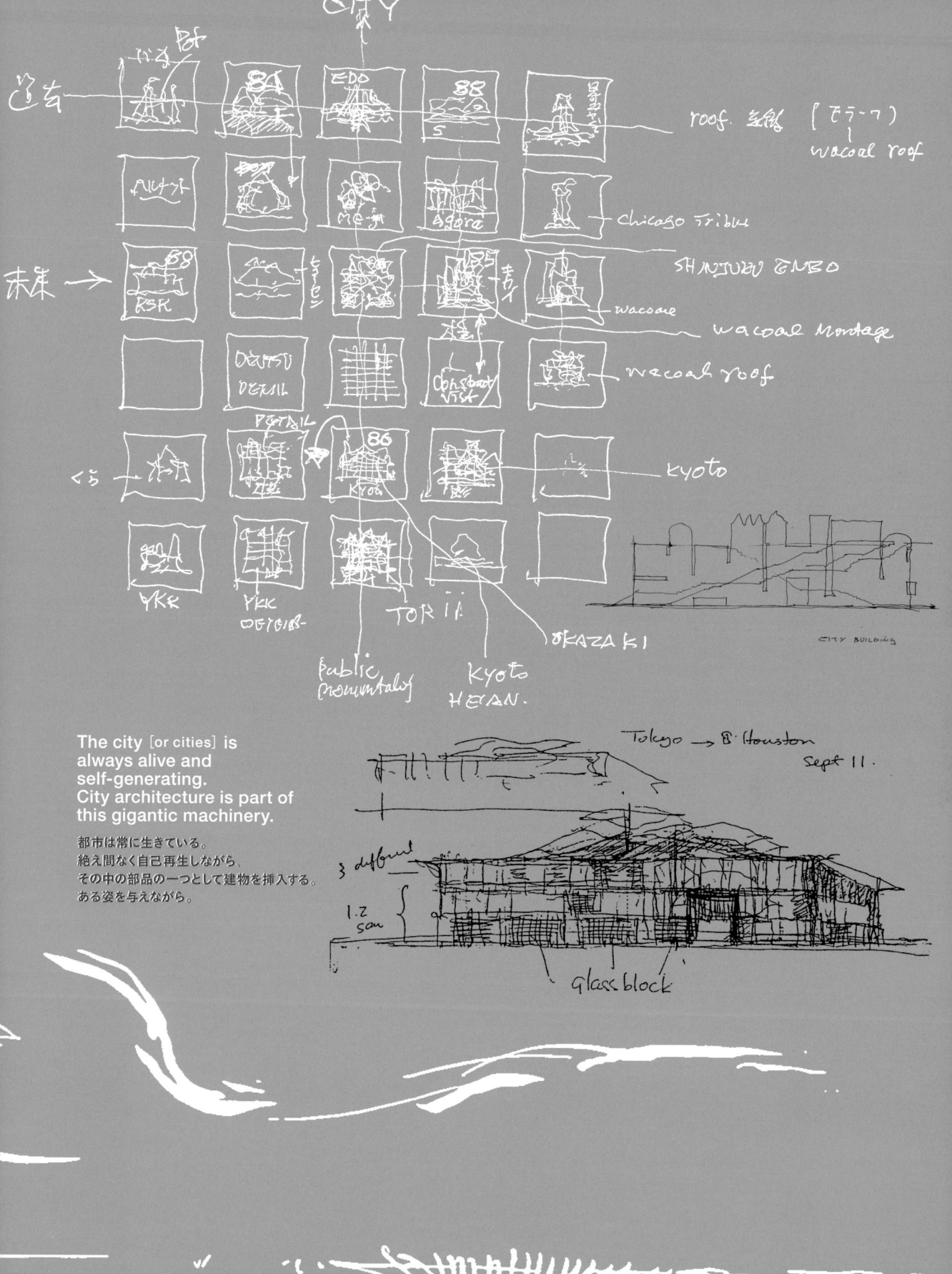

The city [or cities] is always alive and self-generating. City architecture is part of this gigantic machinery.

都市は常に生きている。
絶え間なく自己再生しながら、
その中の部品の一つとして建物を挿入する。
ある姿を与えながら。

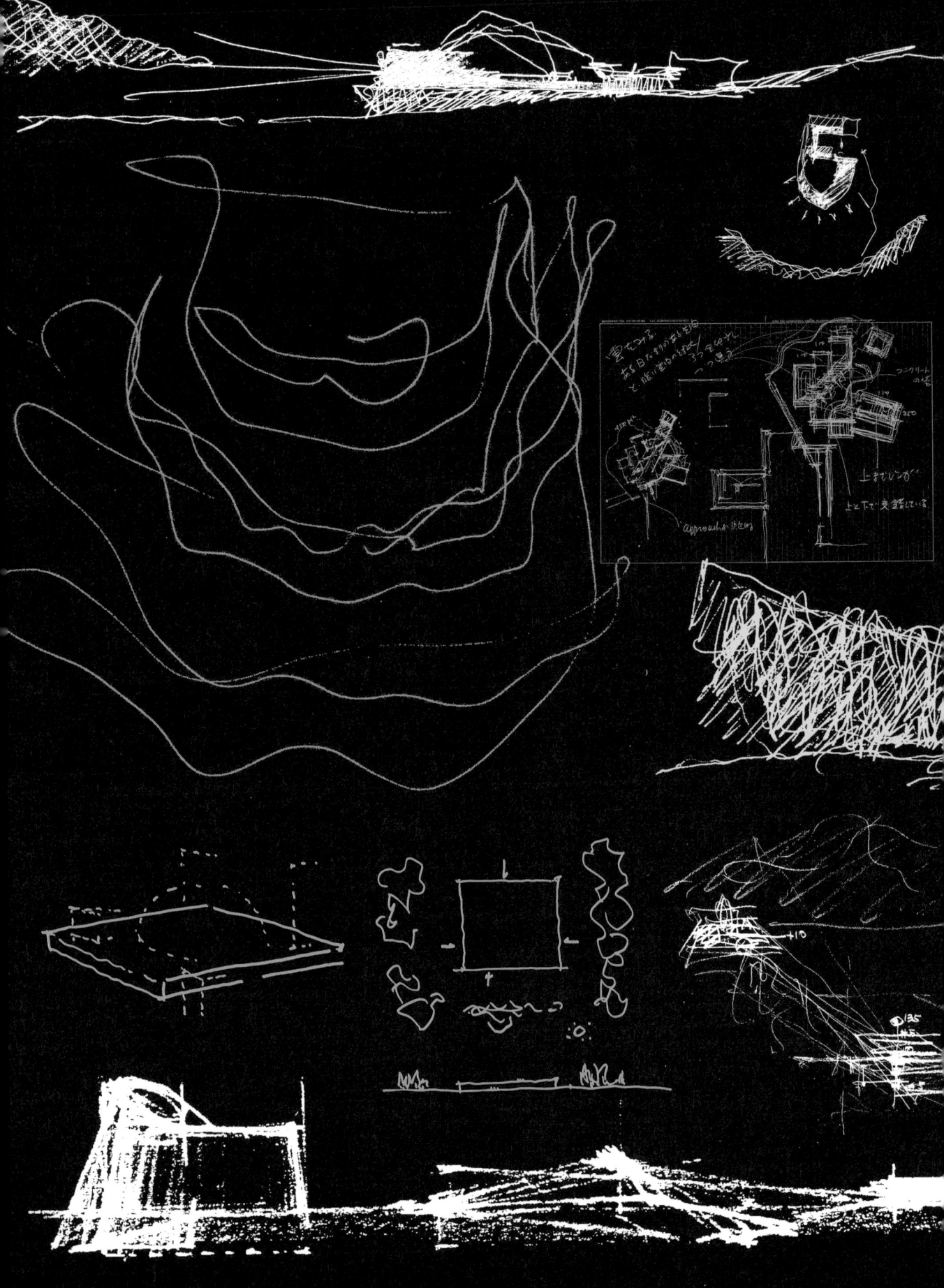

An academic campus is
a unique environment where architecture of
many styles, from
ancient to modern,
claims their own respective identities.

キャンパス。それは特異な環境だ。
何故ならば、そこには様々な時代の様式の建物群があるからだ。
そこでは、自己のアイデンティティーのある姿の発見が重要だ。

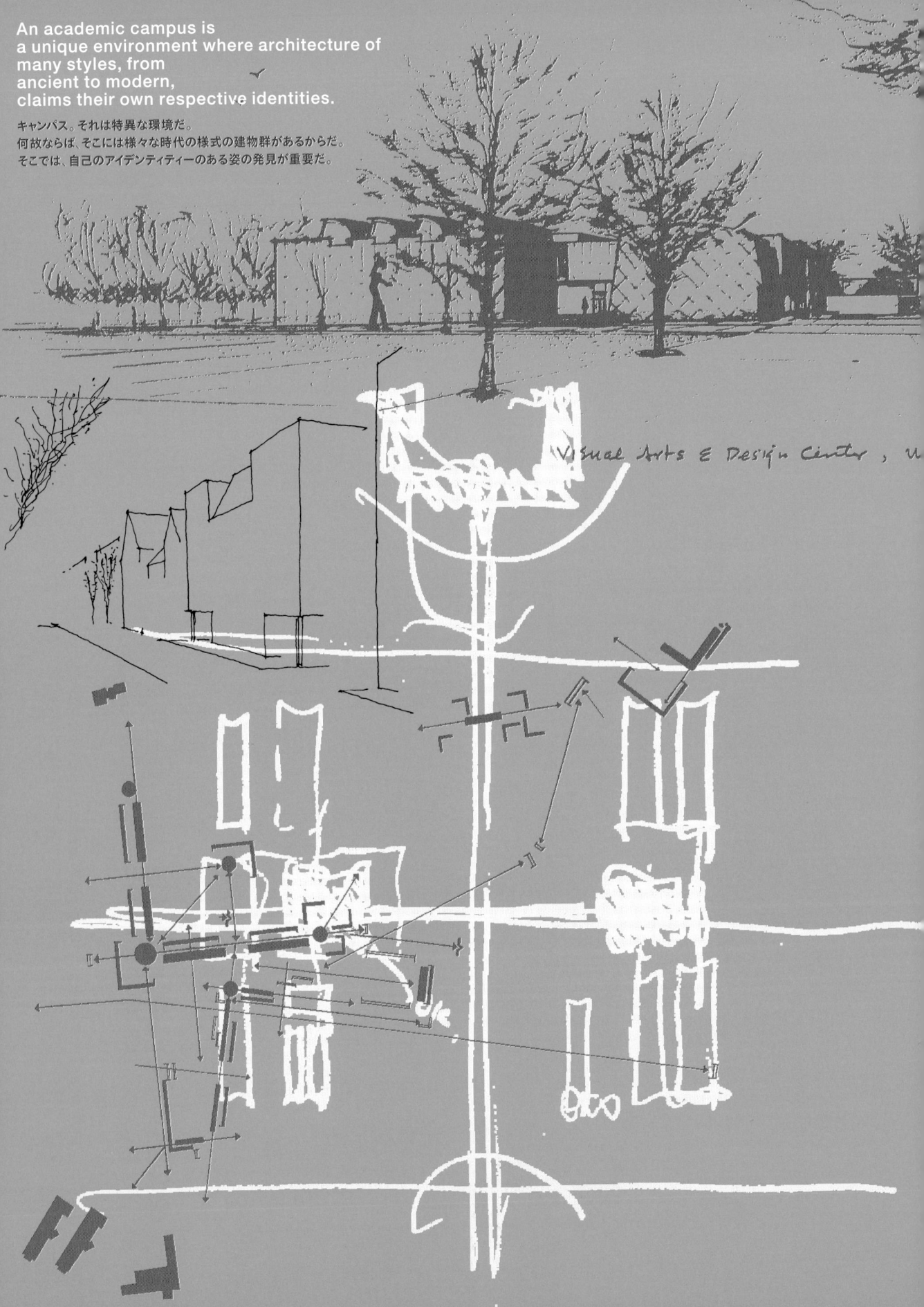

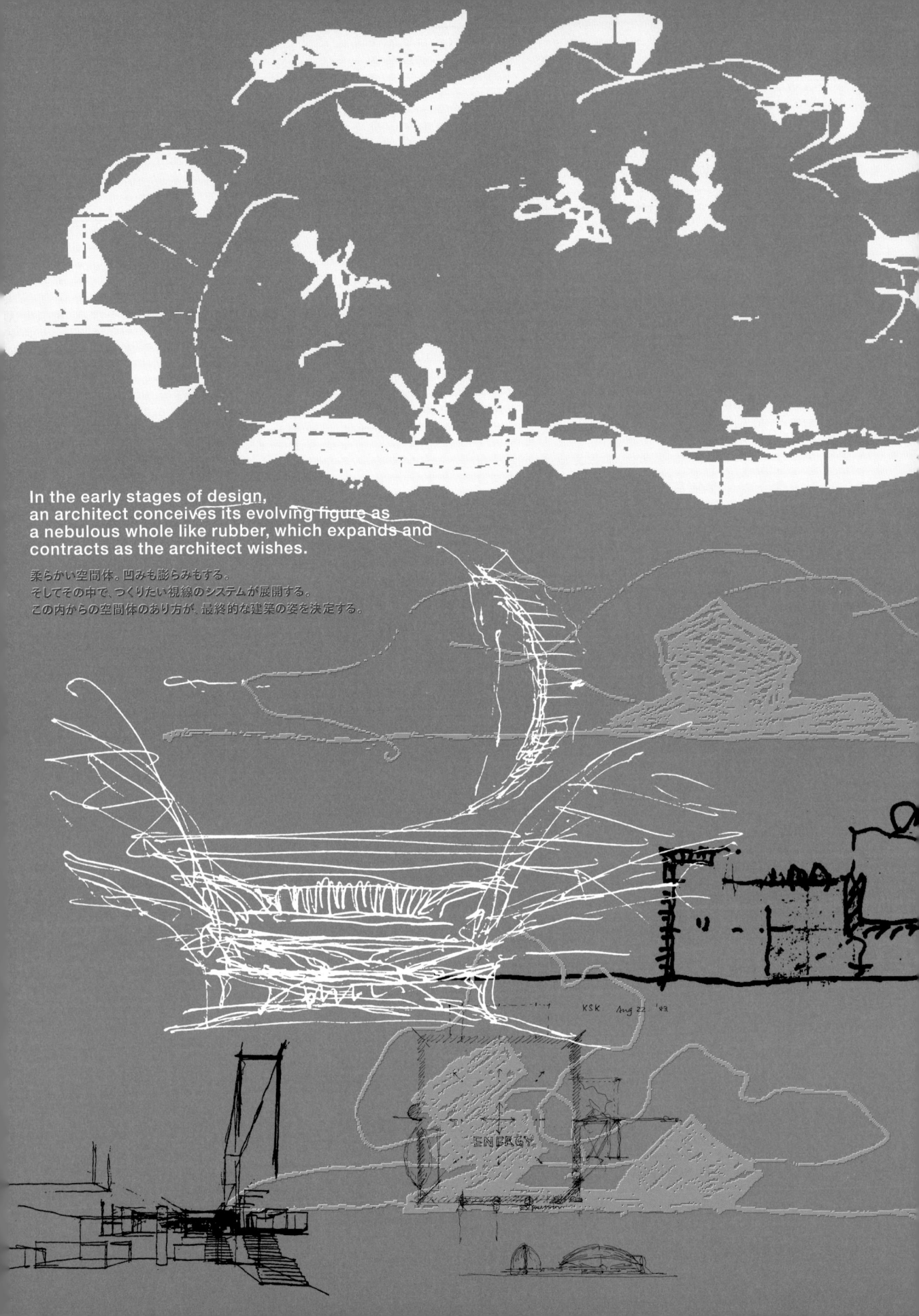

In the early stages of design,
an architect conceives its evolving figure as
a nebulous whole like rubber, which expands and
contracts as the architect wishes.

柔らかい空間体。凹みも膨らみもする。
そしてその中で、つくりたい視線のシステムが展開する。
この内からの空間体のあり方が、最終的な建築の姿を決定する。

F. M
12. 20. 2002

The establishment of
a unique religious axis along mountains,
villages, and rice fields.
A secular axis is
often developed perpendicular to
the religious axis.

Oku is an invisible center.
This concept generates
a design where a sense of depth in space is
sought within a limited area.

山、里、田を結ぶ宗教軸、それに交わる生活軸。
都市の中にも自然との共生が生まれる。
奥の概念とは、見えざる様々な中心の思想。
そこから限られた空間に深みを与える手法が、日本では誕生した。

Figure Ground   Figure Street   Figure Nature

Sky   MA
WATER   FLOW → OKU.

ZERO conversion

— OKU

奥が広がっている

Path

PLAN SECTION

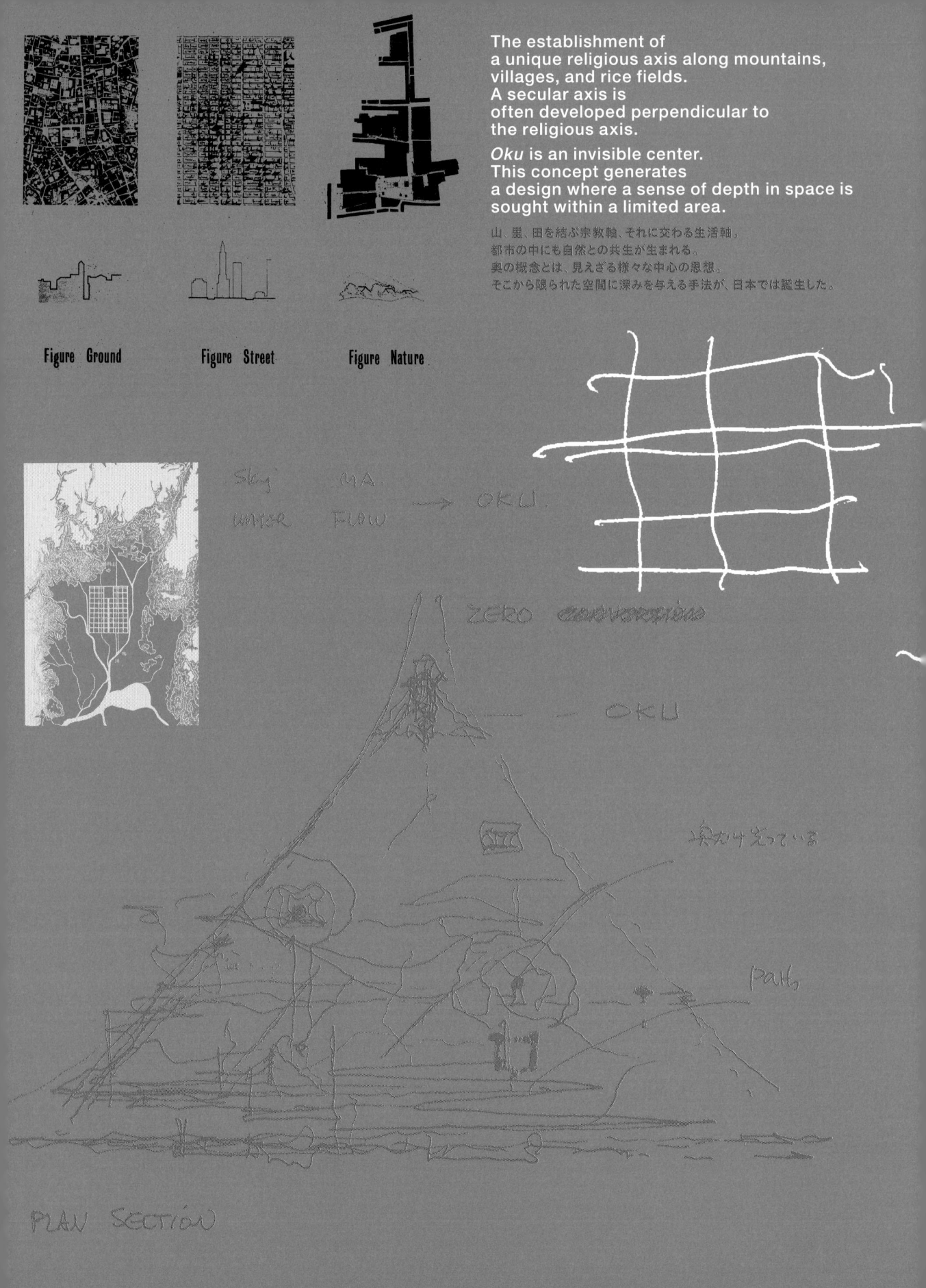

∑ Public Plaza

OKO

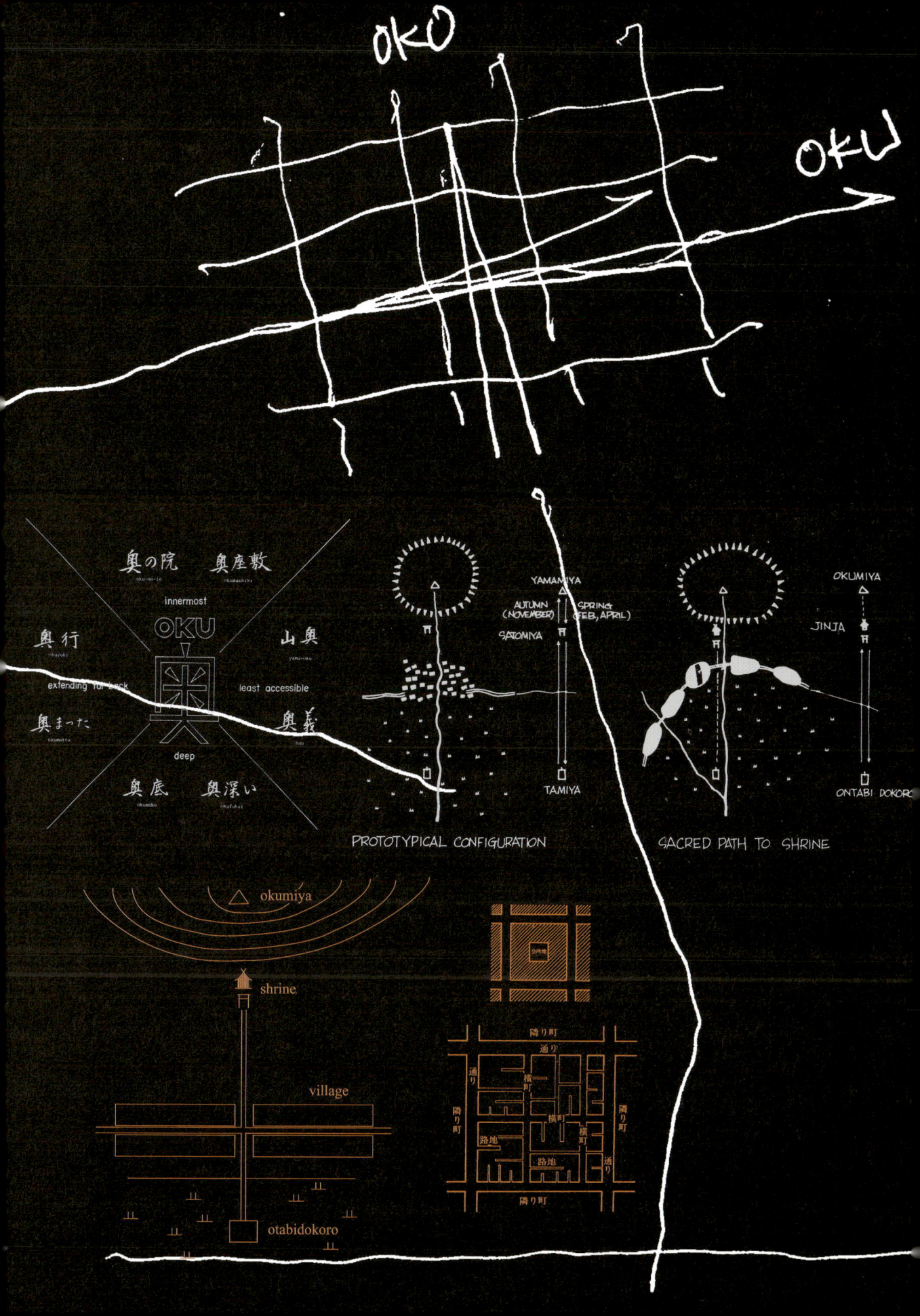

OKU

奥の院　奥座敷
oku-no-in　okuzashiki
innermost
奥行　　OKU　山奥
okuyuki　奥　yama-oku
extending far back　least accessible
奥まった　　　　奥義
okumatta　　　　　ōgi
deep
奥底　奥深い
okusoko　okufukai

PROTOTYPICAL CONFIGURATION

YAMAMIYA
AUTUMN　SPRING
(NOVEMBER)　(FEB, APRIL)
SATOMIYA

TAMIYA

SACRED PATH TO SHRINE

OKUMIYA

JINJA

ONTABI-DOKORO

△ okumiya

shrine

village

otabidokoro

隣り町
通り
通り　横町
隣り町　　　　隣り町
横町
路地
路地
隣り町

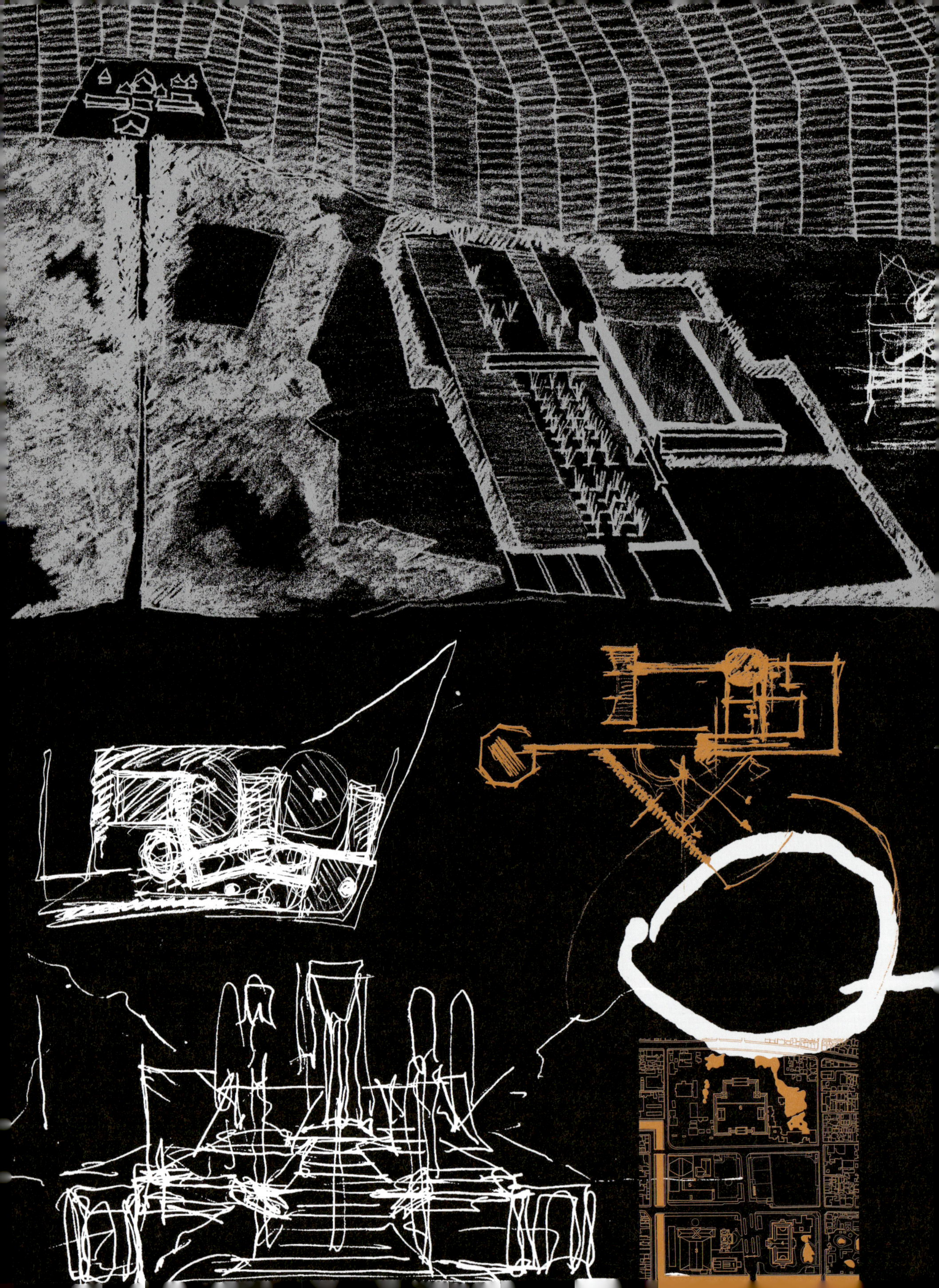

As one of the ways to give
a sense of depth in a given space,
I create several sightline interventions through
walls, screens, and trees.

空間に奥性を与える手法の一つとして、
与えられた空間が示唆する視線の方向に、
壁、スクリーン、時に樹木等で、それをさえぎる層をつくり、
その空間に深みを与える。

Three Paradigms of Collective Form

Linkage performs an important role in connecting heterogeneous elements meaningfully and effectively.

集合体の基本となる三つのパラダイム。
様々なヘテロの形態の集合が、さらに相互の関係性を増大する。
その中でのLinkageの様態の重要性。

- Slab as generator of new urban form for offices

- Use new modern technology. Cantilever.

  Bubble.

- Urban facilities (Communal, Cultural, Entertainment) inter dependent.....

KEIO Fujisawa Campus.

(Fj.).
- Soft spine Dramaturgy.
- 急がず焦らず... 忌む - 8WONT.

- Corner : periphery.

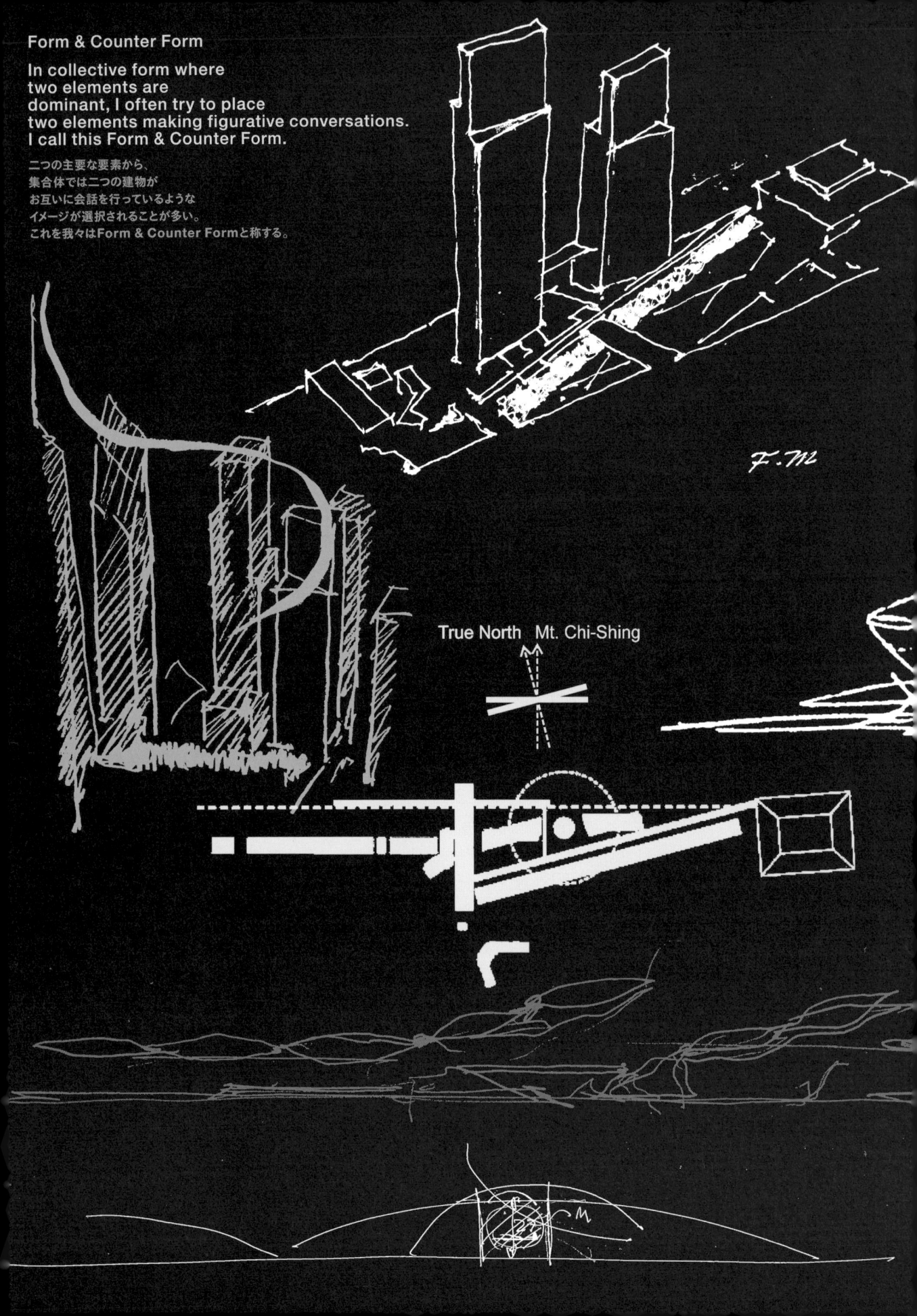

Form & Counter Form

In collective form where
two elements are
dominant, I often try to place
two elements making figurative conversations.
I call this Form & Counter Form.

二つの主要な要素から、
集合体では二つの建物が
お互いに会話を行っているような
イメージが選択されることが多い。
これを我々はForm & Counter Formと称する。

True North   Mt. Chi-Shing

cube

ヒクイ

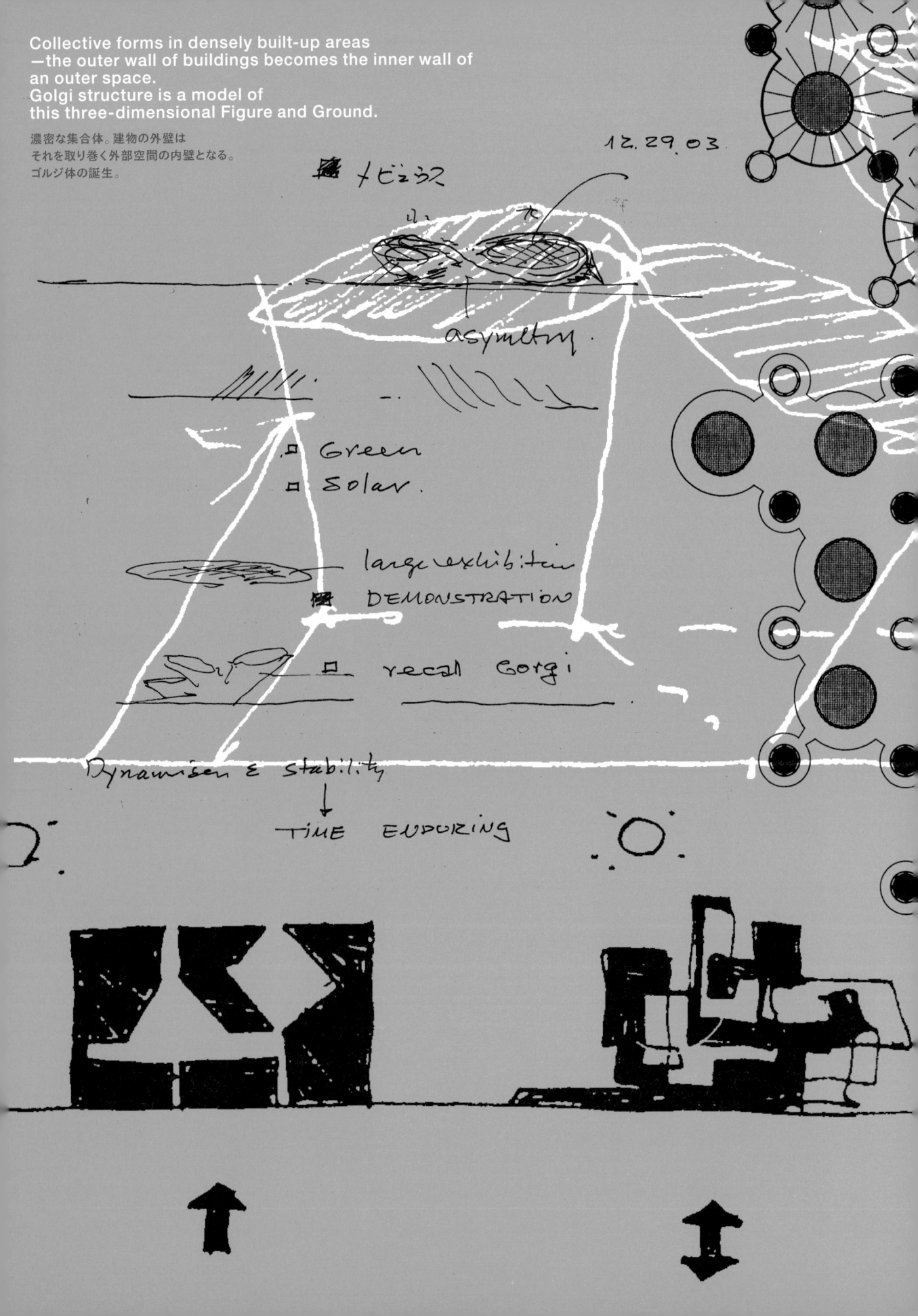

Collective forms in densely built-up areas
— the outer wall of buildings becomes the inner wall of an outer space.
Golgi structure is a model of
this three-dimensional Figure and Ground.

濃密な集合体。建物の外壁は
それを取り巻く外部空間の内壁となる。
ゴルジ体の誕生。

12.29.03

メビウス

asymetry

Green
Solar

large exhibition
DEMONSTRATION

recall Gorgi

Dynamisen & stability
↓
TIME ENDURING

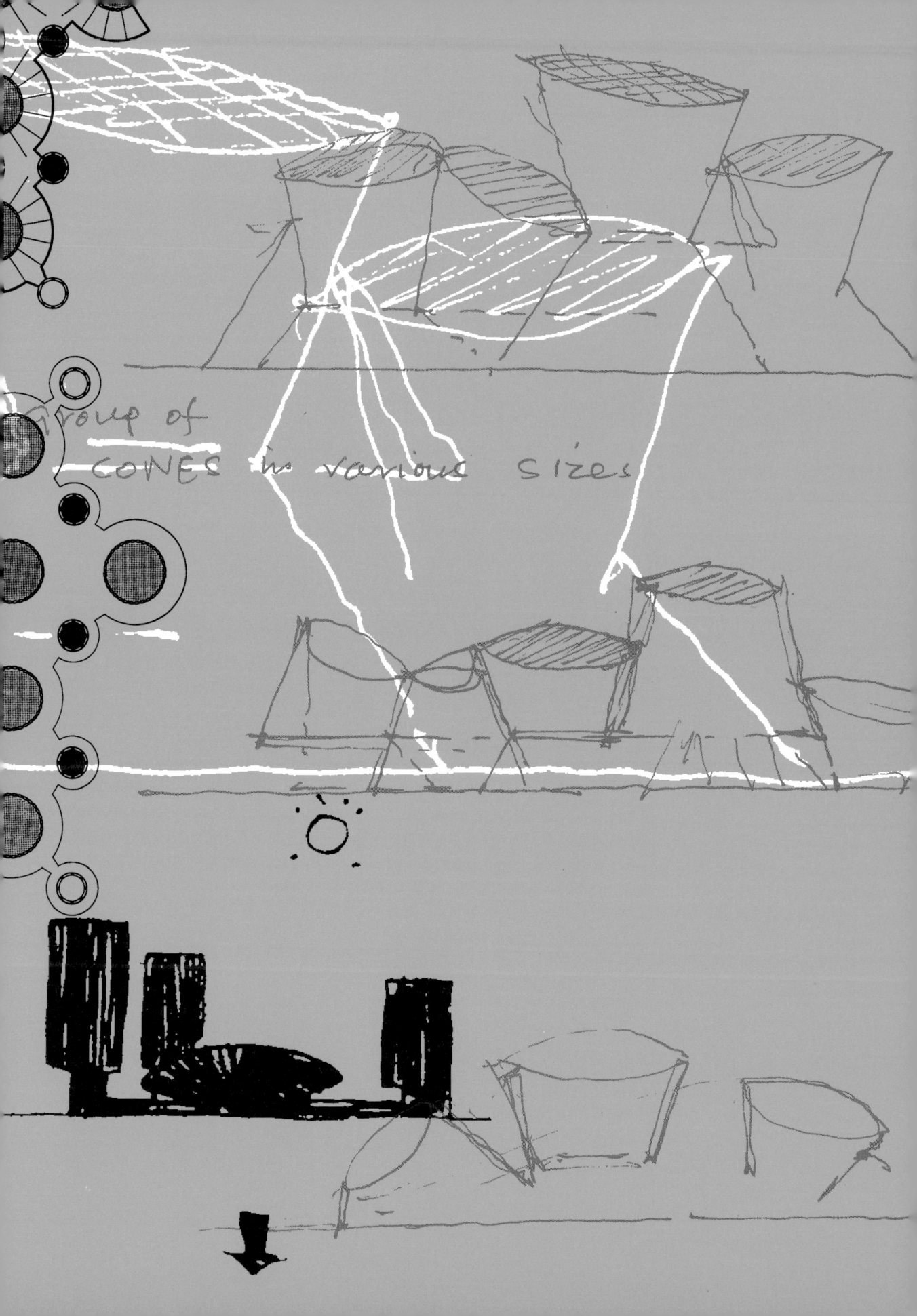

Group of
CONES in various sizes

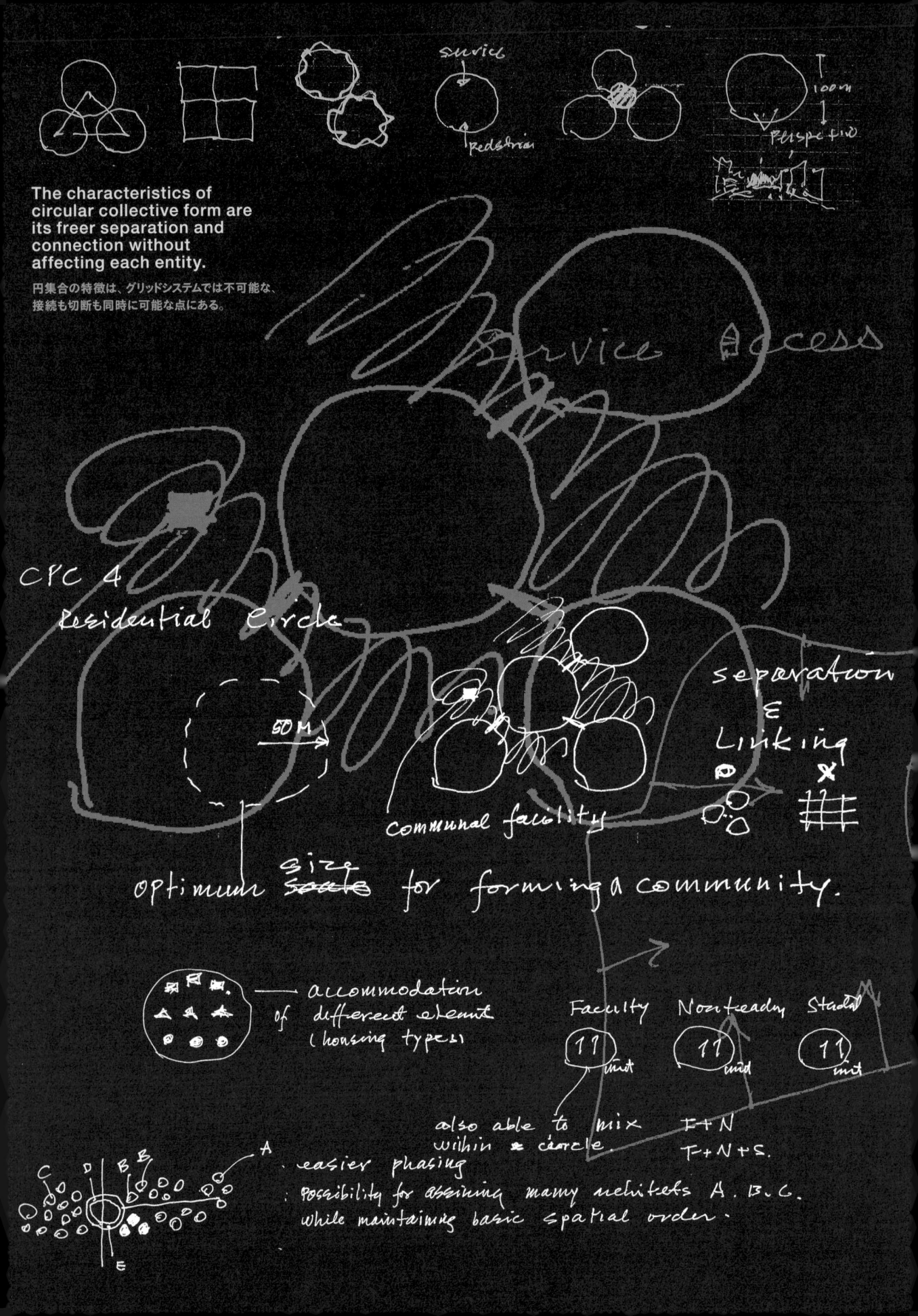

The characteristics of circular collective form are its freer separation and connection without affecting each entity.

円集合の特徴は、グリッドシステムでは不可能な、接続も切断も同時に可能な点にある。

Service Access

CFC 4
Residential Circle

50 M

separation & Linking

communal facility

optimum size for forming a community.

— accommodation of different element (housing types)

Faculty — 11 unit
Non-ready — 11 unit
Student — 11 unit

also able to mix within a circle.   F+N
                                     F+N+S.

· easier phasing
· possibility for assigning many architects A. B. C. while maintaining basic spatial order.

Panorama

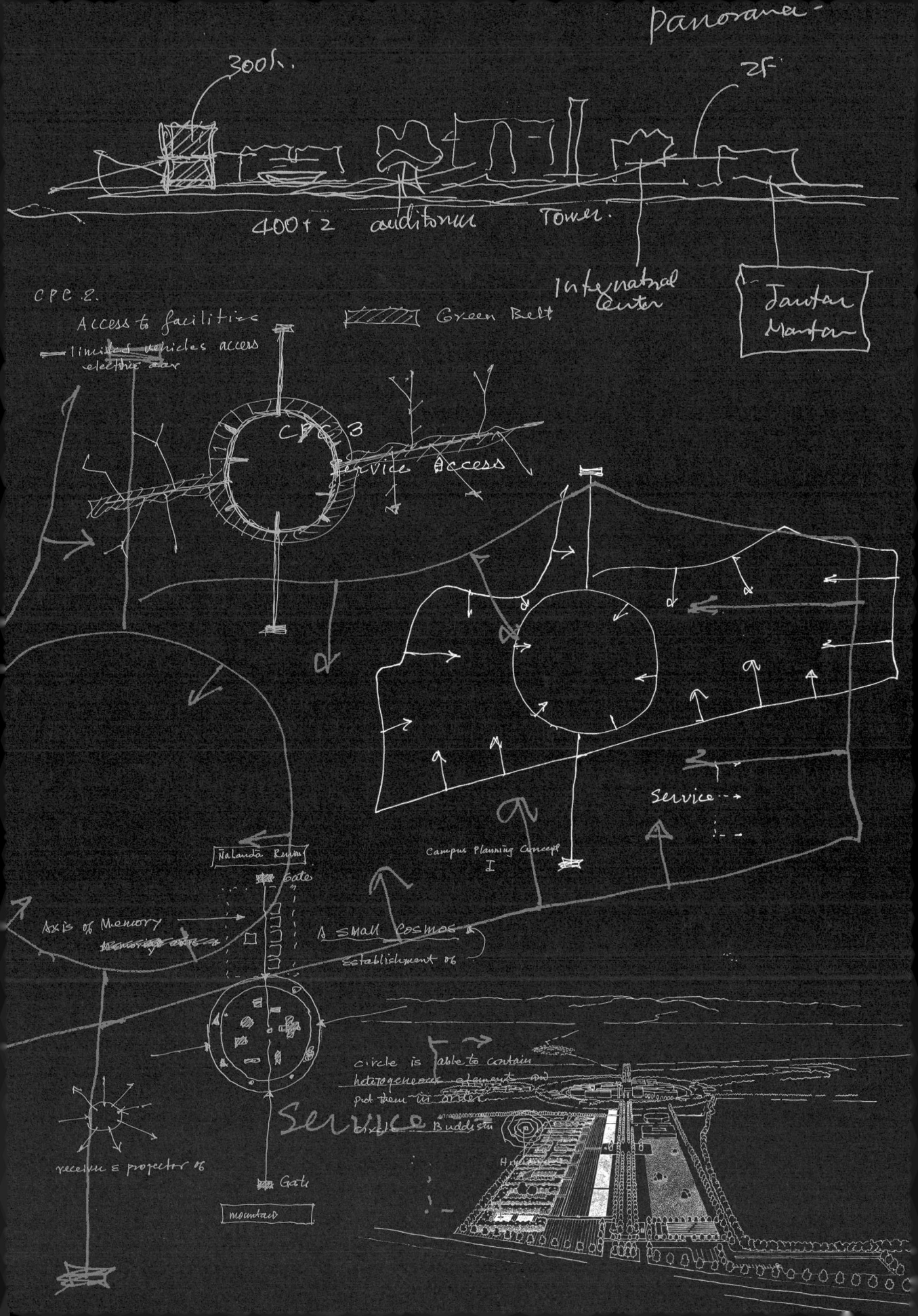

300 ft.

2F

400 + 2   auditorium   Tower.

International Center

Jantar Mantar

CPC 2.
Access to facilities
— limited vehicles access
   electric car

▨ Green Belt

CPC 3
Service Access

Service

Campus Planning Concept I

Nalanda Ruins
Gate

Axis of Memory
Memory area

A SMALL COSMOS
Establishment 06

SERVICE
circle Buddhism

receiver & projector 06

Gate
mountain

circle is able to contain
heterogeneous elements and
put them in order

Collective Form of Open Spaces
The master plan of a city made by open spaces rather than building masses offers a Copernican change in city making.

建築群のあり方が決定する未来の都市ではなく、
広場群が未来の都市の姿を示唆する。
コペルニクス的変革が期待される21世紀。

1 Journey to the West 1959~1960

西方への旅 1959~1960

This was a trip throughout Asia, the Middle East, and Europe more than half a century ago. It was an encounter with cities, architecture, and moreso, with time. Encountering those places again and seeing what has changed and what has remained the same has left a strong impression on me.

今から半世紀以上も前、アジア、中近東、ヨーロッパへの旅。多くのまち、建築との出会いのほか、それは時との出会いでもあった。何故ならばその後、同じまち、建築に再会するたびにその変貌あるいは不変性が強く印象に残っていく・・・。

1959 ——
1960 ╍╍╍

Panathinaikos Stadium and Plaza, Athens
Located at the tip of a T-intersection, the white stadium appears carved out of a hillside from marble. Used in the first Olympiad, its form has not changed since its construction in ancient times.

アテネのパナティナイコ競技場と広場
T字形の車道をいくとその先端に丘をくり抜いた白亜の競技場が現れる。ここで最初のオリンピックが開催された。その姿は今も変わらない。

Chahar Bagh Boulevard, Isfahan
Walkway at the center of a 100-meter wide road. Slightly raised above the level of the road and reserved solely for pedestrians, it seemed like a walkway for the world's most beautiful people.

イスファハンのチャハールバーグ・ブールバード
幅100mの道路の中央を走る歩道。車道より少し盛り上がっている歩行者だけのみち。世界で最も美しい人間のためのみち。

Panathenaikos Stadium and Plaza, Athens, Greece -1960

Chahar Bagh Boulevard, Isfahan, Iran -1959

Hydra Island, Greece -1960

Chandigarh

When I visited, only the office building and the High Court were completed. Strong sunlight was striking the office building's brise-soliel, creating deep shadows.

シャンディガール

私が訪れた時はこの事務棟とハイ・コートのみが建てられていた。強い日射しに事務棟表層のほりの深い陰影が浮び上がる。

Chandigarh, India -1959

Ahmedabad, India -1959

Singapore

I visited Singapore for the first time in 1959. I remember the distinct smells of Chinatown in the center of downtown and the slow rhythm of the ceiling fans in the Raffles Hotel lobby near the waterfront.

シンガポール

1959年、最初に訪れたシンガポール。都心の中国人商店街が発散する特有のすえた臭い。海辺に近いラッフルズホテルのロビーの天井扇風機がゆっくり回っていた。

Singapore -1959

Damascus, Syria -1960

Isfahan, Iran -1959

2 | Memory, Reincarnation, Rebirth
回想・再生・新生

Architecture and human beings share an important similarity: both experience birth and inevitably confront death. However, while human beings cannot avoid their final demise, the life of architecture is sometimes extended— in other words, reincarnated or reborn.

Until a work of architecture is completed, it remains in the hands of architects and builders. But at the instant it is finished, it is handed to its owners, its users, and to society at large— and its fate lies therein. In some cases, life is cut off early (such as the World Trade Center, less than 30 years). In some cases, longer life is ensured via registration as a World Heritage Site. The Parthenon in Athens serves no function today, but has obtained eternal life because of its symbolic value.

I have been lucky to experience several early projects which, after a half century, were either reborn, given new life, or exhibited a graceful maturity through time. My debut work in Japan was Toyoda Memorial Hall at Nagoya University, over 65 years ago. A few years ago, it received a comprehensive exterior concrete refurbishing and interior renovation. In St. Louis, my debut work in the United States (also completed in 1960) was renovated in 1996 as the centerpiece of a larger complex of buildings I also designed— the Sam Fox School of Design & Visual Arts.

The maturing (or "ripening") of a building often occurs where the building maintains a strong relationship to its surrounding context in a natural manner. The Austrian Embassy along a sloping site in Azabu, Tokyo and the Iwasaki Museum in Ibusuki, Kyushu, are good examples.

人間と建築の一生には、似たところがある。そこは生まれがあり、死があるからである。しかし、人間は必ず死を迎えるが、建築は生きながらえるケースは稀ではない。別な言葉でいうならば再生（生きかえる）、新生（生まれかわる）することがしばしばあるからである。

建築は生まれるまでは建築家・施工者の手にあるが、誕生した瞬間、施主のみならずその使い手、さらにはより大きな〈社会〉にその生死が委ねられる。

時にワールド・トレード・センターのように、30年に満たないうちにその生命が断ち切られる。あるいは世界遺産に登録され、より長い生命が保証されるし、アテネの廃墟パルテノンは利用価値はなくてもその象徴性ゆえに永遠の生命を持続している。

ここに収められた私の蒼生の時代のプロジェクトの多くは半世紀を迎えるものも多いが、再生、新生、あるいは成熟と様々な生きざまを示している。

私の日本での処女作、名古屋大学の豊田講堂は完成後、65年目を迎えるが、数年前、外部の打放しコンクリート、内部改装により新しい生命が与えられた。また同じ1960年にセントルイスに誕生した米国での処女作は、その後建設されたSam Fox School of Design and Visual ArtsのComplexの中心的施設の一つとして新しい生命を与えられている。

時に〈成熟〉という表現があてはまる場合もある。それは多くの場合、周縁の環境に自然に融合している場合を指してよいだろう。

東京、麻布の坂道に建てられたオーストリア大使館、あるいは指宿の岩崎美術館はそのよい例として挙げてよい。

University of Tokyo Thesis Project | 1952
I fondly remember locking myself up in my apartment to complete my thesis project—an Art Community Center—submitted in the spring of 1952. The drawings are currently stored at the University of Tokyo's Architecture Library.

東京大学卒業設計 | 1952
1952年春に提出された卒業設計アート・コミュニティー・センターは、一人で自宅の一部屋に閉じこもって仕上げた思い出の多い作品である。現在、東京大学建築学科図書室に図面が保管されている。

Projects at Harvard University Graduate School of Design | 1953
This is a housing project for university staff members, located along Congress Avenue near Harvard University. In contrast to thesis projects at the University of Tokyo, all projects at the GSD required models in various scales. Studio professor, Josep Lluís Sert.

ハーバード大学GSD時代の作品 | 1953
ハーバード大学に近いCongress Avenueのsiteに想定された大学関係者のためのハウジング。東京大学の時と違って、すべての課題に様々なスケールの模型が要求された。指導教官、ホセ・ルイ・セルト。

Picnic with students at Washigton University -1958

Maki with model at Harvard University Graduate School of Design -1953

Studio discussion at Washington University -1958

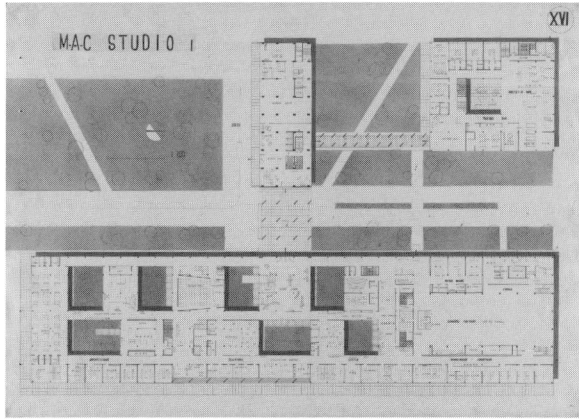

Thesis project at the University of Tokyo -1952

Nagoya University Toyoda Memorial Hall | 1960
This was my first project in Japan. At the time, Nagoya Station could be seen in the distance on the horizon. The design creates a gateway connecting to an open green spine on both sides.

名古屋大学豊田講堂 | 1960
日本における最初の作品。当時、キャンパスのこの場所に立つと、遙か彼方に名古屋駅付近が霞んで見えた。門型のデザイン。両側のオープンスペースを介して後背の緑豊かな空間へと続く。

Aerial view from the north -1960

Maki and building at completion -1960

Concept

Nagoya University Toyoda Memorial Hall Renovation | 2007
This refurbishment was completed 47 years after the building opened. 30mm of the exterior concrete was scraped off and a new 55mm finishing layer with reinforcing was added—reviving the beauty of the original concrete design. The interior was also renovated and upgraded to modern standards.

名古屋大学豊田講堂改修 | 2007
竣工後、47年を経て改修が行われた。外装の打放しコンクリートはその表層を30mm削り、新しいメッシュ筋の上に55mm打増しを行い、竣工時の美しさを取り戻すことに成功。同時に内部も各施設の充実化を図った。

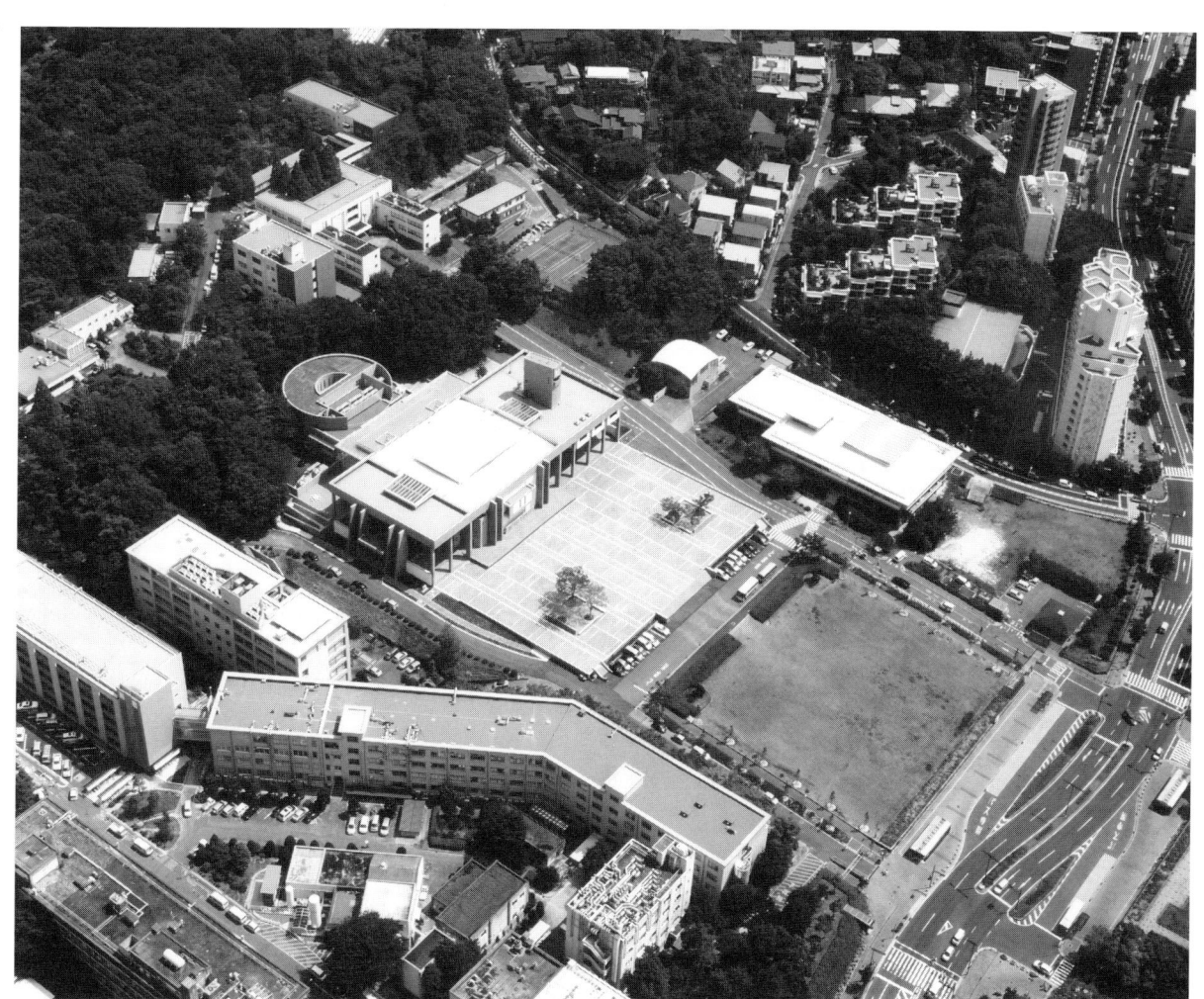

Aerial view from the north -2007 [T.K.]

Exterior view of north plaza -2007 [T.K.]

Washington University in St. Louis Steinberg Hall |1960
This was my first project in the US. It was sited between two Neo-classical buildings. The building is characterized by its folded plate roof with deep overhangs, giving its silhouette the impression of flight.

セントルイス・ワシントン大学　スタインバーグ・ホール |1960
米国における最初の作品。2棟のネオ・クラシックの建物の間に挿入されている。折板構造の屋根が深い軒を形成し、建物のシルエットに飛翔性を与えている。

South entrance to Steinberg Hall -1960

Maki and his drawing of Steinberg Hall -1958

Steinberg Hall during construction

Structural model of Steinberg Hall roof

Aerial view from the west -2006

Model of campus with Sam Fox School in white [T.K.]

Katoh Gakuen Elementary School | 1972
This was the first open school in Japan. On opening day, colorful balloons were released into the blue sky. The interior has not changed to this day.

加藤学園初等学校 | 1972
日本最初のオープンスクール。開校の日、無数の色とりどりの風船が青空に向かって打ち上げられた。その内部の姿は今も変わらない。

Exterior view -1972

The school in use -1972

The school in use -2014

Brasilia Japan Embassy | 1972

I first visited the Brasilia capital city in 1969. In the morning from my hotel, I could see the Plaza of the Three Powers— a modernist utopia. At that time, the embassy surroundings were empty and somewhat desolate.

在ブラジリア日本大使館 | 1972

1969年、最初の首都ブラジリア訪問、朝ホテルからサンクン広場を見る。モダニズムのユートピア。大使館敷地の周縁はまだ荒涼とした領域に過ぎなかった。

Exterior view -1972

Maki's visit to Brazilian National Congress -1969

Interior view of entrance hall -2008

Iwasaki Museum | 1978
This project is near the ocean in southern Japan. It was conceived as a pavilion highlighting the contrast between massive exposed concrete, more delicate lighter concrete, and cross frames that mark openings.

After 30 years, the landscape has matured around the building.

岩崎美術館 | 1978
海に近い南国のプロジェクト。Massとしての打放しコンクリートとCrossのフレームを形づくる繊細なコンクリートの対比のパヴィリオン。Crossはオープニングの象徴。

そして30年後の成熟した建物の風景。

Exterior view -1972 [J.A.]

Exterior view -2010

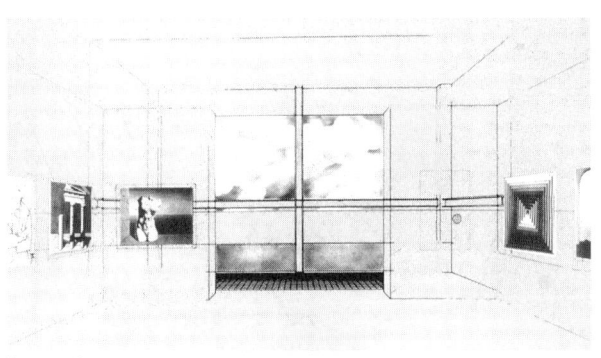

Perspective

Rissho University Kumagaya Campus | 1967, 1968
This was the first example of group form by Maki and Associates.

Several heterogeneous buildings define a plaza. The Station Building along the east edge houses University information and communications, a City Room.

立正大学　熊谷キャンパス | 1967, 1968
槇事務所の最初の集合体。

広場を囲むヘテロな建築群。その東端にあるステーション棟は、大学のすべての情報の発信地、City Roomでもある。

Aerial view from the north -1968 [S.K.]

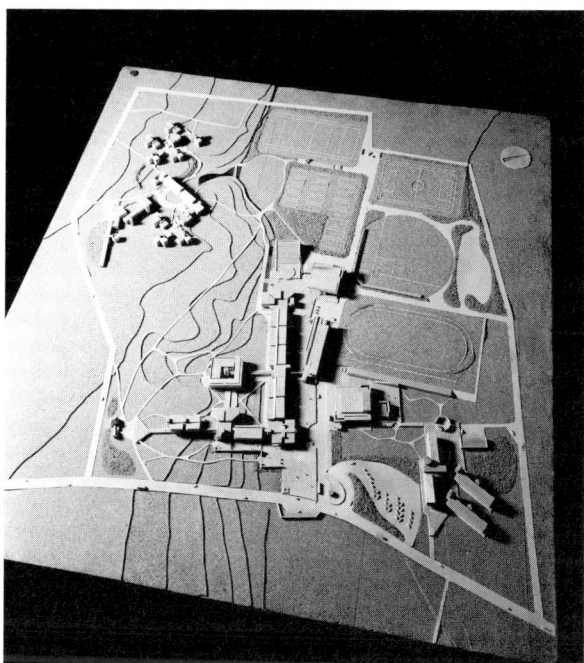

Model of campus -1968 [O.M.]

Exterior view -1968

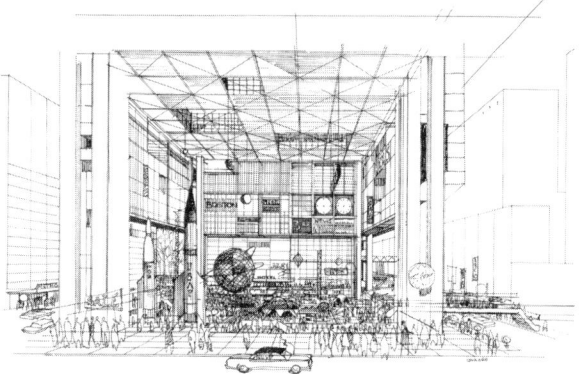

City room concept drawing -1965

National Aquarium, Okinawa | 1975
The building is a collection of arcades enclosing the aquarium functions and a large central tank. Its white block walls shade the strong Okinawan sun, while the pre-cast veranda gives it connections to local traditions. (A portion of the arch assembly has been recreated at the Memorial Park in 2014.)

沖縄国際海洋博　水族館 | 1975
魚の美術館とも称すべき大水槽を中にもつアーケード群。それは沖縄の強い日射しをさえぎりながら、一方特有のローカリティーを示すプレキャストコンクリートでできた縁側でもある。
（2014年に記念公園のパヴィリオンとして一部が再生された。）

Aerial view -1975

Pavilion preserved after demolition -2014

View of the sea -1975

Austrian Embassy in Japan | 1976
An embassy is a large house. The entertainment spaces form the nucleus of planning. Remaining spaces are organized to connect sequentially, including the office block.

在日オーストリア大使館 | 1976
大使館は大きな住宅。接待の客間がその核にある。オフィス棟も含め、空間の回遊性を重視している。

Exterior view of entrance -1976

Interior view -1976

Maki with the ambassador

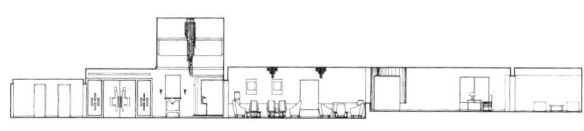

Interior elevation

Exterior view from north -1976

Toyota Kuragaike Memorial Hall | 1974
This is a pavilion in nature. Interior spaces are organized to view and connect to rich greenery outside. The scenery remains intact to this day.

トヨタ鞍ヶ池記念館 | 1974
田園のパヴィリオン。内部の主要空間の視線はすべて豊かな周縁の風景へ向けられている。幸いその風景は今も変わらない。

Aerial view -1974 [T.M.]

Interior view of dining room -1974 [J.A.]

Exterior view of garden -2008

Isar Büropark | 1995

I first learned of the Black Forest in Southern Germany in my middle school geography class. The fact that a green forest was called "black" is mostly what stuck in my memory. A half century later, I was given the opportunity to design an office park in the suburbs of Munich and visited the Black Forest for the first time. The office complex is integrated with a striped landscape that connects it to the Black Forest.

イザール・ビューロパーク | 1995

中学の地理の時間に、ドイツの南部には黒林（Black Forest）があると習った。林は緑なのに何故黒なのかそれだけが妙に記憶に残っていた。半世紀後、ミュンヘン郊外にオフィスセンターを設計する機会を得、その時初めて黒林を訪れた。オフィスコンプレックスのリボン状のランドスケープがそのまま地平線上の黒林につながる。

Isar Büropark and a view of Black Forest beyond -1995 [J.A.]

Black Forest -1989

United Nations Consolidation Building

In the 1970s, one of our good friends had a full view of the United Nations complex from their Beakman Hill residence to the north. Though most people experience the view of the UN from the east, the tall white office building was equally impressive when viewed from the north. Twelve years ago, while considering the expansion plans for the UN, that view helped me understand how a U-shaped plan would result in a better balanced office building than a simpler square building on the given site.

新国連ビル

70年代、ニューヨークの我々の定宿の一つがBeakman Hillsの丘から南に国連コンプレックスの全貌を見下ろせるところにあった。多くの人々は東からその全貌を見ることが多いが、北から見る時事務棟の白い直立した棟が印象的であった。そのゆえか、12年前、オフィスの拡張計画があった時、その棟に凹みのある姿を与えるほうが四角の棟より事務棟とのバランスがよいのではないかと考えた。

View from the East River -2003

View from the Rockefeller's apartment -1970s

4 World Trade Center | 2015

Immediately after the original World Trade Center was completed, I took this photograph of the twin towers silhouetted in red along the Hudson River from the train to Philadelphia. This was before the financial center to its west was built. The strong impression of its simple silhouette remained in my mind when first conceiving the design of 4WTC as a glass sculpture— an homage to the original towers. 4WTC sometimes disappears from view due to the reflective glass used. This reminds us of the original WTC and its short life of less than 30 years.

Twin towers from across the Hudson River -1973

4 ワールド・トレード・センター | 2015

ニューヨークのワールド・トレード・センターが完成直後、フィラデルフィアからニューヨークに向う電車の中から偶然2本のタワーのその赤いシルエットが、ハドソン河に写り込む姿を撮ることができた。左上の写真はまだ西側のフィナンシャル・センターが建設される以前である。その時、印象に残った単純なタワーのシルエットはガラスの彫刻のような4WTCのオマージュと考えてもよいだろう。4WTCは日光のリフレクションによって時に眼前から消える瞬間がある。それは30年に満たない短命の生涯を終えたWTCを慈しむように。

Exterior view of 4WTC by Maki and Associates -2014 [TE.]

Old-Yamate street -1957

Hillside Terrace | 1969-1992

When I was asked by the Asakura family to develop a small corner of their property in 1967, it was just a quiet residential district in Tokyo with light vehicle traffic and a wealth of trees. The site is an elongated property that stretches along Yamate Boulevard over 250 meters, which was a rare piece of land in Tokyo even at that time. The zoning for the site allowed only 150% of the land area to be constructed as gross floor area with a maximum height of ten meters. The site was zoned for first class residential property, which was unique at the time given the 22 meter width of Yamate Boulevard. This was rare for any city in Japan, where the density and land use is typically proportional to the width of the street. As proven later, the entire development was an incremental process, both in time and in program, which took almost a quarter-century to complete the six phases.

In retrospect, I must say that the results of the first phase must have given some suggestion of the forthcoming developments that would occur on the Hillside Terrace property, but nobody, including myself, could have predicted the final results that exist today. Even though the materials and methodologies changed over the years, many of the original design strategies are evident in the later phases of the Hillside Terrace project, which includes humane environments, heterogeneity of expression, corner entrances, circuitous walkways and interplay with trees.

Old-Yamate street -1957

Exterior view of Phase I -1969 [J.A.]

Interior view of Phase I -1969 [K.M.]

The Kameki Tsuchiura House -1935

Coner plaza of Building A -2015

Exterior view of Building A, B -2015

Sarugaku mound -2015

Exterior view of Building C -2015

Courtyard of Building F, G -2015

Exterior view of Building F, G -2015

ヒルサイドテラス | 1969-1992

1967年に朝倉家より小さな角の敷地に設計を頼まれた時、まだそこは閑静な東京の住宅地で、車の通りも少なく、樹木が生い繁っていた。敷地は旧山手通り沿いに250m長く広がっており、当時の東京でも珍しい土地であった。敷地の容積率は150％と小さく、高さ制限も10mと規定されていた。前面道路である旧山手通りの幅員が22mなのに対し、敷地は第一種住居地域に指定されていることも特殊であった。のちにわかることだが、全体の開発は時間・プログラムともに段階的に行われ、全6期が完成するのに約四半世紀かかった。

振り返ってみると、第1期で完成した建物の生み出した結果が、のちのヒルサイドテラスの開発に何らかの影響を与えたことはいっておきたいが、私を含め、誰もが今日ある最終形を予測することはできなかったであろう。使われる材料や手法は時を経て変化していったが、ヒューマンスケールを重視した環境、多様な表現、コーナーエントランス、回遊性のある歩道や樹木との連動といった原点となるデザイン手法の多くは、ヒルサイドテラス後期においても反映されているといえよう。

Alfred Roth: Doldertal Apartment Houses, Zurich -1936

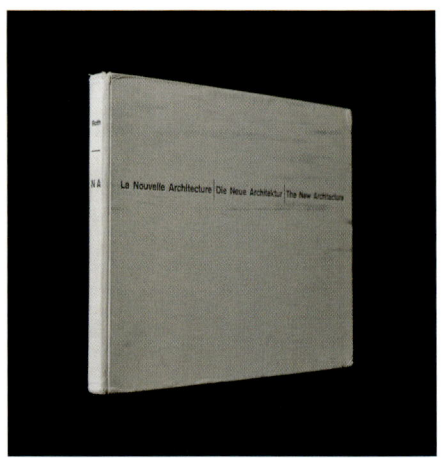

Alfred Roth
"The New Architecture" (1940)

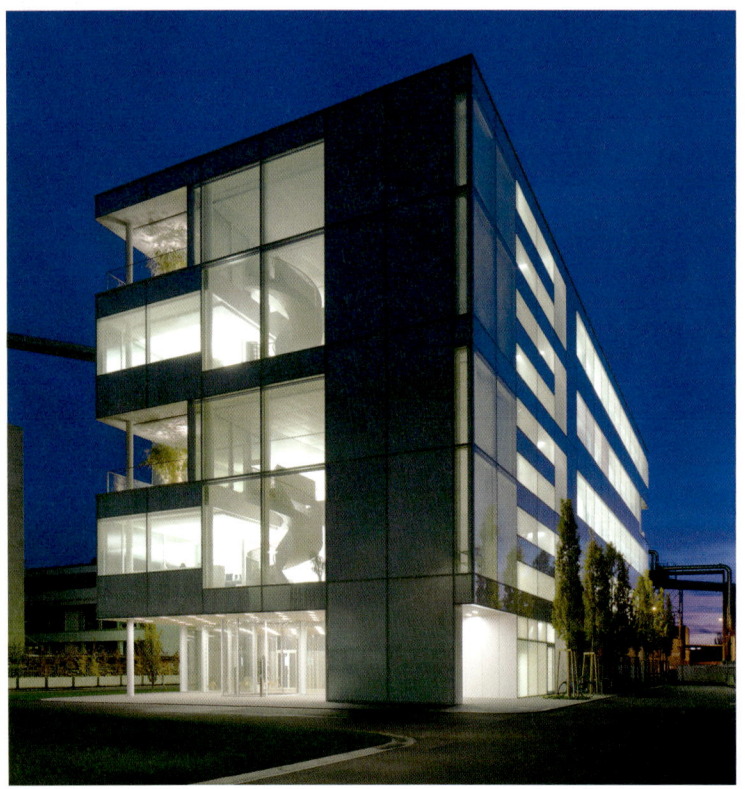

Square 3, Novartis Campus | 2009
As a student of architecture, there were a number of books that served as our bibles – including the works of LeCorbusier and another Swiss book on young architects working in 3 countries across Europe. Amongst the works published there was Junzo Sakakura's Japanese Pavilion for the 1937 Paris Exhibition. Another that left a strong impression among was a mid-sized apartment complex by Alfred Roth in Zurich. Years later, after completing a building for Novartis in Basel, I realize the high level of construction excellence has not changed in Switzerland, keeping the spirit of modern architecture alive.

スクエア 3　ノバルティス　キャンパス | 2009
大学在学中、コルビュジエの作品集と同じように我々のバイブルであった建築書に、スイスから3カ国語で発刊された当時のヨーロッパを中心とする著名な建築家の作品集があった。その中には1937年パリ万博における坂倉準三の日本館も掲載されていた。中でも強い印象を残したものがアルフレッド・ロートのチューリッヒの中層集合住宅である。後年、バーゼルにNovartisの建物を建てたが、この二つの作品を並べてみると、スイス近代建築の背後にある優れた施工精度とそれを支えるスピリットは全く変わっていないことを発見する。

Evening view of Square 3, Novartis Campus -2009 [L.R.]

Chiba University Inohana Memorial Hall | 1963
Similar to the Nagoya University Toyoda Memorial Hall Renovation, this project was refurbished after 51 years with new exposed concrete on the exterior as well as interior upgrades.

千葉大学ゐのはな記念講堂 | 1963
名古屋大学豊田講堂と同様、築後51年、劣化の激しい外装の打放しコンクリート、内部機能の低下に対して改修を行った。

Exterior view -1963 [J.A.]

View of entry -2014 [T.K.]

Yokohama I-Land Tower | 2003

The building that occupies the eastern edge of this triangular site is a section of the 1929 Bank of Yokohama Head Office Annex, originally located several hundred meters away. The Bank was relocated, with a few sections of the exterior and the Bank Hall faithfully reproduced to complete the space, which serves as a multi-purpose hall and community center in Yokohama.

横浜アイランドタワー | 2003

この三角形の敷地の東端を占める建物は、現敷地より数百米離れたところにあった旧横浜銀行本店別館(1929)の尖端部分を移築し、後部の外装部分と1階の銀行のホールを忠実に再現している。現在内部では横浜市のコミュニティー・センターとして多角的な活動が行われている。

Exterior view -2013 [hpb]

Exterior view of original building -1929 [C.Y.]

Interior view of original building

Interior view -2003 [hpb]

Interior view -2014 [YU]

Site plan (original location shown in dotted lines)

PREVI Low-Cost Housing in Lima, Peru | 1972
This is a UNESCO sponsored low-rise housing complex in Peru's capital Lima. The housing project utilized a Self-Aid system, which allows for open development and expansion as family needs change. 40 years later, only one house remains as it was, with other exhibiting a variety of infills, updates, and extensions.

ペルー低層集合住宅 | 1972
UNESCO主催によるペルーの首都リマにおける低層集合住宅。セルフ・エイドのシステムが発達しているこの地域で、家族の発展とともに、増築可能な案が要求された。40年後、1棟を残し、全棟の建増し、外装の更新が行われている。

Exterior view -1972

Exterior view -2014 [KMDW]

Meeting during competition, James Stirling in center

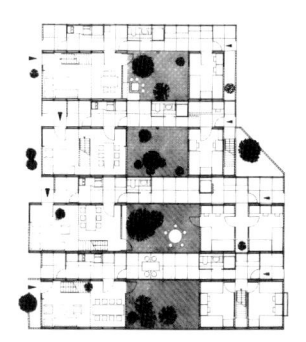

Unit plan

Maki with Kiyonori Kikutake

Floating Pavilion | 1996

The City of Groningen, Netherlands (population approx. 170,000), which once belonged to the Hanseatic League asked us to design the Floating Pavilion. It is used seasonally for many of the city's creative ventures, ranging from festive musical/theatrical performances to tranquil poetry readings. This non-site-specific architecture possesses a commanding presence because of its dynamic and unique form. Transfiguring itself in relation to one's vantage point, it may appear as a snail, a heron or a cluster of clouds. In 2015, the Pavilion was handed to a local maritime school to be used for training and cultural performances.

Floating Pavilion traveling through the countryside -1996

Area plan (route shown in red)

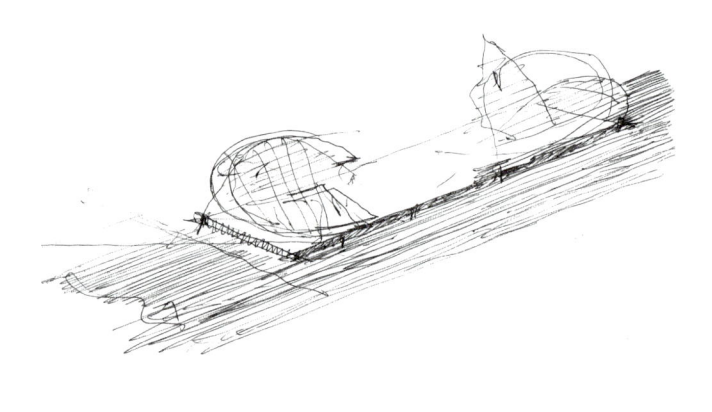

浮かぶ劇場 | 1996

浮かぶ劇場は、ハンザ同盟の加盟都市の一つであったオランダのフローニンゲン市（人口約17万人）から依頼された。期間限定で使用することができるこの劇場では、ミュージカルや劇といった賑やかなパフォーマンスや、静かな詩の朗読といった様々な創作活動が披露された。このパヴィリオンのダイナミックな形態は、サイト・スペシフィックではない建築として、強い存在感をもつ。これは見る者の視点によって、ある時はカタツムリや鷲、またある時は雲のかたまりというように、異なった姿を生み出す。2015年、商船学校の実習船として再生された。

Evening view -1996　　[J.S.]

Night view -1996　　[B.L.]

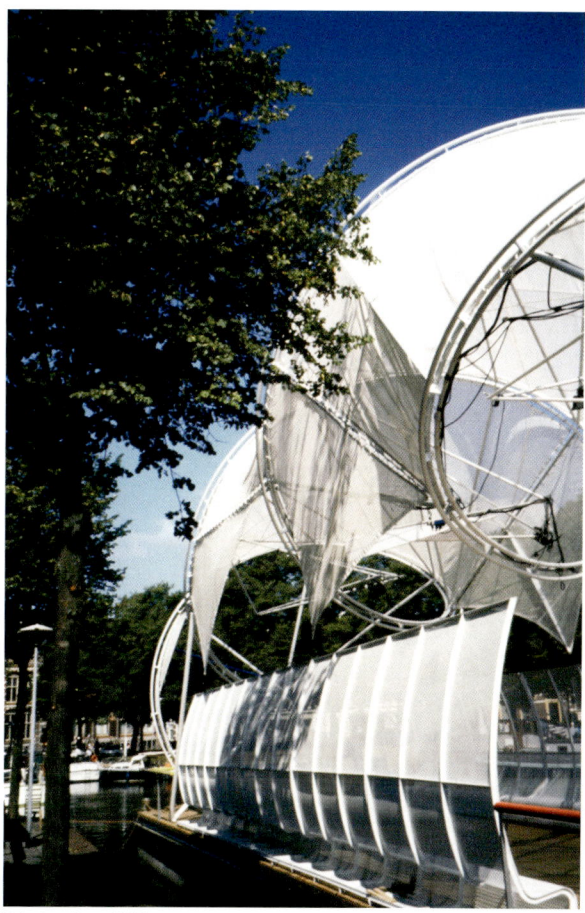

Exterior view -1996

Exterior view -2015　　[Y.Y.]

SPATIAL ENTITY, FIGURE, SIGHTLINES

空間体・姿・視線

Continuous space

Square 3, Novartis Campus

A NEBULOUS WHOLE

SIGHTLINES

Cafe & Atrium
SPIRAL

[T.K.] Esplanade
SPIRAL

Sequential sightlines
Kaze-no-Oka Crematorium

Entrance   Entry porch   Courtyard   Enshrinement room   Forecourt   [T.K.]
Kaze-no-Oka Crematorium

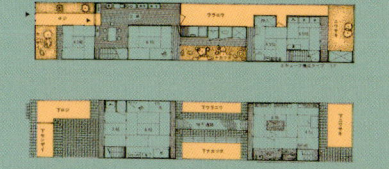

設計の初期段階において、空間体は、内外からの視線によって、ゴムのように伸縮自在である。

Plan of machiya in Kyoto.
Exterior spaces highlighted in orange.

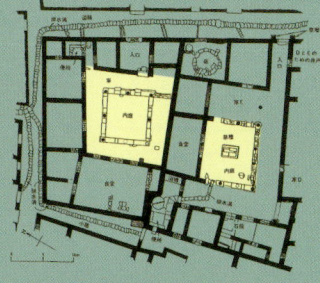

Two houses in the second sector of Delos Island. Inner courtyards highlighted in yellow.
(Leonardo Benevolo. *The History of the City*, 1980)

A spatial entity conceived at the beginning of planning is still elastic, like rubber, expanding or contracting according to pressures by sightlines from both inside and outside.

Agora space
Republic Polytechnic Campus

Central Court
Aga Khan Museum

Centrifugal sightlines
Shenzhen Sea World Cultural Arts Center

Entrance corridor
International College for
Post-graduate Buddhist Studies

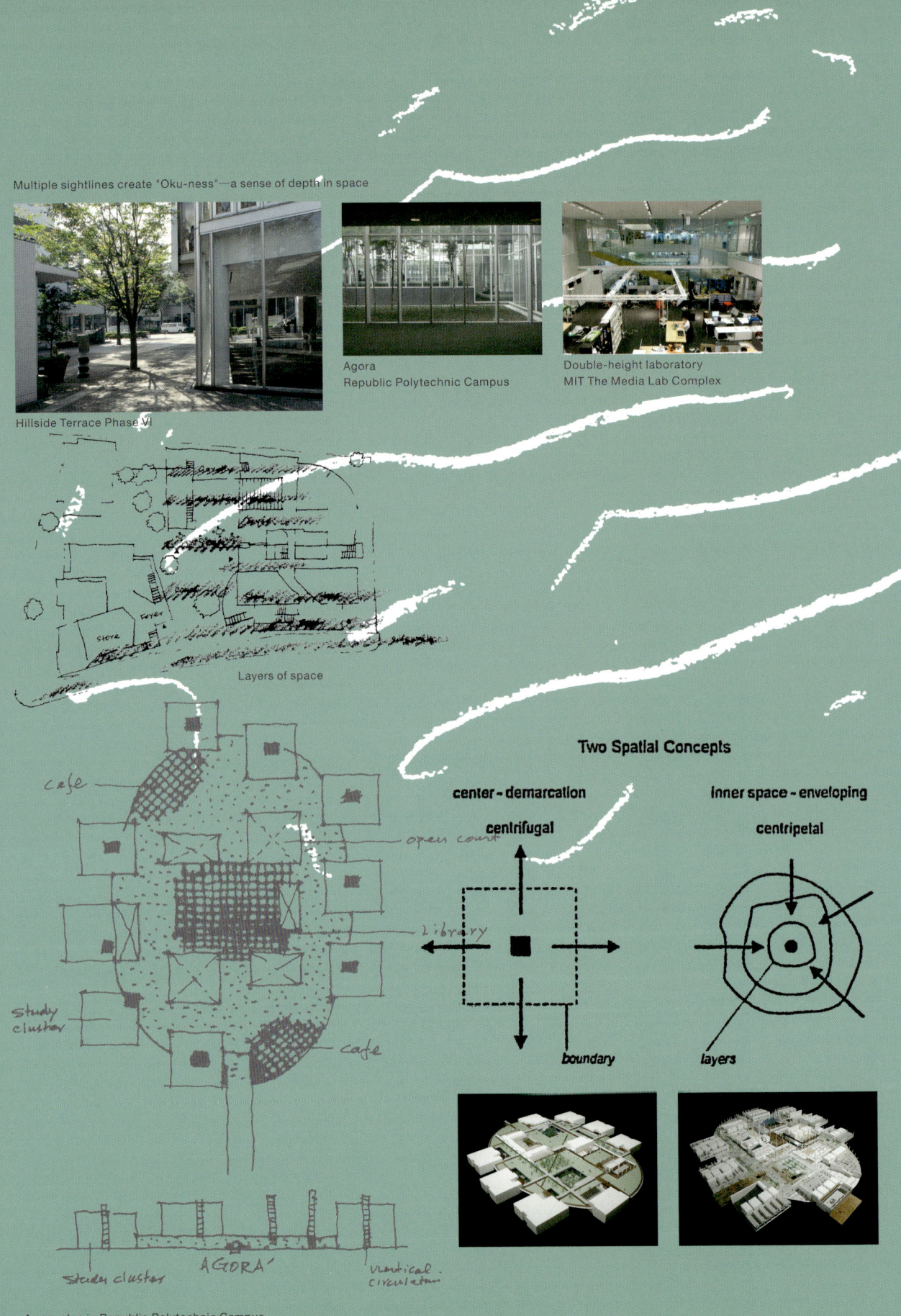

Multiple sightlines create "Oku-ness"—a sense of depth in space

Hillside Terrace Phase VI

Agora
Republic Polytechnic Campus

Double-height laboratory
MIT The Media Lab Complex

Layers of space

Two Spatial Concepts

center - demarcation
centrifugal

boundary

inner space - enveloping
centripetal

layers

Agora plan in Republic Polytechnic Campus

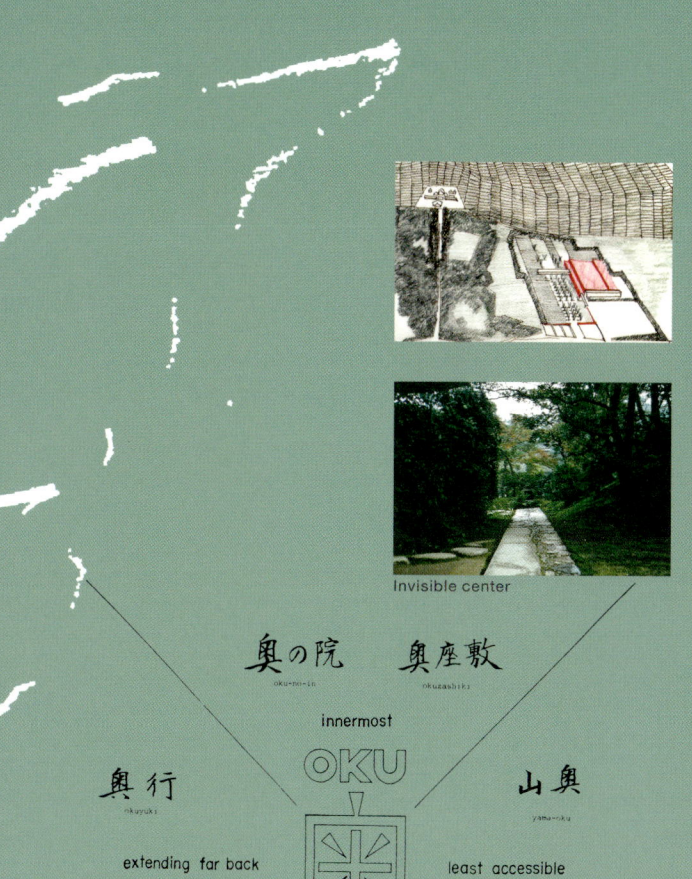

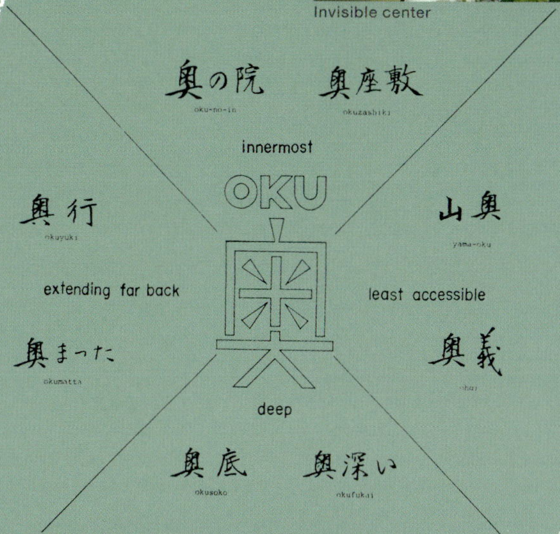

Invisible center

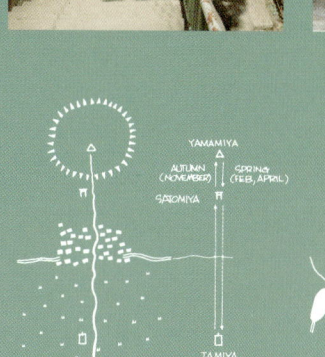

奥の院　奥座敷
oku-no-in　okuzashiki

innermost

奥行　　　OKU　　　山奥
okuyuki　　奥　　　yama-oku

extending far back　　least accessible

奥まった　　　　　奥義
okumatta　　　　　ougi

deep

奥底　　奥深い
okusoko　okufukai

PROTOTYPICAL CONFIGURATION 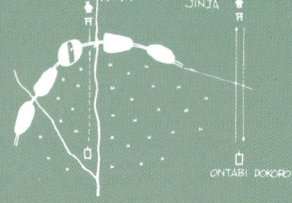 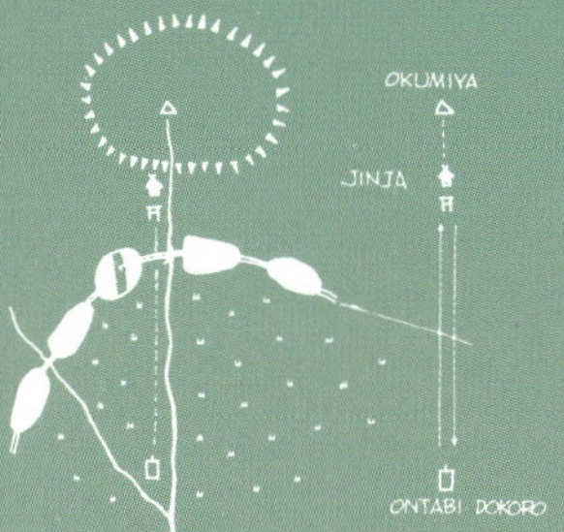　　SACRED PATH TO SHRINE

YAMAMIYA / AUTUMN (NOVEMBER) / SPRING (FEB, APRIL) / SATOMIYA / TAMIYA

OKUMIYA / JINJA / ONTABI DOKORO

OKU = INVISIBLE CENTER
Inner space vs. Center
Envelopment vs. Demarcation

A typical Japanese village at the foot of mountains

間 MA

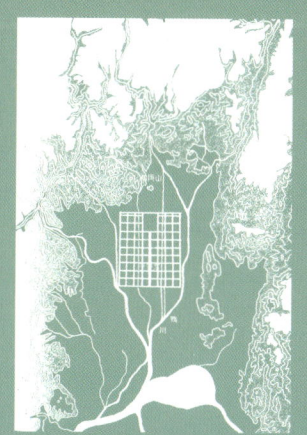

Kyoto in ancient times

TRIAD site model

3 | Spatial Entity, Figure, Sightlines

空間体・姿・視線

In the initial stage of design, I do not think of the building in question as something with a clear form. I think of it as a "spatial entity" (*kūkantai*)—meaning a space wrapped in a closed, curved surface. In my mind, the closed, curved surface is still elastic like rubber; the spatial entity has not yet crystallized into anything definite.

This is because a spatial entity is determined not only from its outer surface but also by the extent and character of the space it encloses. I call this a "nebulous whole". Its manipulation is not done formally, but spatially.

. . .

The important task in this process of spatial manipulation is to construct appropriate sightlines within the spatial entity. Why construction of sightlines? Human beings are unique in the way they feel and act as a result of their spatial experiences. For example, children's behavior is universal, regardless of cultural background or generation. As humans mature, their behavior is controlled more and more by the spatial culture in which they are immersed. It is an enjoyable process for an architect to understand the unique conditions and construct appropriate sightlines within a spatial entity.

In Kaze-no-Oka Crematorium, a set series of rituals is conducted in respective assigned spaces. Here one can experience the construction of sightlines that leads visitors from one space to the next.

In other cases, such as the MIT Media Lab Complex or the Agora at Republic Polytechnic Campus in Singapore, an open environment is sought—such that one can easily recognize location in relation to the whole. In such a case, it is important to construct sightlines in multiple layers. The architecturalization of these sightlines is facilitated by maintaining transparency as much as possible and strategically locating each space.

In "Modernism on the Open Sea", I have mentioned Aldo van Eyck's Amsterdam Orphanage as a good example of construction of sightlines and place.

設計の初期の段階において、私はたびたび対象となる建築の全貌を一つの明確な形態としてとらえるのでなく、ある広がりをもった空間体としてアプローチすることから出発する。この場合、空間体とは一つの閉曲面に包まれた空間を意味しているのだが、意識の上ではその閉曲面はゴムのように伸縮自在であって、決して形態として結晶化されてしまったものではない。空間体を単に外側から決めるだけでなく、そこに包まれた空間は、どのような広がり、性格をもたせるかも重要であるからである。私はこれを「曖昧な全体（Nebulous whole）」と呼ぶ。空間体の操作は形態操作ではなく空間操作なのである。

. . .

その空間操作で重要なことは空間体の中にどのようなふさわしい視線の構築をつくりだすかにある。

何ゆえ視線の構築なのか。

人間は空間の中で見ることによって、何かを感じ、そして振る舞うという特性をもっている。たとえば子供の振る舞いは文化、時代を問わずユニヴァーサルである。その人間が次第に成長するにつれて彼がおかれた特別な空間文化によってその振る舞いが制御されていくこともよく知られた事実である。そうした視線構造の特殊性を前提にとらえられた空間体の中に望ましい視線を構築していくことは建築家にとって楽しい作業である。

風の丘葬斎場ではその中で一定の儀式がそれに対応する空間の中で行われる。一つの空間から次の空間を認識させる視線の構築がそこに現れる。一方、MITメディア研究所、あるいはシンガポールのRepublic Polytechnic Campusのアゴラのように、広がりのある空間の中で常に自分のいる場所と全体の関係が容易に認識されることが好ましいとされる環境では、多層の視線の構築が重要となり、その層に各空間同士はでき得る限り透明な仕切りをもたせ、同時に各空間の上下関係に対しても特別な配置を行うことによって、上述の多層の視線の構築を完成させている。それがそのまま建築化（architecturalization）の作業への移行を容易にしている。『漂うモダニズム』で特にアルド・ファン・アイクの孤児の家における視線と場所の構築を取り上げたのは、その優れた例だからである。

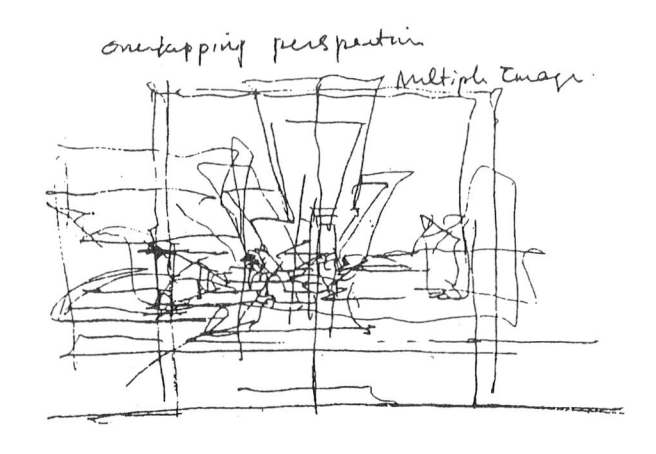

◎Toward Cities　　　　　　　　　　　　SPIRAL | 1985
◎都市へ　　　　　　　　　　　　　　　スパイラル

Elevation facing Aoyama Boulevard　　　　　　　　　　　　　　　　[T.K.]

Before construction

Elevation of Aoyama Boulevard -1960

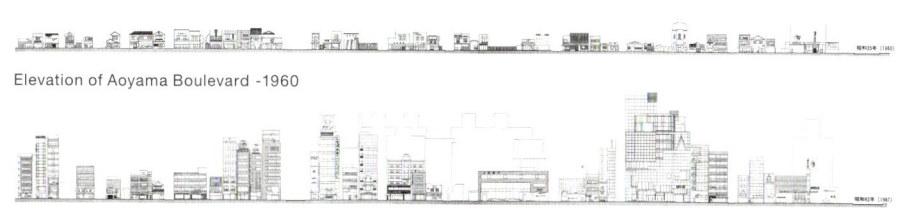

Elevation of Aoyama Boulevard -1987

Since World War II, the Wacoal Corporation has grown into one of Japan's largest manufacturers of women's lingerie. As part of a campaign to improve its corporate image in the early 1980's, the company expanded its marketing program to include fashion, art, and music. SPIRAL was commissioned as part of this effort, intended to serve as an arts center for corporate-sponsored cultural activities while designed to be itself a work of art.

Each floor and space in this complex has its own distinctive character, both in its interiors and facade expression. The first floor opens up to a dimly-lit entrance lobby and café at the center. Past this low-ceilinged promenade, the stepping floors gradually lead to the main installation space at the rear. Skylit by natural light, this semi-cylindrical multi-storied atrium is defined by a gently sloping ramp, resembling a piece of floating sculpture, gradually leading the visitors to the second floor. Visitors may also reach the upper floors

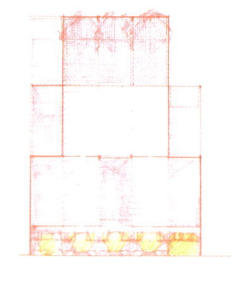

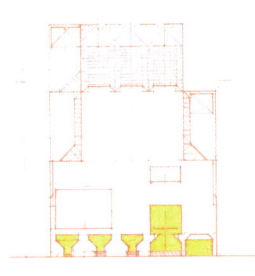

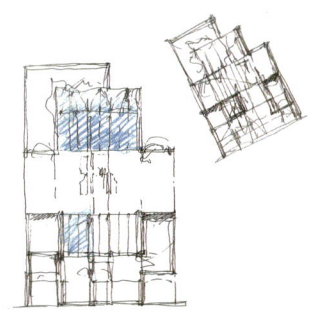

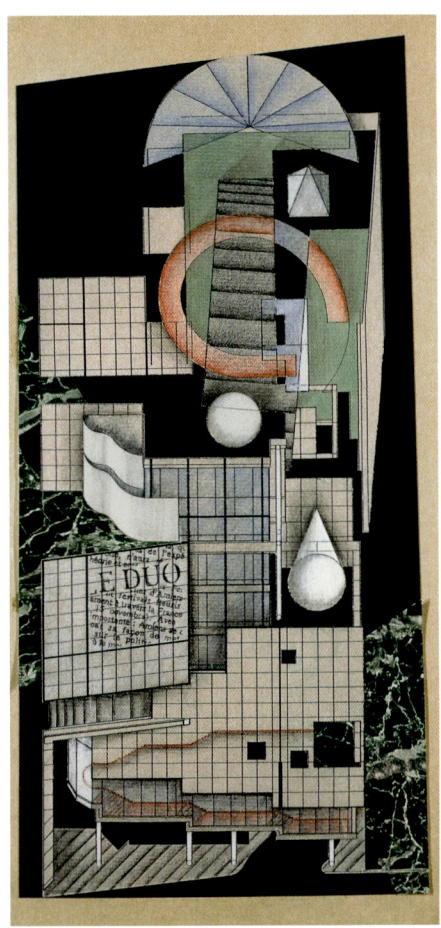

Collage of the facade

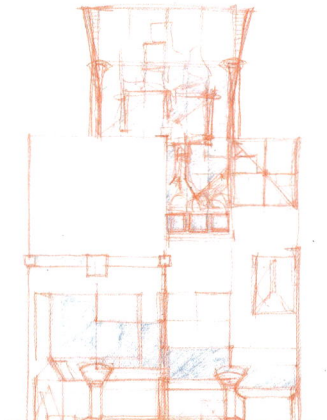

from the "esplanade," a cascade of stairways and landings overlooking the street that continues upward through a high-ceilinged space to the third-floor theater.

Rather than striving for unity through homogeneity, SPIRAL achieves unity through collage. At the very top of the building is the thin lighting rod that completes this ascending movement. The stepped piloti on the ground floor, third floor balconies with sculptures and the cone on the framed terrace create projections and recessions within an otherwise taut building membrane. A variety of materials (aluminum, glass, and stainless steel) are used, but unity is maintained through their honest and direct expression.

The facade provides a comfortable, human scale, yet at the same time the building as a whole stands with strong presence, fitting its location along Aoyama Avenue, one of the most fashionable streets in cosmopolitan Tokyo. This

Roof garden on the fourth floor [T.K.]

Aerial view [S.M.]

Film *L'Année dernière à Marienbad* (1961)

building houses a variety of spaces, but its essential spirit is expressed in its facade. Unlike the facade of a classical building which is usually contained in a set framework, this spirit is borderless, continuously seeking to extend itself.

Stairs ascend from the entrance hall

Esplanade

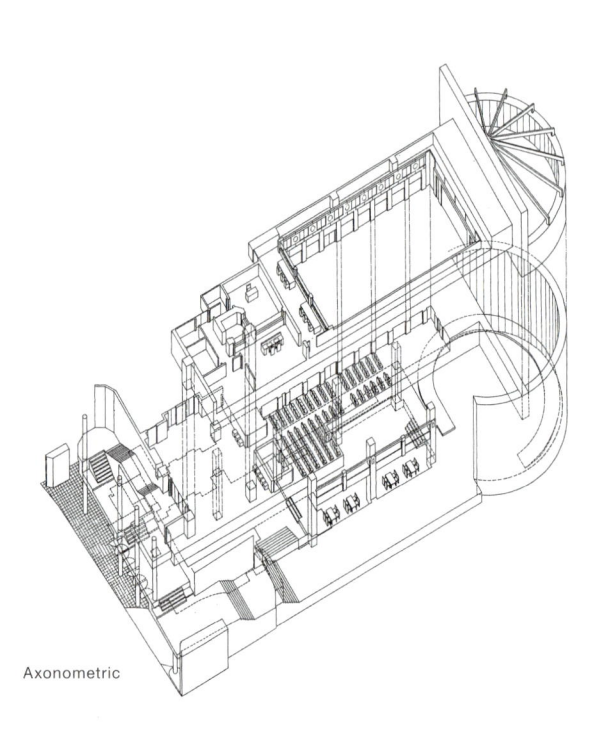

Axonometric

Kozo Nishino Exhibition "空のかたち" (2004) [K.I.]

Thonik Exhibition "en" (2009) [Y.W.]

Fujiwo Ishimoto Exhibition
"Flowers blossoming in textile and ceramics" (2010) [K.I.]

Perspective of atrium

Main gallery and Atrium beyond [T.K.]

第二次大戦後より、ワコールは日本最大の女性下着メーカーの一つとなるまでに拡大した。1980年代にその企業組織のイメージを改善するキャンペーンの一環として、ワコールはそのマーケティング部門を、ファッション、芸術、音楽へと拡張した。スパイラルは、このキャンペーンの一環として依頼され、企業主催の文化活動のためのアートセンターでありながら、建物自体もアートの一作品となるように設計された。

建物の各階、各空間は、それぞれに異なるファサード、内装のキャラクターをもっている。1階には薄暗いエントランスロビーが広がり、中央にカフェが設けられている。この天井の低いプロムナードを過ぎると、階段状にステップする平場が奥のメイン展示スペースへと導く。スカイライトから射す自然光で照らされたこの半円錐状の吹抜けアトリウムは、浮かぶ彫刻のような緩やかな傾斜路によって特徴づけられ、訪問者を2階へと導いていく。また、訪問者は「エスプラナード」と呼ばれる階段と平場の連続する空間を介して上階へ行くこともできる。ここからは外の大通りを垣間見ながら、高天井の空間を上って、3階のシアターに辿り着くことができる。

スパイラルは、均一性によって建物の一体感をつくりだすのではなく、コラージュによってそれをつくりだしている。建物の頂部にある細い避雷針は、建物全体が上昇していくイメージを完結している。1階のピロティ、3階の彫刻バルコニーやフレームされたテラスの中の円錐などは、建物の表層に出っぱり引っ込みをつくりだす。多様な材料（アルミ、ガラス、ステンレス）が使用されているが、このような実直でダイレクトな表現により、建物の一体感が保たれている。

外装は、威圧感のないヒューマンなスケールでデザインされているが、同時に、建物全体として強い存在感があり、青山通りのように東京のもっともファッショナブルな通りにふさわしい装いをしている。スパイラルは、様々な空間を収容しているが、その主要な精神はそのファサードにあるといえよう。クラシックの建物のような定められた枠組みにはまるのではなく、この建物のファサードは自由で、常に拡張しようとしているかのようだ。

National Museum of Modern Art, Kyoto | 1986
京都国立近代美術館

Okazaki Park in Kyoto, marked by the Heian Shrine, houses a number of the city's cultural facilities. Each building is designed in a style reflecting a certain architectural period, and here the New National Museum of Modern Art holds a unique presence in the existing historical context.

As opposed to Tokyo's chaotic sprawl, Kyoto's streets largely follow the patterns of an orthogonal city grid—recalling the city's origin as a new capital, laid out based on models from

South elevation

Perspective diagram

imperial China. The clarity of this grid provided inspiration for organizing the facade of granite-faced precast panels and a curtain wall system composed of both transparent and translucent glass, resembling shoji screens. The 20-meter-tall exterior walls are composed of three layers: rusticated granite base reminiscent of traditional Japanese monumental masonry, pre-cast concrete panels with granite veneer, and aluminum cornice and roof. A hint of classicism can be found in this tripartite division.

The transparent corner towers also hold much significance in establishing the building's identity. When viewed from the canal running south of the site, the corner towers establish a clear separation between the museum and the adjacent Industrial Hall. Such material composition represents various dualities: horizontality and verticality, the present and the past, transparency and solid mass, Japan and the West.

View along canal [J.A.]

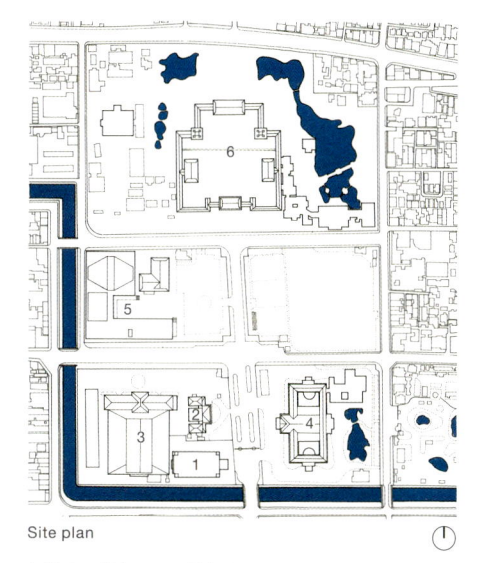

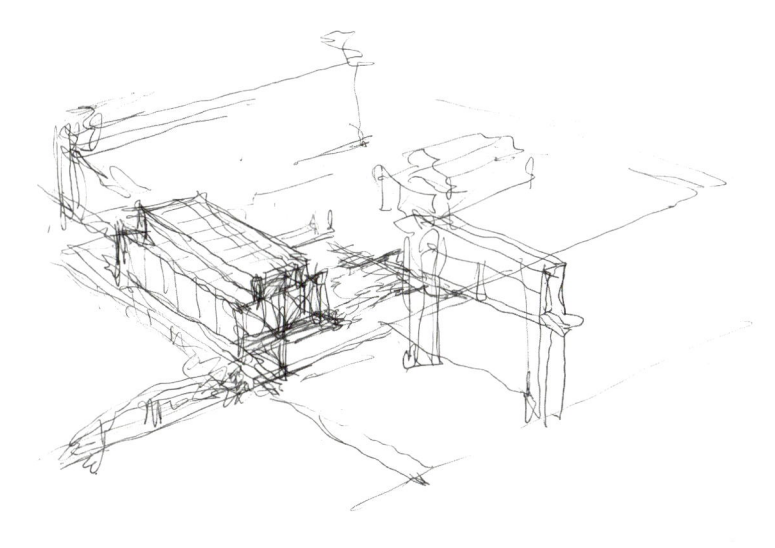

Site plan

1 National Museum of Modern Art
2 Prefectural Library
3 Exhibition Hall
4 Kyoto Municipal Art Museum
5 Kyoto Hall
6 Heian Shrine

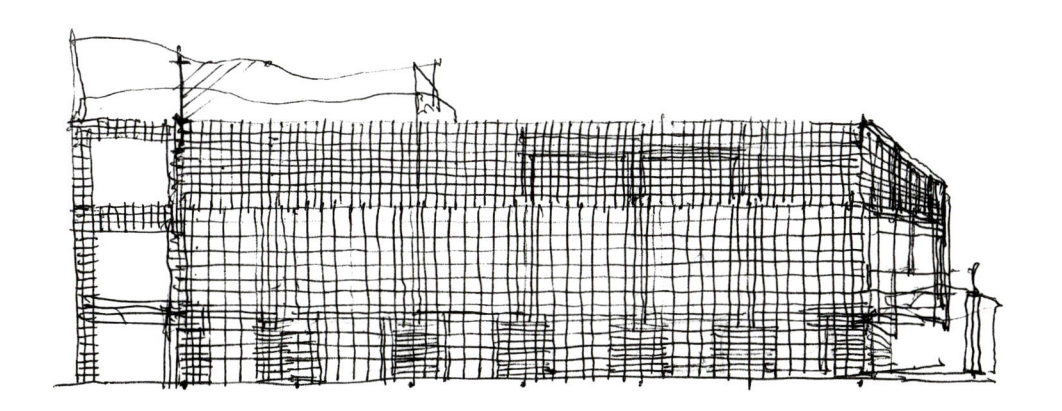

京都の主要な都市文化施設の多くは、平安神宮によってよく知られる岡崎公園の中にあり、それぞれの建物は建設された時代特有の様式をもつ。新しい国立近代美術館は、そうした歴史的文脈の中で新たな独自性を獲得すべく計画された。

無秩序にスプロールした東京とは対照的に京都のほとんどの街路は直交グリッドに沿っており、中国王朝の町割をモデルに新都市として建設された歴史を感じさせる。ファサードを構成する花崗岩仕上げのプレキャストパネル、そして障子を連想させるような透明と半透明のガラスを組み合わせたカーテンウォールシステムは、京都の明快な街路グリッドを一つの手掛かりとしている。高さ20mの外壁は三つの層で構成されている。粗面仕上げの花崗岩による基壇、日本の伝統的な石組みを連想させるような、平滑な花崗岩で仕上げられたプレキャスト・コンクリート・パネル、そしてアルミ製のコーニスと屋根である。こうした三層構成に古典主義建築の美学を感じることもできるだろう。

Main stair in the entrance hall

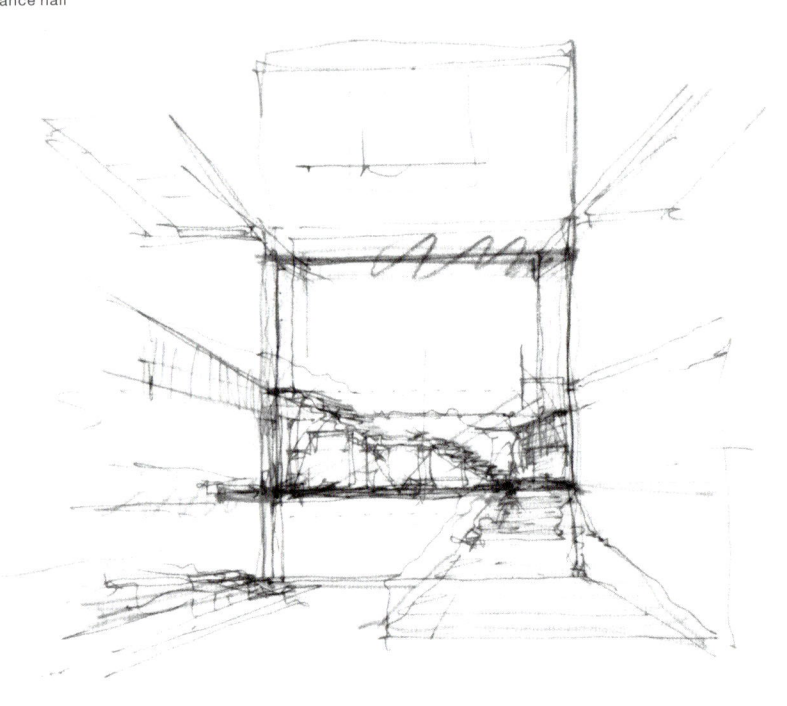

コーナーの透明なタワーは新しい美術館の独自性を主張するうえで重要な役割を果たしている。敷地の南に流れる疎水越しにファサードを見ると、コーナーのタワーは隣接する勧業館と美術館を明確に区分していることがわかる。こうした材料の構成は、水平と垂直、現在と過去、透明と量塊、日本と西洋といった様々な両義性を表現している。

Lobby on the third floor overlooking Heian Shrine -2014

View from the third-floor gallery to stair atrium below

[T.K.]

Tokyo Metropolitan Gymnasium | 1990
東京体育館

The Tokyo Metropolitan Gymnasium is a reconstruction of an older sports facility which had become inadequate in accommodating growing contemporary demands. The grounds for the Tokyo Metropolitan Gymnasium is part of the Meiji Jingu Park, bound by Sendagaya Station to the north, residential and commercial complexes to the south and west, and the National Stadium to the east. Finding such large parcel of open land in densely built Tokyo was quite rare even at this time, and the design takes advantage of its unique

Aerial view [T.K.]

setting by treating the entire site as an urban park.

While the volumes of the individual buildings are constrained, the roof form of each building is given a significant architectonic role— thus continuing the investigations of a symbolic roof that began with the Fujisawa Municipal Gymnasium (1984) and Makuhari Messe (1989). While the Main Arena, Sub-Arena, and Indoor Swimming Pool are all independent in size, shape and form, they are dynamically knit together through the use of modern materials— primarily metal, glass, and concrete.

Model photo collaged on to the city skyline

East elevation

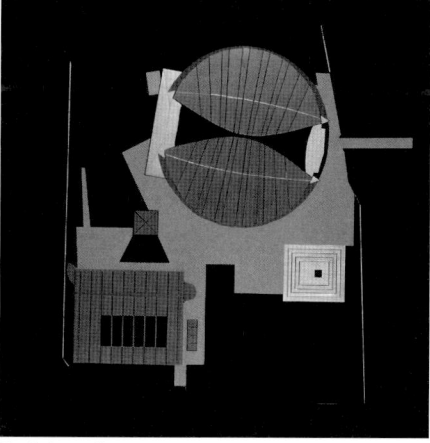

Roof plan collage

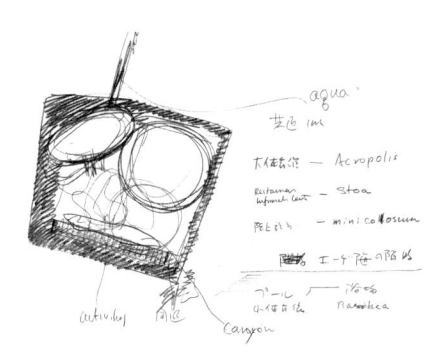

東京体育館は、既存の体育施設が新たな時代の要請に応えられなくなったために、その改築として計画された。敷地は明治神宮の一画にあり、北に千駄ヶ谷駅、南と西に住宅地と商店、そして東に国立競技場がある。密集した都心部においてこれだけの空地を見つけることはこの計画当時ですら困難であったので、空地であるという環境を活かすために敷地全体を都市公園ととらえてデザインした。

地上に現れる建物のヴォリュームをなるべく小さく抑えながら屋根形態に重要な建築的役割を与え、藤沢市秋葉台文化体育館（1984）に始まり幕張メッセ（1989）へとつながる、象徴的な屋根をどのようにデザインすべきかという検討をさらに進めている。メイン・アリーナ、サブ・アリーナ、室内水泳プールは、その大きさ、姿や形態すべてが異なりそれぞれ独立している一方で、金属、ガラス、コンクリートといった現代的な材料を共通して使うことにより各施設をダイナミックに結びつけている。

Interior view of Main Arena

Model

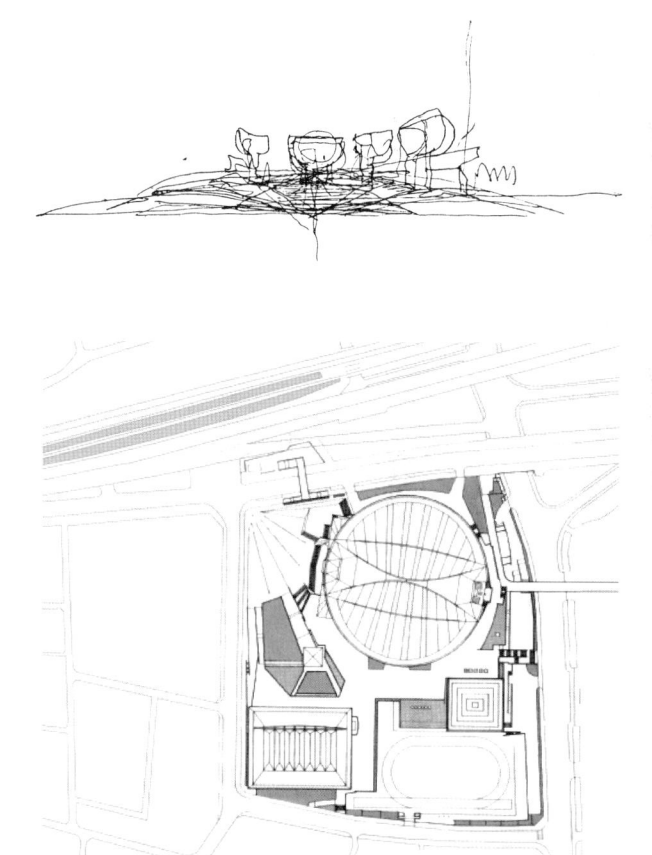

Site plan

Yerba Buena Center for the Arts | 1993
イエルバ・ブエナ芸術センター

Yerba Buena Center for the Arts is Maki and Associates' first building in the United States since Steinberg Hall (1960), and is a part of a major mixed-use redevelopment complex south of Market Street, aimed at creating a new hub of cultural activities as a venue for local artists. Its particular mission is to showcase San Francisco's ethnic and cultural diversity through a variety of art disciplines, providing space for changing exhibitions, installations, and performances of an experimental nature.

View from the public park

Site plan

The building is located atop the Moscone Convention Center with its long span structure; therefore, it has been designed with a steel ductile moment frame to minimize imposed loads and cladded in lightweight materials using roll-formed corrugated aluminum in combination with flat panels. In reference to the industrial spaces to which the participating artists' studios reside and exhibit, the Center takes on an image of an "elegant factory."

The building also aspires to recreate another image rooted in the consciousness of San Francisco and its origins as a port town; its low-profile horizontality, metallic skin, and sculptural elements such as light steel stairs, handrails, and flagpoles all suggest the image of a ship harbored in the gardens, gleaming in the California sunlight.

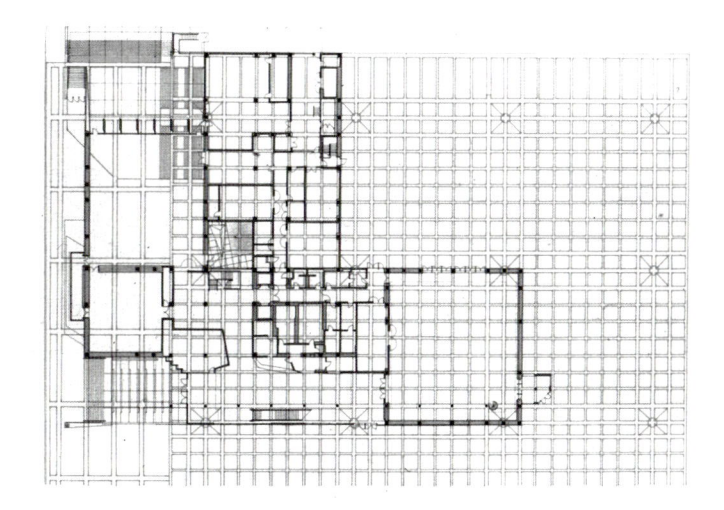

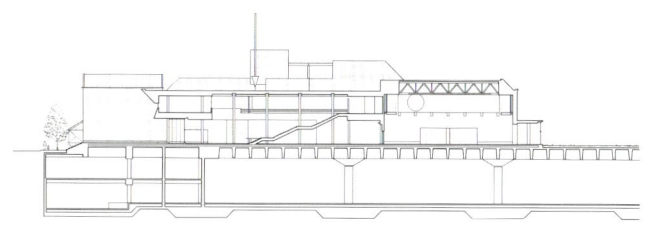

First floor plan and structure grid plan and section

Visitors resting at the entry plaza

スタインバーグ・ホール以降初めて我々が米国で設計したイエルバ・ブエナ芸術センターは、マーケット・ストリートの南に計画された複合用途の大規模再開発の一画にあり、サンフランシスコのダウンタウンにおける新たな芸術活動の中心として計画された。実験的性格をもつ企画展示やインスタレーションを開催し、パフォーマンスも展開できるようなスペースをつくることにより、芸術の多彩な可能性を示し、サンフランシスコの民族的、文化的多様性を表現するという特別な使命を担っている。

モスコーニ・コンベンション・センターの屋根スラブの上に建てられたこのロング・スパンの建物は、構造荷重を最小限に抑えた鉄骨のモーメントフレームの主体構造と、軽量化を図ったアルミの平板とコルゲートパネルの外装によって構成されている。建物内に設けられたアーティストのスタジオや展示のために設けられたインダストリアルな空間から、この建物は〈優雅な工場〉といった雰囲気を感じさせる。

そして、この建物はサンフランシスコの港町としてのイメージも喚起するように

Entrance lobby

計画されている。建物の水平性を強調した低いシルエット、メタリックな表層、そして軽やかな鉄骨階段や手摺、旗竿といった彫刻的要素、これらすべてが庭園に停泊しカリフォルニアの陽光をきらきら反射させた航海客船のイメージを連想させるだろう。

Protruding passage [J.A.]

Gallery 1 [P.P.]

Anteroom to galleries [R.B.]

Tokyo Church of Christ | 1995
東京キリストの教会

Tokyo Church of Christ was designed to rebuild the 40-year old wooden church in conjunction with road expansion for traffic improvement. The church's most urgent need was a significant increase in seating capacity. Over the years the congregation had clearly outgrown the old building, and, hoping to accommodate further growth, the church requested a main hall

Aerial view of the church showing its dense urban context [T.K.]

Site plan

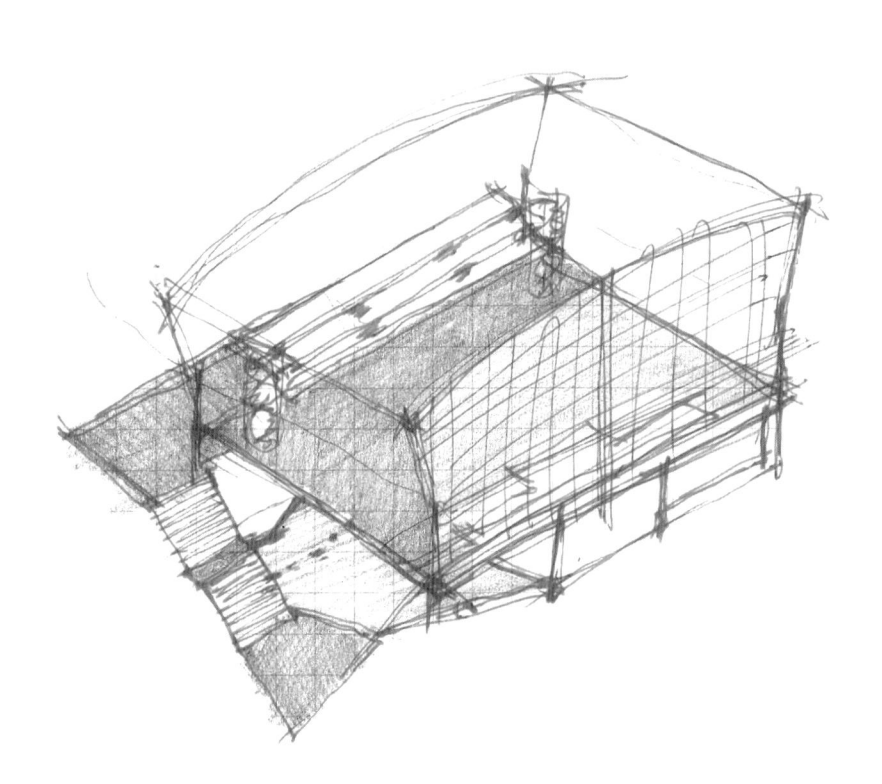

space that would seat 700 people. Requiring a tall volume, the Main Hall was raised up to the second-floor level where its ceiling space could expand freely to create a symbolic roof line for the building. A simple, shallow arch shape appeared in the early sketches as a way of expressing a metaphor for the celestial vault.

The Main Hall was to be filled with natural light. However, the visual chaos of the surrounding city—similar in certain ways to the urban chaos we celebrated in the SPIRAL's facade— here provided unsuitable scenery for a space of spiritual reflection. In order to catch abundant light that would enhance the quiet mood of the hall interior, a translucent wall of light across the front of the Main Hall was devised. Recalling the image of a large *shoji* screen on the interior, the "light-wall" is revealed as a double-layered modern curtain wall on the exterior.

Main Hall [T.K.]

このプロジェクトは、道路の拡幅整備による敷地縮小に伴い、40年間富ヶ谷に建っていた木造の教会を改築するべく依頼された。この計画にあたって最優先された条件は、メインの礼拝堂の収容席数を700席にまで増やすことだった。大空間を要する礼拝堂を2階に上げることにより、空間を自由に拡張できるようにし、それが生み出した屋根線も建物をシンボルづけるものとした。設計初期のスケッチに見られるシンプルでやや扁平したアーチの形状は、天空のヴォールトを表現するメタファーの一つとして考案されている。

メインの礼拝堂は、自然光あふれる空間とすべきであった。しかし、周辺の街がもたらす視覚的なカオスは―スパイラルのファサードで祝した都市のカオスと似てはいるが―ここでは、精神的な瞑想の空間をつくりだすにあたりふさわしくない情景であった。メインの礼拝堂正面に半透明な光の壁を設けることで、礼拝堂内部の静寂なムードを演出するための十分な光を確保することができた。この〈光の壁〉は、内部からは大きな障子スクリーンを思わせるイメージをつくりだしながら、外からはモダンなダブルスキンのカーテンウォールとして現されている。

Evening view of the Main Hall [J.A.]

Jewish Community of Japan | 2009
日本ユダヤ教団

The Jewish Community of Japan is the center of Jewish life in Tokyo. The Community first purchased a house and pool on its current site in 1953, and made an extensive addition in 1979. After thirty years there, the community (with members from over a dozen countries and a fifty-year history) became concerned with structural, mechanical, security, and accessibility issues, and decided to rebuild on the same site.

The site is long and thin (20 meters along the north facing

Evening view from the north elevation

Site plan

Original estate, acquired in 1953

Previous JCJ building, built in 1979

street front and 50 meters in depth) sloping upwards towards the rear. "A light-filled interior" was a strong wish of the client, and became a primary theme of the design. The main approach wraps around the building and up one story, leading to a bright, double-height entrance hall. The exterior is cedar board formed concrete, with the north and south facades clad in patterned tiles. The south garden includes a generous wooden terrace for gatherings.

Programmatically, the basement houses parking and a ceremonial bath. The first level houses a 200 person capacity multi-purpose space, and a formal lounge adjacent to the wooden terrace. The second level houses an 86-seat synagogue, classrooms, library space, as well as the Rabbi residence.

Synagogue looking towards the bimah

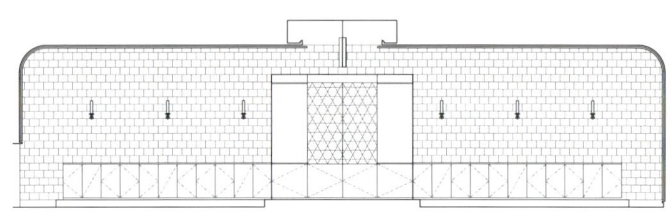

Synagogue elevation

Synagogue in original JCJ -1979

Bracket light

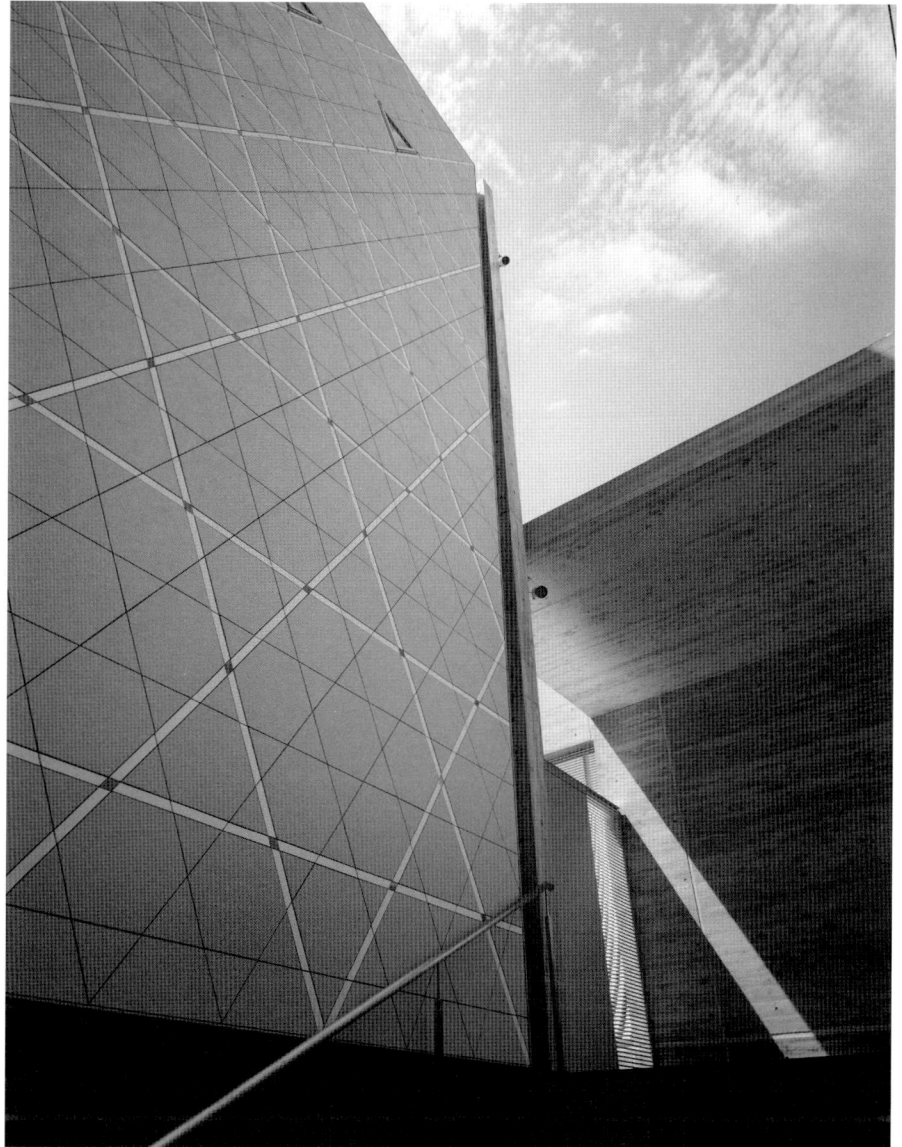

Entrance canopy [T.K.]

日本ユダヤ教団は50年以上の歴史をもつ、日本におけるユダヤ教のコミュニティー・センターであり、コミュニティー・メンバーの出身国は、12カ国以上におよぶ。1953年、現在の場所に住居とプールを購入し、1979年には増築部が完成した。それから30年が経ち、構造・設備の老朽化、身障者対応、セキュリティーなどの問題を解決するため、建て直しが決まった。

「光あふれる明るい室内としたい」という施主の強い要望が、この計画の大きなテーマになった。敷地は北側が前面道路で接道間口は約20m、奥行きは約50mの細長い形状である。メインアプローチは建物の外周を巡って1階の明るいエントランスロビーに至るようにした。外装の主要な部分は杉板本実型枠の打放し仕上とし、北と南のファサードは大判タイルでパターンを構成している。南側の庭はすべて木製でシンプルに構成したガーデンテラスとなっている。

建物のプログラムとして地下には駐車場と洗礼室、1階には200人を収容する多目的室とそれに隣接する厨房、南側のガーデンテラスに面するラウンジが設けられている。2階には86席の固定席をもったこの建物の中心的存在のシナゴーグと、日曜学校のための教室や図書室などがあり、ラビ（宗教指導者）の住居もある。

Rolex Toyocho Building | 2002
ロレックス　東陽町ビル

As a new base of operations in Tokyo, the Rolex Toyocho building includes general office space, watch maintenance and repair facilities, and a school for training maintenance and repair staff. A solid central core ("spine") and a contrasting steel skeleton ("ribs" - consisting of 22 pairs of thin round columns at the perimeter) were utilized to create a clear architectural hierarchy. The thin "ribs" give the building an appropriate spatial rhythm while preserving transparency at the perimeter. The double-skin glazed curtain wall utilizes

North elevation

tempered glass stanchions, adding depth to the facade while maintaining transparency and lightness.

Work space [T.K.]

[T.K.]

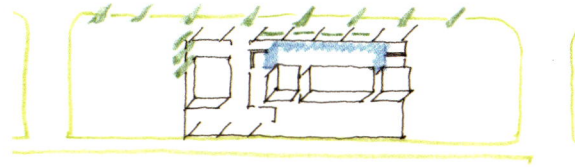

ロレックスが新たな拠点として計画したこの建物には、一般の事務スペースのほかに、時計の修理やオーバーホールのための作業室と、その技術を習得するためのスクールが収められている。この建物の場合、コアの構造体と窓周りの丸柱で骨格には明確なヒエラルキーがある。22対の肋骨は鋼管の独立柱によって極めて細身につくられている。肋骨には空間にふさわしいスケールが要求されるとともに、ガラス皮膜の透明性を大きく減少しないことが望ましい。細い骨には軽やかで薄い被膜がふさわしい。ダブルスキンのガラスウォールは方立てに強化ガラスを使用することで斜め奥行き方向にも透明感と軽さが生まれる。

Cafeteria on the seventh floor

Rolex Nakatsu Building | 2009
ロレックス　中津ビル

The Rolex Nakatsu Building in Osaka is a technical facility serving Western Japan, similar in program to the Rolex Toyocho Building in Tokyo. Watch maintenance and repair require extreme concentration, so there is a corresponding need for scheduled break time. In response to these requirements, the building includes both tightly controlled work spaces and open break spaces. The standard floor plate accommodates the work areas, while the top floors include café, gallery, and open terraces for relaxation.

Evening view from the northeast [T.K.]

Project site before construction

Similar to Rolex Toyocho, Nakatsu has a tripartite structure (base - entrance / body - workspaces / top – break spaces), but also responds to its unique context. The site is tightly bound by buildings on three sides and the Midosuji elevated highway in front, making it essential to limit views from interior to exterior. In response, the glass curtain wall alternates clear glass bands and white ceramic fritted bands, controlling sight lines and field of vision while still admitting ample natural light. A random transparent circular pattern on the white bands adds life to the interior and a sense of expression and movement to the facade as a whole.

Entrance

Cafeteria

Work space [T.K.]

Two-storey atrium [T.K.]

大阪に完成したロレックス中津ビルは東京のロレックス東陽町ビルと同様に時計に関するテクニカルサービスのための施設であり、その西の拠点として計画された。時計のメンテナンスや修理は極度の集中を必要とする作業であり、それゆえに一定のインターバルで休養し、リラックスする時間が要求される。そしてこうした業務の様態に対応し、集中と開放のための相反した空間を用意している。精密作業のスペースが基準階である胴部となり、一方、開放的なカフェやギャラリーがトップの屋根階をつくる。エントランスの基部を含めたこのような3層構成は「東陽町」と相同であるが、その姿の違いは周囲の状況、すなわち場所のコンテクストに起因する。

三方を建物で囲まれた奥に長い敷地と前面に走る高架の新御堂筋を考慮すると、作業に集中するためには視線をある程度制御したい。そのための表層が白いセラミックプリントと透明ガラスのカーテンウォールであり、十分な天空光を取り込みながら視界を限定する。白い帯に穿たれた丸穴は風景をつなぎ、内部での閉塞感を緩和すると同時に、ファサードに表情や動きをもたらす。

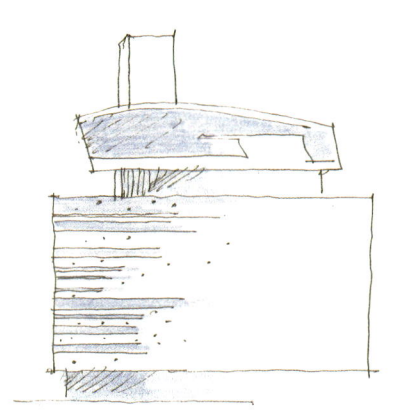

Skyline Orchard Boulevard | 2015
スカイライン・オーチャード・ブールバード

Skyline Orchard is commissioned by Far East Organization, a private developer in Singapore whose aim is to offer bespoke residences for luxury living at a coveted address. This project, perched on a small hill one block from Orchard Boulevard, is a 33-storey residential tower that rises to 147 m.

The building makes use of the site's maximum height allowance by raising the tower 20 m off the ground, ensuring the best views for all units. All four corners have balconies

Exterior perspective

Site plan

designed as outdoor rooms extensions of living, dining and bedroom areas to suggest an open environment that responds to the tropical climate of Singapore.

The first and second floors are layered through a sequential series of unfolding indoor and outdoor spaces reaching into the inner depths of the site. These are organized by the landscape design utilizing a wide variety of plant material, stone, timber and water.

The entire tower is clad in silver aluminum panels providing a sense of luxury and elegance, shimmering in the tropical sunlight. The protruding bay windows and carved corner balconies cast deep shadows on the silver panels to create a distinct character and silhouette that distinguishes the building.

Exterior perspective

Exterior perspective of base

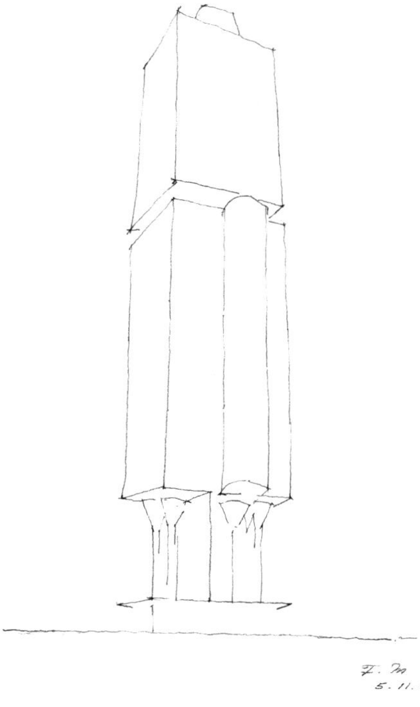

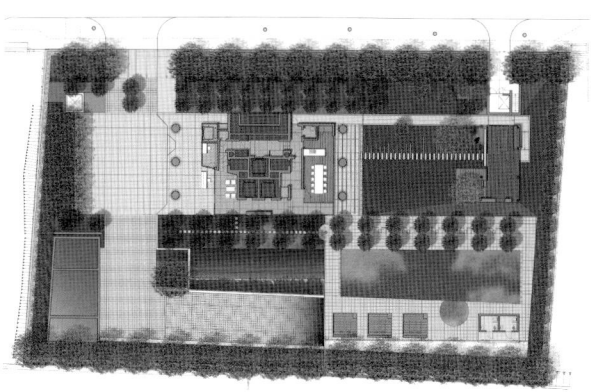

Ground floor plan

このプロジェクトは、シンガポールのディベロッパーから新しい最高級マンション・ブランドを立ち上げるために依頼された。我々の建物は、オーチャード大通りから1ブロック入った小高い丘に位置する、高さ147m、33階建てのレジデンシャル・タワーである。

建物の構成としては、敷地の高さ制限を最大限活用するために住居部分を20mほど持ち上げた形態とし、低層階の住居にも見晴らしのよい眺望を確保している。また、各階4方向のコーナーにバルコニーを設け、その周りにリビング・ダイニング・スペースを配置することにより、屋外リビングとして住人の多様なニーズに対応することができる。

1階では様々な空間が層状に連続する緑豊かなランドスケープを施し、タワーの垂直方向に連続するバルコニーも緑で取り囲むことにより、森の中からそびえ立った緑のタワーとなるよう計画している。また、シンガポールにあるレジデンシャル・タワーの多くが、プラスター吹付け仕上げのファサードとなっているが、この建物は、全面シルバー色のアルミパネルで覆うことで、その存在

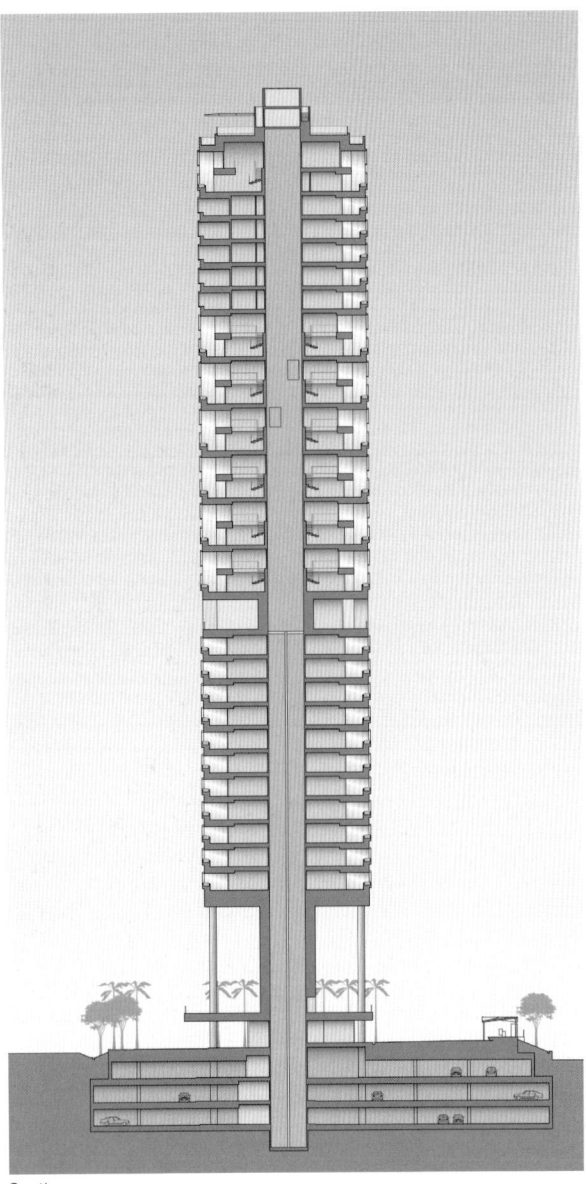

Section

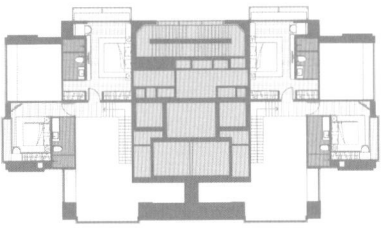

Type C (second floor plan)

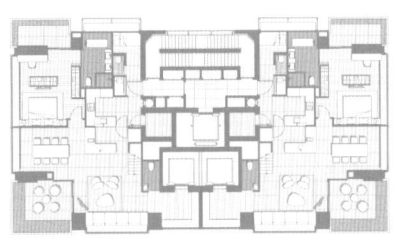

Type C (first floor plan)

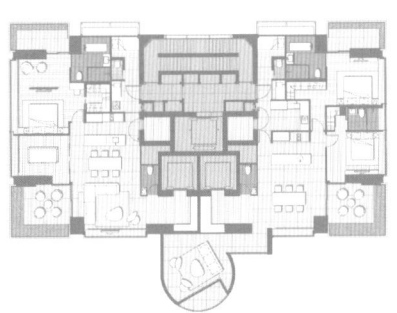

Type A & B (typ. floor plan)

Dining room

感をより際立たせると同時に、移ろいゆく日の光により、様々な表情を醸し
だしてくれることであろう。

Model room photograph

Construction photograph

Nagano City Hall and Nagano Performing Arts Center | 2015
長野市第一庁舎・長野市芸術館

The site is located along a large boulevard defining one of the major urban axes of Nagano City. The building is designed with low eaves along the boulevard and a rhythmically divided facade, in order to establish a human-scale streetscape. Visual transparency creates an active interplay between interior and exterior. This "seeing / being seen" relationship is established via open views of building activity from the boulevard, and open views of the adjacent plaza greenery and the cityscape

Aerial view from the northeast

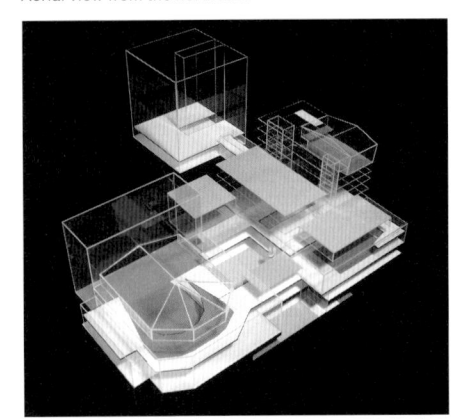

Conceptual model

建設地は長野市の都市軸の一つである大通りに沿っており、通り沿いの軒の高さを抑え、ファサードの分節化によってヒューマンスケールの街並み形成を目指している。通りからは中の様子が垣間見え、中からは広場の緑や街の風景が望める開放的なしつらえであり、建築の内と外で〈見る-見られる〉の関係性をつくっている。また、周辺の公共敷地を含めた整備を念頭に置き、緑豊かで落ち着きのある〈現代の境内〉のような外部空間を市民広場として整備する。

建物は庁舎とホールの複合施設であり、両者は庭をはさんで一体的に連携しつつも、それぞれの特性が読み取れる形態と表情をもたせている。合築の相乗効果によって、より賑わいが生まれるよう、庭を巡る回遊路を設けて相互に利用可能な構成とした。芸術館には、音楽を主目的とする1300席の大ホール、生音の響きを重視した300席の音楽専用ホール、それに演劇を主体とするスタジオ型の小ホールというように特性を明確にした三つのホールと市民の芸術活動を支援する練習室や制作室などがつくられる予定である。

from the interior. In harmony with the public surroundings, we have also designed an adjacent civic plaza as a serene modern "keidai (open space)", rich in greenery and echoing that of the nearby Zenkoji Temple.

The building houses the new City Hall and an Art Wing, organized around a shared courtyard that enhances their respective form and expression. A circulating corridor around the courtyard connects the two towers and further energizes the space. The Art Wing houses three types of halls, each distinct in character: a 1,300-seat music hall, 300-seat music hall designed for live music, and small studio-type hall for plays. Rehearsal rooms and studios are also included, supporting activities of local artists.

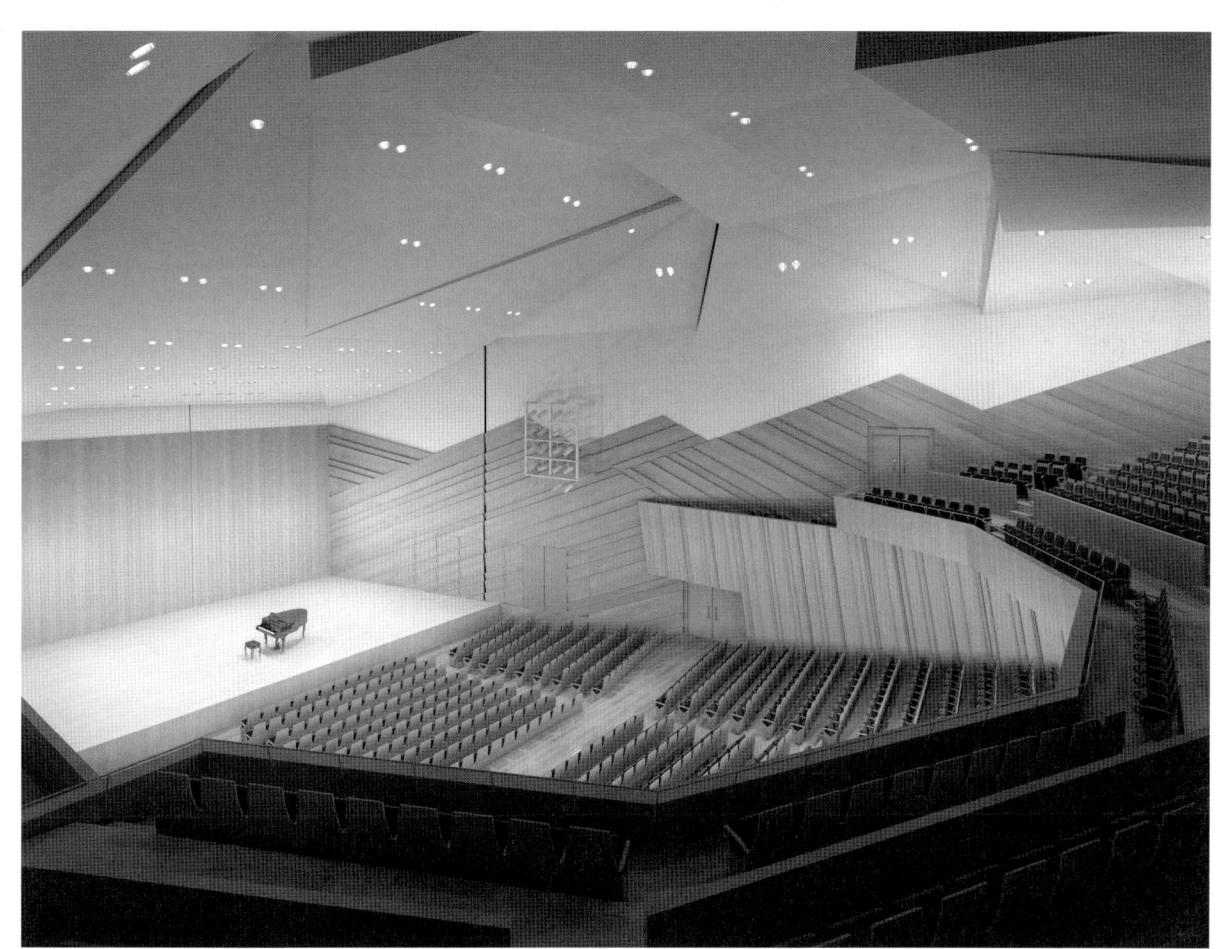

Main Hall

Assembly Hall

Lobby

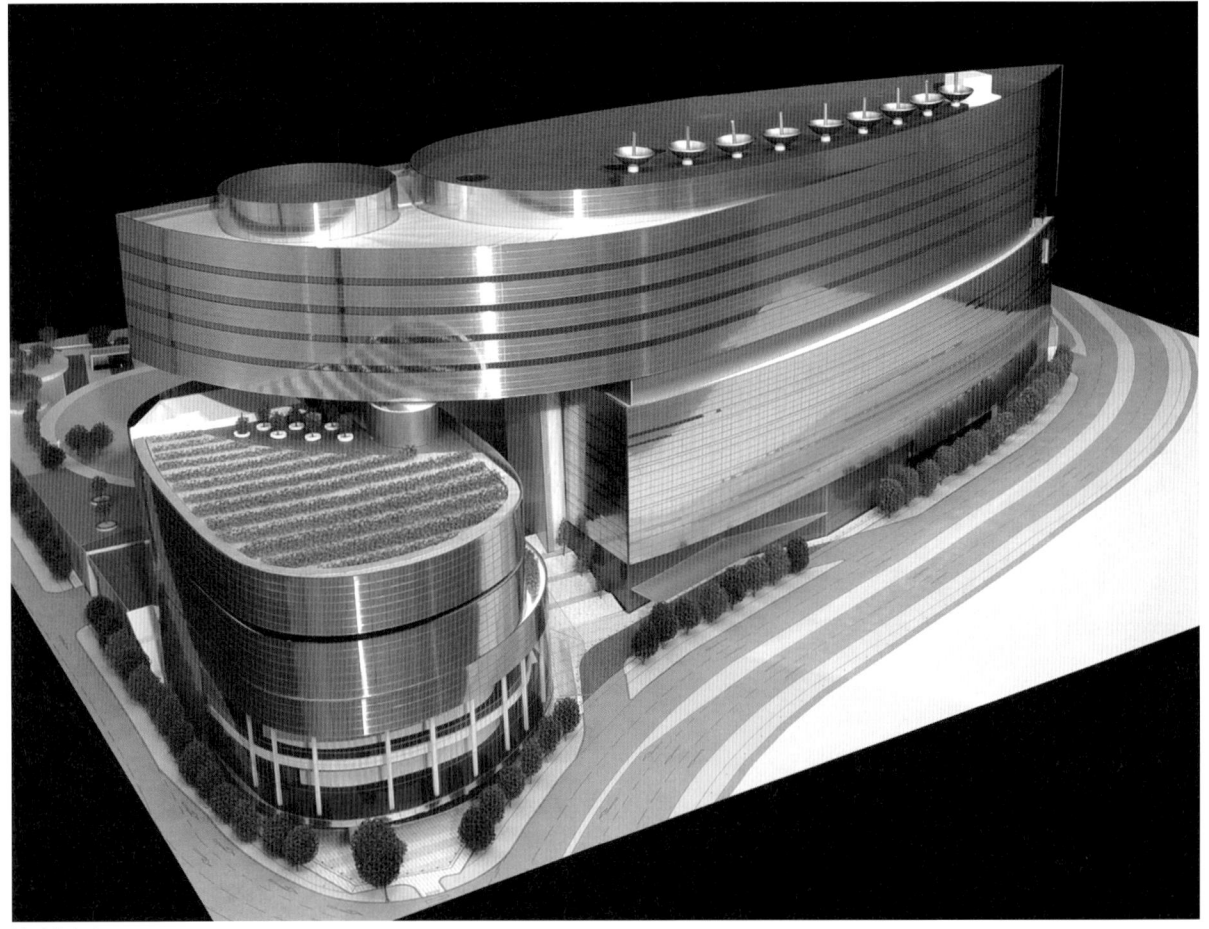

Singapore Mediacorp | 2015
シンガポール・メディアコープ

Model photo

Site plan

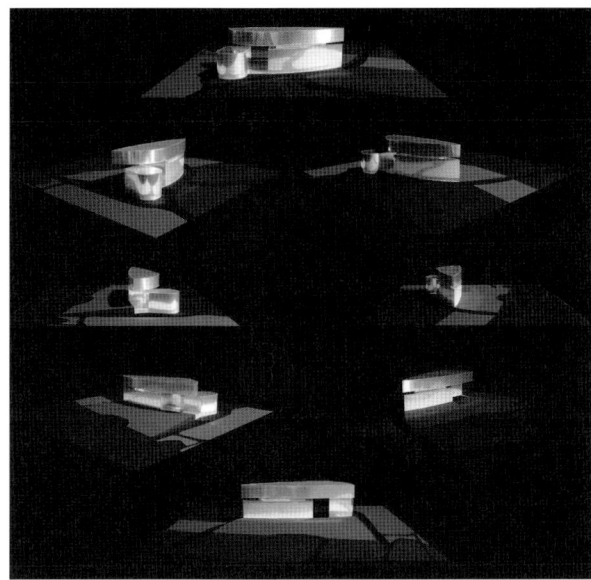

Concept model

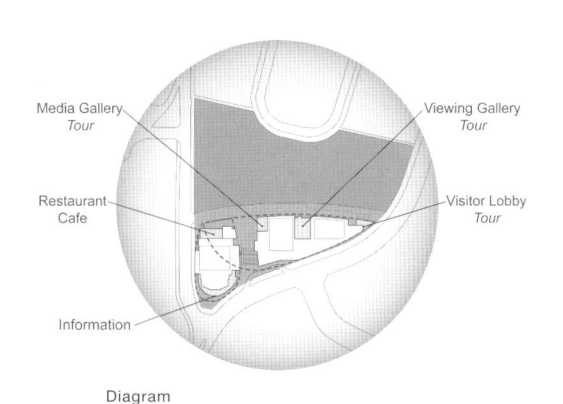

The design for Mediacorp, Singapore's National Broadcast Company, is the winning scheme of an international competition in 2011. Located on a long triangular site at the prominent corner of Ayer Rajah and Stars Avenue, Mediacorp is designed as a gateway to the Mediapolis master plan by Zaha Hadid. The site is also adjacent to a National Park with which the project is fully engaged and integrated to foster synergy.

In addition to traditional broadcast facilities, Mediacorp uniquely integrates active public engagement through a 1,500-seat Broadcast Theatre, Media Galleries, Exhibition spaces and public tours through its studios, newsrooms and radio stations. The Theatre is strategically located on axis from the Fusionopolis MRT Station at the intersection of two cross roads. The formal design strategy provides a unique form and place to each of the three primary programs: 1,500-seat Broadcast Theater, Broadcast Studios and Corporate Offices composed to create a "gateway," a "View Corridor" to the park beyond. The View Corridor is a multi-level public plaza with a Town Stage lined with a Café, Bar, Restaurant, Viewing Room, Theatre Foyer and the Corporate Office Lobby. The central element is grand stairway of 50 steps commemorating Singapore's 50th Anniversary at the time of the opening.

The Broadcast Center is organized vertically on 12 levels above grade and 3 floors below. The two large four-storey tall studios are located at grade level stacked on top with Control Rooms, Editing Suites, Post Production Studios, Media Operations Centre, News & Radioplex and 4 levels comprising the Corporate Offices hovering above. Aimed to become a leading international media company in the production of creative content, the offices for 1,600 are designed as an open collaborative workplace encircling a four-storey atrium.

The building is designed to uniquely be recognized as a facility for media. In addition to its distinctly simple composition and forms, it is clad in specially treated stainless steel intended to reflect and project the surrounding environment, climate, activities and people into its facades. As in the evolution of media itself, the image of the building is dynamic and constantly in motion. At pedestrian grade level, the building is highly transparent with its large glass facades showcasing the activities within to become seamless with the sidewalks, plazas, terraces and park.

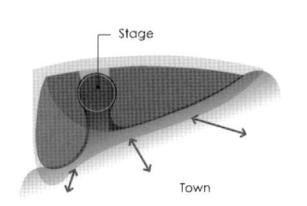

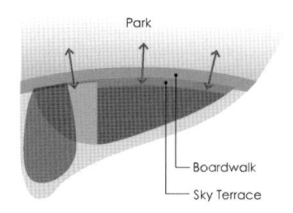

Diagram

Landscape as stage of town

Landscape connecting to the park

Corporate office

Media gallery

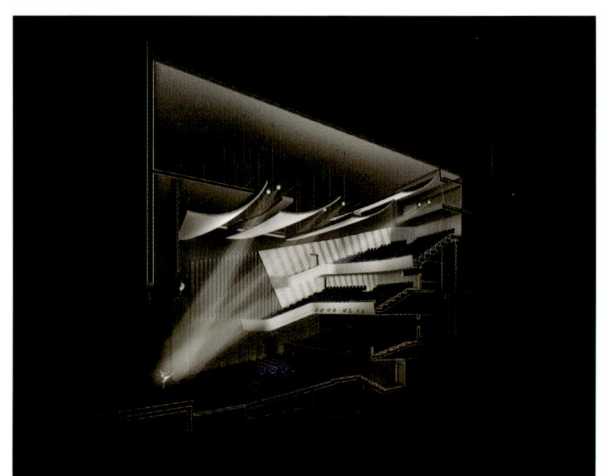

Newsroom

Auditorium

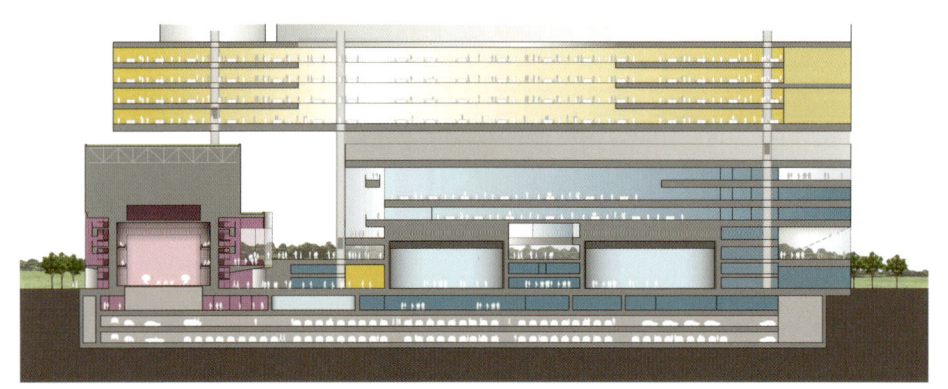

Section

Construction photograph

1 Stainless steel panel
 t=3mm
 bead blasted finish
2 IGU
 8+A12+8mm
3 Low-e coating
 Aluminum coping
 t=3mm
 PVDF, maki silver
4 Weather sealant
 aluminum grey
5 Thermal insulation
6 Structural sealant
 black
7 Weather sealant
 black
8 Extruded aluminum pelmet
9 Extruded aluminum mullion
 powder cated, traffic white
10 10 Aluminum panel
 t=2mm
 PVDF, maki silver
11 Extruded aluminum trim
 PVDF, maki silver
12 Aluminum strip ceiling
 light grey

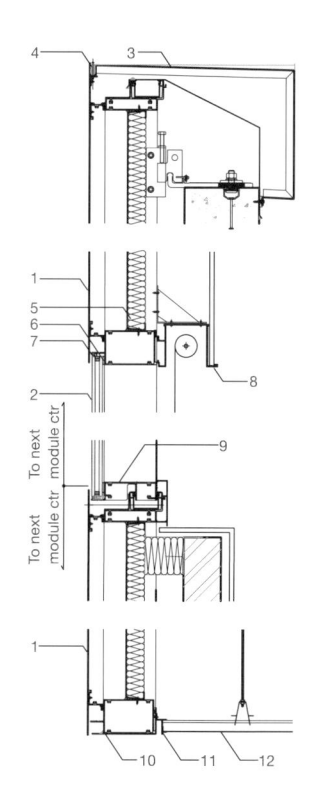

Typical facade detail (scale:1/20)

シンガポール・メディアコープは、国際設計コンペの優勝案である。建物はアヤ・ラジャとウェセックス・リンク通りの角に位置する細長い三角形の敷地に建ち、ザハ・ハディドがマスター・プランナーとして参画したメディアポリスへの門として計画されたものである。また、敷地はナショナル・パークに隣接し、建物と一体的に新たな相乗作用を生みだすことも目的とされている。

従来の放送局施設に加え、メディアコープは1500席のブロードキャスト・シアター、メディアギャラリー、展示スペースを設け、またスタジオ、ニュース・ルーム、ラジオ局等を回遊するパブリックツアーを開催することで、その建物の公共性を積極的に表現している。シアターは、2差路の交点に位置するMRTのフュージオノポリス駅からの軸に沿って、戦略的に配置されている。

形態デザインは、ブロードキャスト・シアター、放送スタジオ、オフィスが、それぞれ独自の形態と場をもち、建物一体として、隣接する公園につなぐ「ビュー・コリドア」と名付けられた門を構成している。この「ビュー・コリドア」は大きな吹抜け空間のプラザと、カフェやバー、レストラン、展望室、シアターのホワイエ、オフィスロビーなどが集まるタウン・ステージで構成されている。またこの空間の主たる要素として、建物オープニング年であるシンガポールの独立50周年を記念し、50段の大階段が計画されている。

放送センターは、地上12階、地下3階に垂直方向に配置さている。二つの4層スタジオが1階に計画されており、その上に調整室、編集室、ポストプロダクション・スタジオ、メディア・オペレーション・センター、ニュース&ラジオ・プレックスと、4層にわたるオフィス階が設けられている。国際的で創造性豊かなメディア・プロダクション企業を目指し、1600人収容のオフィス空間が、4層吹抜けのアトリウムを介して広がり、共同作業にふさわしいメガ・オープン・スペースとなっている。

外装はシンプルな構成と形態に加え、特殊加工が施されたステンレスパネルで仕上げることで、周囲の環境や自然に彩られた景観、さらには気候やそこを歩く人々などの風景を写しだし、それがメディアに従事する建物であることを表現するようなデザインとした。その極めて彫刻的な表層は、光や変化する周囲の状況により刻々と動き続ける。歩行者の行き交う地上レベルでは、大きなガラスファサードによって透明性が保たれ、歩道やプラザ、テラス、公園から建物内の活動を垣間見ることができる。

Shenzhen Sea World Cultural Arts Center | 2016
深圳海上世界文化芸術中心

China Merchants Property Development Co., Ltd. (CMPD) is one of the most revered real estate companies with the longest history in China. The company has been energetically developing in the Shekou peninsula area in Shenzhen for over the last few decades.

In late 2011 we were invited to undertake our first project in China: a cultural center that would serve as the core of Sea World's comprehensive office, retail, and residential

Aerial view from park

development. The site of Shenzhen Sea World Cultural Arts Center is one of the most spectacular ones in Shekou peninsula with beautiful views of Hong Kong Island over the frontal waterway. The Center is intended to house an exhibition space, a theatre, museums, private galleries, and members clubs with retail facilities related to cultural activities.

The formal composition of the project suggests its dynamic relationship with the water, the adjacent park, and the mountains to the northwest. The total floor area is approximately 70,000㎡ and the project is expected to be complete in 2016.

Site plan

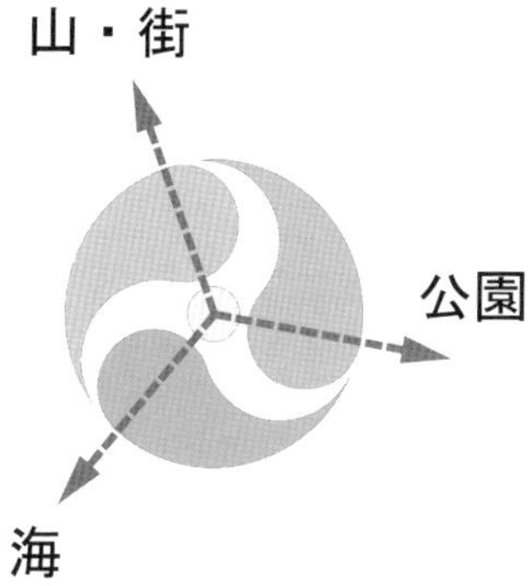

Concept diagram

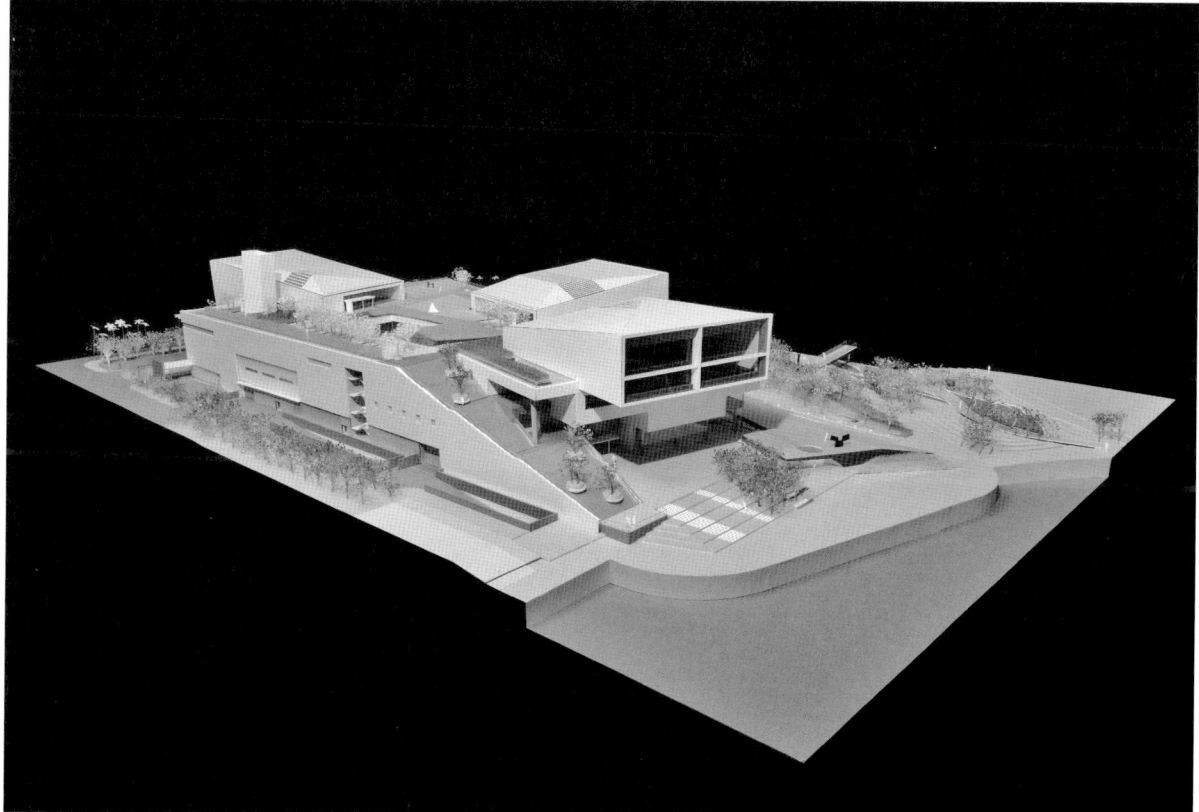

Aerial view from Shekou Bay

招商局地産控股股份有限公司は、中国においてもっとも歴史をもつ不動産開発企業の一つである。招商局は深圳の蛇口エリアを数十年にわたって精力的に開発してきた。

2011年の末に、蛇口の「海上世界」地域における業務・商業・住宅などの開発の核をなす文化施設の設計を依頼された。これは我々にとって、中国での最初のプロジェクトである。

深圳海上世界文化芸術中心の敷地は、蛇口半島の南東に位置し、そこからは眼前に広がる海の向こうに香港島が浮かぶ雄大な景色を望むことができる。この施設は、展示場・劇場・美術館・ギャラリー、さらに文化的活動に関連した商業空間などを含む複合施設である。

また、その形態的構成は、海、隣接する公園、そして北西に構える山との、それぞれの力強いつながりを示唆するようなものとして構想された。延床面積がおよそ7万㎡のこの施設は、2016年に竣工する予定である。

Main Museum

Culture Plaza

Central Plaza

Aerial view from park

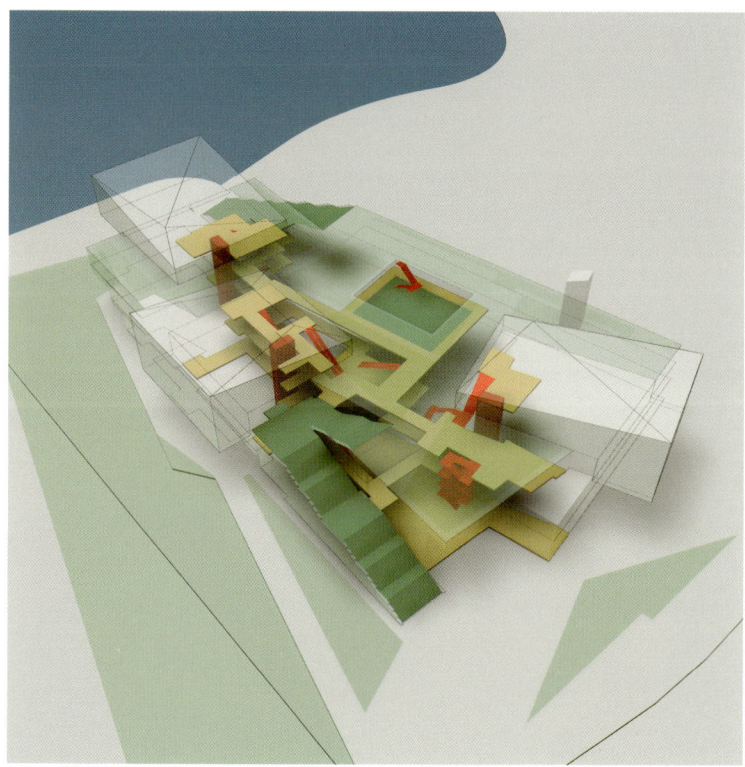

Diagram model

◎Toward Countryside

YKK Guest House | 1982
前沢ガーデンハウス

◎田園へ

View from the south [O.M.]

In the early 1980s the YKK company, a leading manufacturer of zippers, asked us to design a guest house to provide lodging and conference spaces for their distinguished visitors. This guest house, situated on a wedge-shaped site bordered by a small hill is designed in the image of a large house. The multi-story space facing the south garden is the heart of this building, by which all elements of the building are visually linked. This is a center of what is not only a house but a facility with a public character as well.

One can look down on this structure from all four directions, in particular from a road running along a hill, so that the composition had to be designed with many different viewpoints in mind. The central public space, the guest room wing with the chimney and the conference room wing in particular form an orderly composition.

View from the south -2012

View from the north [O.M.]

10.22.80 MAEZAWA, KUROBE

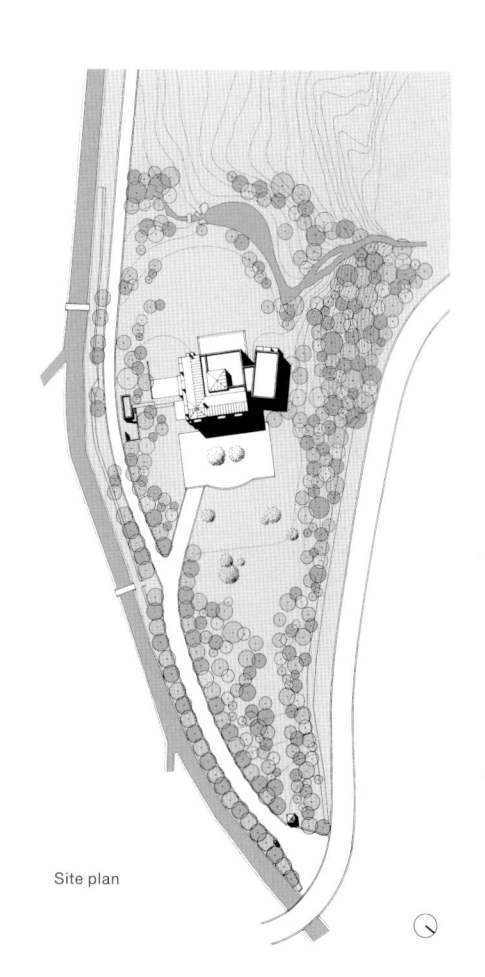

Site plan

1980年代のはじめYKKより、訪問者が宿泊し集会できるゲストハウスを設計するよう依頼があった。小高い丘から見下ろせるくさび型の敷地に置かれたこのゲストハウスは、完結した〈一つの大きな家〉というイメージに基づいて設計されている。南側の庭に面した吹抜けの空間は、この建物の中心である。この空間を介してすべての諸要素が視覚的に関連づけられている。

また、この建物は四方から、あるいは崖上の道路からも見下ろされる位置にあるために、そこに様々な視点・視線に耐え得る明快な全体像が求められた。特に南側の庭から見ると、中央のパブリック・スペース、煙突を軸にした客室棟、そして会議室棟の、三つの諸要素が一つの構成された秩序をつくり上げている。

Seminar room [O.M.]

Lounge [O.M.]

Living room -2004

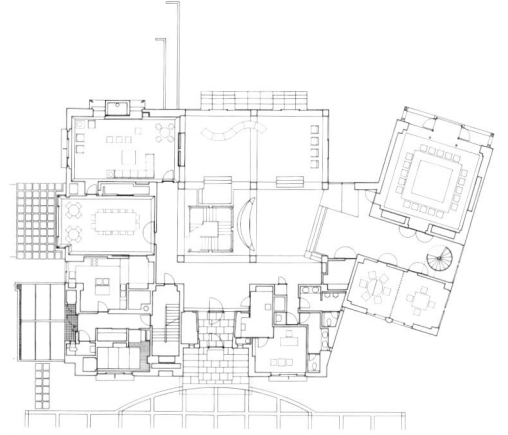

First floor plan

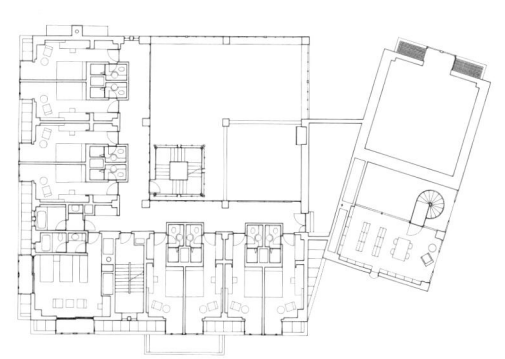

Second floor plan

Fujisawa Municipal Gymnasium | 1984
藤沢市秋葉台文化体育館

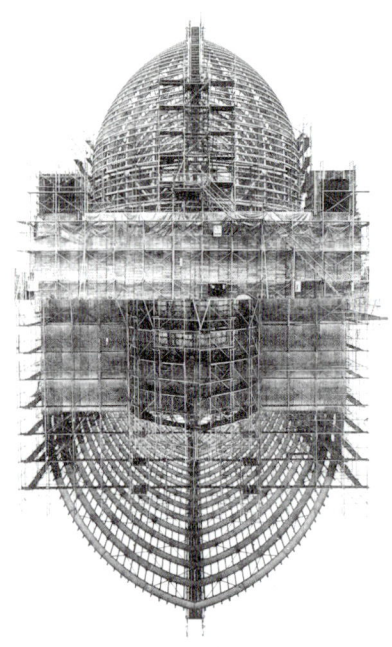

Collage of structural framing

Japanese warrior helmet [T.I.]

Arena skyline

Fujisawa Municipal Gymnasium is a public facility combining a main arena and sub-arena, along with a variety of support facilities. The two main volumes are contraposed at a slight angle to one another and linked by a central entrance hall. Together, they create a variety of silhouettes and transform with changing light throughout the day.

The primary element that embodies the spirit of this project is its unique roofscape – both in form and material. The roofs are covered with 0.4 millimeter thick stainless steel sheets, which required a great deal of technical refinement prior to execution. Studies for the working (manufacturing, cutting, and welding) and assembly of the thin metal pieces took two years, and the actual construction took another two years.

Stainless steel responds very sensitively to light and shadow. It can appear soft at times and at other times hard-edged. As dusk approaches, the outline of the roof merges beautifully with the sky. Since ancient times, metals have suggested a variety of images, due to their precise forms, hardness, and sharpness. The roofs at Fujisawa may resemble beetles, blimps, helmets, or even medieval armor. At the same time, their lightness, thinness, and shiny quality are decidedly forward-looking, like a UFO. The Fujisawa Gymnasium expresses both the "past" and the "future" and, in doing so, equally succeeds in expressing the "present".

Exterior view from the north

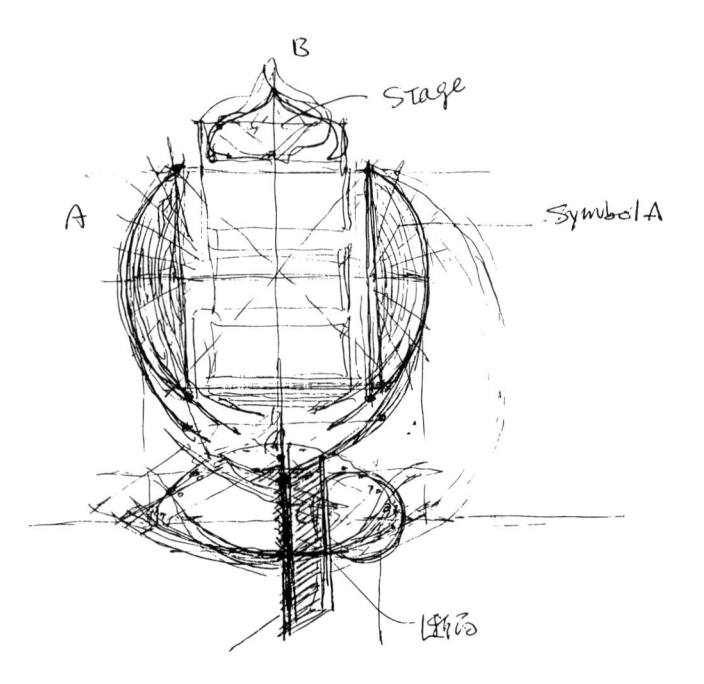

藤沢市秋葉台体育館は大アリーナと小アリーナ、その他のサポート施設によって構成されている。二つのアリーナは中央のエントランスホールでつながれ、それらを包む曲面体の屋根は、互いに相呼応し、様々なシルエットを展開する。

このプロジェクトの設計の基本は、屋根にあるといってよい。屋根は0.4mm厚のステンレスの皮膜によって覆われており、この薄い金属片の製作、切断、溶接を含む加工と構成に関する研究と設計に2年、施工期間にさらに2年を要した。

ステンレスは光の陰影に敏感に反応する。時に穏やかに、時に鋭く。特に薄暮に近づくとその空と接するエッジは、美しく背景に溶け込んでいく。金属はその材質がもつ性格のゆえに、正確さ、硬さ、鋭さを通して、古来より様々なイメージを喚起してきた。この屋根も時にカブトムシのように、または飛行船のように、あるいはヘルメットのように見えてくる。じっと凝視していると、何か中世の騎士の甲冑を思わせる。しかし一方で、現代においては飛翔するような軽やかさ、薄さ、そしてきらめきのゆえにUFOを想起させるのである。そうした〈過去〉と〈未来〉という二つの時が交錯する点として、藤沢の体育館は〈現在〉を表明している。

Main approach to the gymnasium [H.K.]

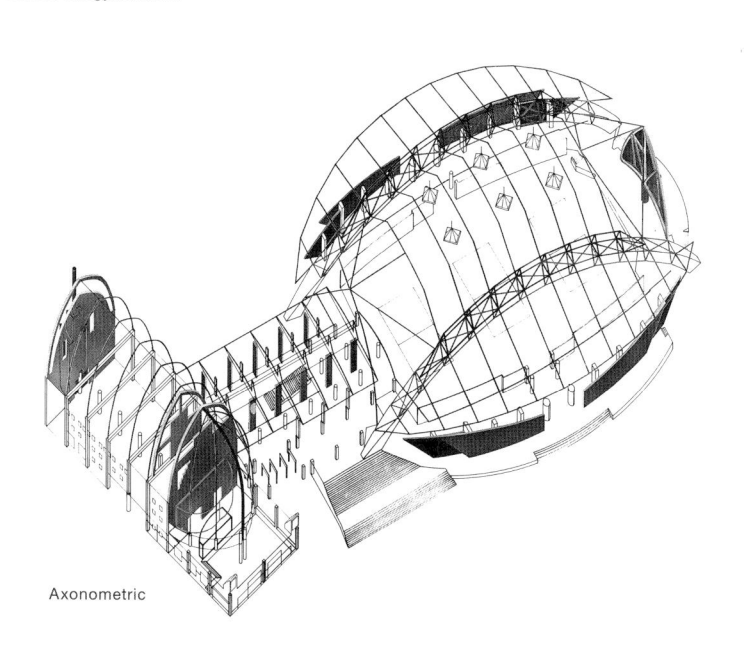

Axonometric

Main Arena

Model

Photograph during construction

Maki assessing models with project staff

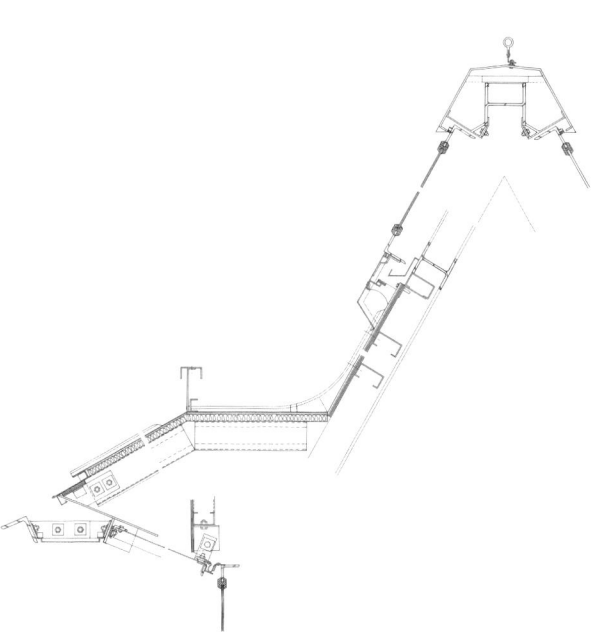

Detail of roof

Kirishima International Concert Hall | 1994
霧島国際音楽ホール

Kirishima International Concert Hall sits within a gently sloping plateau among a range of volcanic mountains in southern Kyushu. The site yields to a superb panorama of the Kirishima peaks to the east and Sakura Island to the south. In response to the growing reputation of its music festivals and heightened activity of the local musicians, the government of the Kagoshima Prefecture decided to establish a permanent home for these music activities in this beautiful rural context.

霧島国際音楽ホールは、南九州に広がる霧島高原の一角に位置し、敷地は緩やかなくだり斜面をもつ。東に霧島連峰が連なり、また南方には桜島を望むことができる雄大な景観が展開する。地元の音楽祭やミュージシャンの活動が評価され、鹿児島県はこれらの音楽活動のための永久的な建物をこの美しい田園のコンテクストの中に計画した。

この施設は、800席のコンサートホール、4000人を収容できる野外音楽堂、サポート機能を担う練習室やリハーサル室から構成されている。コンサートホールは、メタリックな多面体の屋根に覆われ、周囲の角ばった連峰の形状を思わせる。

Kirishima Concert Hall with volcanic Sakura-jima in the background [T.K.]

音楽ホールの周囲を巡るホワイエは、次第に上昇しながら、眼前に霧島連峰が見えるようにしつらえられていて、音楽鑑賞に対する期待や祝祭性を高めるような計画としている。メインホールは小規模なオーケストラおよび室内音楽を主とするクラシック音楽の演奏に適した空間として設計されている。シューボックスを変形した木の葉型の平面形と、三角形で構成された船底型の天井面によって、客席と舞台に視覚的に一体感のある空間となっている。

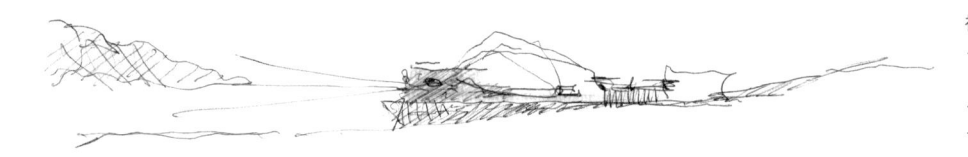

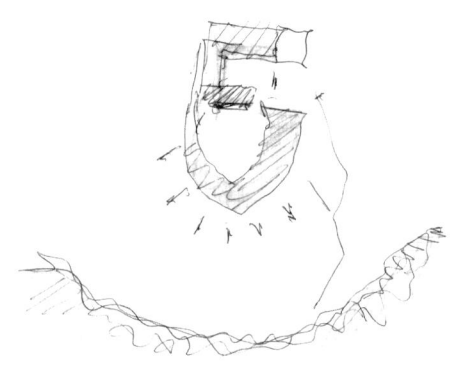

Interior view of foyer [T.K.]

The complex houses an 800-seat concert hall, an outdoor amphitheater hosting 4,000 spectators, and a support building containing practice and rehearsal rooms. The concert hall is signified by a metallic polyhedral roof, which echoes the angular forms of the surrounding mountains.

As visitors ascend the stepping foyer space leading to the main hall, a beautiful silhouette of the Kirishima Range rises directly ahead, increasing the sense of anticipation and festivity. The main hall is used primarily for classical music, with a special focus on performances by chamber ensembles and small orchestras. A deformation of the classic rectangular concert halls, the leaf-shaped plan of this main hall brings the audience closer to the stage and establishes a sense of unity between the performer and the audience.

Exterior view at twilight

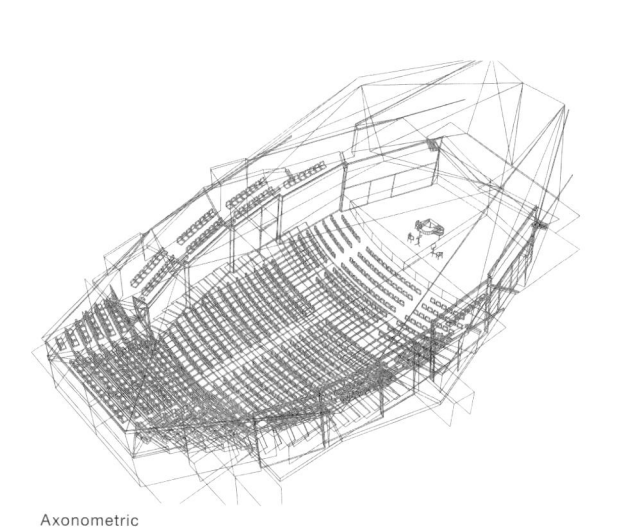

Axonometric

Interior view of concert hall

Kaze-no-Oka Crematorium | 1997
風の丘葬斎場

The Kaze-no-Oka Crematorium sits on the outskirts of Nakatsu, a small city of 70,000 people in southern Japan. The grounds, named "Kaze-no-Oka" (Hill of the Winds), serve as a public park that incorporates an existing cemetery and a group of ancient burial mounds. The park is designed as an elliptical field, dipping at the center to form a basin. As one descends, the surrounding landscape disappears from view, creating a place embraced only by the earth.

Aerial view

Seen from this park, the crematorium appears as a partially submerged earthwork with a few architectural fragments that appear as free-standing sculptural forms in an abstract landscape. Our main intention was to design buildings that blend with this scenic environment and to provide an atmosphere of sympathy and dignity for the bereaved through careful designing of spatial sequence.

The crematorium is comprised of three loosely connected but distinct zones—a ceremonial area where funerals are held, a cremation area where final respects are offered, and a waiting area for the family, friends and relatives of the deceased to spend time between ceremonies.

Throughout the building, natural light plays a critical role in conveying appropriate characteristics of each space and in heightening the ritualistic experience of transition. Spaces with highly ceremonial purposes are dignified and

View of the north facade [T.K.]

Funeral hall interior [T.K.]

Detailed wall section of Funeral hall (scale:1/20)

dramatized, while linking spaces are designed to create a natural flow and a sense of repose between consecutive activities. The cremation area is placed around an interior courtyard with a reflecting pool, whose surrounding walls are designed to limit the outside vistas and focus the awareness of visitors inward.

The light entering these spaces is reflected upon primordial materials— wood, concrete, cor-ten steel, brick, and slate.

This ensemble of natural materials and natural light give the architecture a sense of serenity and dignity, creating a place of lasting memories.

Since the crematorium's completion in 1997, many people even from outside the city have visited the place, and as I understand, many of them have expressed a wish to be cremated there if possible. Perhaps this is one of the most unexpected compliments I have ever received as an architect.

Entry porch

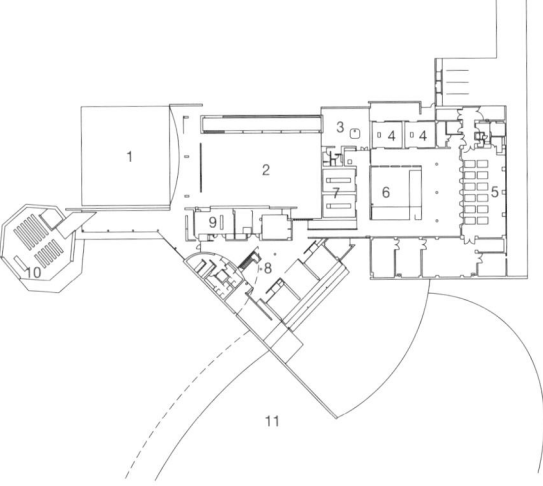

1 Porte-cochere
2 Forecourt
3 Entry porch
4 Oratory
5 Crematory
6 Courtyard (reflecting pool)
7 Enshrinement room
8 Waiting area
9 Office
10 Funeral hall
11 Park (Kaze-no-oka)

First floor plan (scale 1/1600)

Courtyard [T.K.]

Oratory [T.K.]

Enshrinement room [T.K.]

Passage

風の丘葬斎場は、人口7万人の小都市、大分県中津市の郊外の丘に計画された。既存の墓地と近年発掘された古墳群とが一体となったこの土地は、「風の丘」と名付けられている。まず公園の部分は楕円形の野原として計画され、真ん中には窪地がつくられている。この野原を進むにつれ、周囲のランドスケープは視界から消え、まるで土のみによって覆われたような場を体験することができる。

公園から見ると、葬斎場は部分的に埋まったアースワークのように現れ、ところどころに建築の要素が、抽象的なランドスケープの中に独立した彫刻のように突き出している。我々は、周囲の景観の中に溶け込みながら、慎重に計画された空間のシークエンスによって死者へのお悔みや尊厳の念を促すような建築をつくることを、設計の主旨とした。

葬斎場は、葬式が行われる斎場、最後の別れの場となる火葬棟、親族や友人が火葬の間に使用できる待合といった三つの要素から構成されており、これらは緩くつなげられながらも、それぞれ明確に個別のゾーンとして設けられている。

この建物では、それぞれの空間に適した特性を表現し、変化という儀式的な体験を誇張するよう、自然光が重要な役割をもっている。祝祭性の高い空間は尊く、演出された計画とする一方で、つなぎの空間は、連続するアクティビティーの合間を自然な流れでリンクし、平静感ある空間とした。火葬場は水が張られた中庭を巡る回廊に沿って配列されており、周囲の壁は外のヴィスタを断ち切り、訪問者の意識を内側に向けるよう計画されている。

このような光によって演出された空間は、木やコンクリート、コールテン鋼、煉瓦、スレートといった原始的な材料によって仕上げられている。この自然の材料と自然光の調和は、平静で威厳のある建築をつくり出し、永遠の記憶を刻む場所としてふさわしい空間としている。

葬斎場が完成した1996年より、市内外を問わず多数の訪問者がこの場所を訪れ、多数の方々がこちらで火葬されたいとおっしゃっているとのことである。これは、建築家にとって思いがけぬ賛辞の一つといえよう。

Kaze-no-Oka park

[N.P.]

TRIAD | 2002
TRIAD

Designed as a multi-use complex for Harmonic Drive, TRIAD consists of three independent buildings— a Guardhouse, a Gallery, and a Laboratory. Since establishing its main company in Hodaka in 1990, Harmonic Drive manufactures precision decelerators and other instruments used in satellites, spacecraft, and telescopes. The owner also holds a collection of the well-known Japanese artist Yoshikuni Iida, with whom he has a long acquaintance. The unique program of TRIAD emerged from the owner's wish to build a gallery

Elevation of Laboratory with Japan Alps beyond

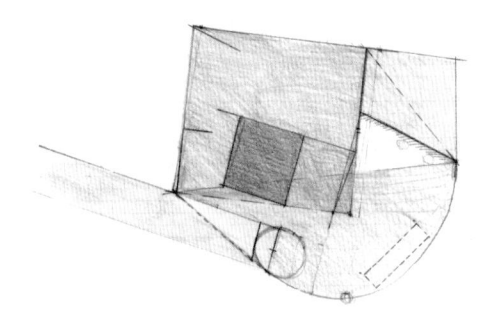

Gallery in winter -2012

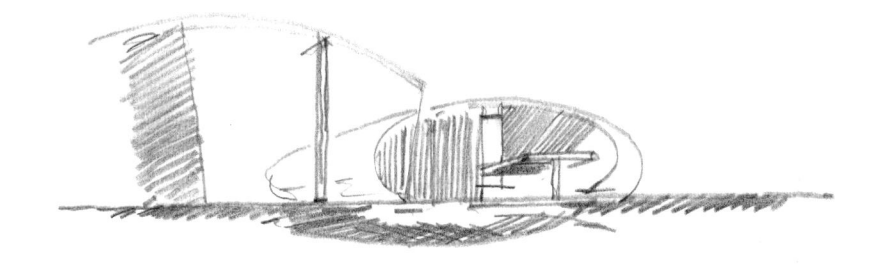

displaying Iida's work, while still addressing the issues of technology and security.

At TRIAD, a dynamic formal relationship between three buildings is sought. While the Laboratory uses a curved sectional profile, the Gallery uses curved forms in plan, surmounted by a pitched roof. The Guard House is rectilinear, but projects a sense of forward movement with its cantilever. A landscape of elliptical grass mounds and steel plates enforce this sense of movement through the site. Careful attention was given to delineation of roof edges, as this complex is always seen against a natural background of sky, mountains, and vegetation. The thin, protruded edge of the Laboratory and Gallery canopies are comprised of honeycomb cores, sandwiched by 6mm prefabricated steel plates joined together on site. Such results can only be obtained through careful detailing and sophisticated technology, done in the same spirit of the work of Harmonic Drive Co. itself.

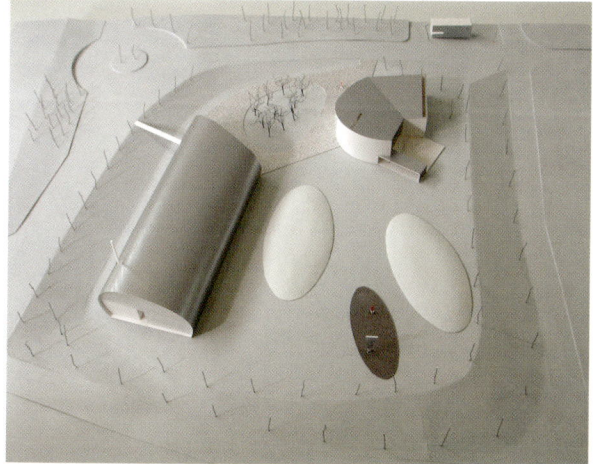

West elevation

Site model

ハーモニックドライブの複合施設としてデザインされたTRIADは、守衛所、ギャラリー、研究棟の三つの独立した建物によって構成されている。1990年に穂高山麓に本社を設立したハーモニックドライブは、衛星や宇宙船、望遠鏡などに使われる精密可動部品を扱う会社である。また、施主は長年の友人でもある飯田善国氏のコレクションを所持している。TRIADのユニークなプログラムは、飯田氏の作品を展示するギャラリーを設けると同時に、テクノロジーやセキュリティーというテーマも表現したいという施主の要望によって生まれた。

TRIADでは、三つの建物のダイナミックな形状とそれ同士の関係性がスタディーされた。研究棟はカーブがかった断面形をもつのに対し、ギャラリーは平面的にカーブの形状を採用し、傾斜屋根によって覆われている。守衛所は直方体であるが、キャンチレバーによって前方に突き出すような躍動感をもっている。ランドスケープは楕円形の緑地のマウンドや、スチールのプレートで構成されており、このような躍動感がさらに敷地全体で感じられるように計画されている。また、この施設は常に空、山脈、緑といった自然の景観を背に見られることから、屋根の形状には注意が払われた。薄く突き出した研

Sculpture gallery [T.K.]

Gallery entrance [T.K.]

Model of Gallery

究棟とギャラリーのキャノピーは、ハニカムコアを6mm厚のプレファブのスチールプレートで両側からはさみ、現地で接合された。このような結果は、精密に計画されたディテールと、洗練されたテクノロジーによって初めて実現されるものであり、ハーモニックドライブの精神そのものを誇張しているといえよう。

1. Built-up Steel Member H-500X250, Oil Paint
2. Steel Deck t=1.6, Oilpaint
3. Urethane waterproofing (sprayed on, t=50-100)
4. Steel 4.5t L=100
5. Steel C, 100x50x20x2.3t
6. Insulating Spacer
7. Welded Stainless Steel Standing Seam Roof
   SUS 304, t=0.4
   Waterproofing PEF sheet t=4
   Acoustic Insulation, t=12
   Fiberboard
   Underlayment, t=25
8. Asphalt Sealer
9. Seal
10. Seismic Expansion Joint

Guard House [T.K.]

Interior staircase of the Laboratory [T.K.]

Detailed wall section of the Laboratory (scale:1/30)

Mihara Performing Arts Center | 2007
三原市芸術文化センター

The Mihara Performing Arts Center takes the place of the former cultural center and gymnasium in Miyaura Park, not far from the center of Mihara City. Like any park with a baseball field and a playground in a small city, it is frequented by local residents of all ages.

When I first saw the program and context of the project, I imagined a pavilion in the park. With a population of 100,000, it seemed unlikely that a 1,200-person theater and its

East elevation

adjoining foyer would be in constant demand. At the same time, the city wished to have local residents use the rehearsal and practice rooms, along with the main stage, on a regular basis. I therefore thought of an approachable foyer with an intimate scale, avoiding typical tropes of grandness associated to big theaters. Here, local residents and visitors could rest and enjoy the occasional event or planned exhibition. To enhance its public character, a cafe and a courtyard is added. The courtyard is an inner garden that could be opened when the weather is nice, and accommodate larger events when required.

Concept

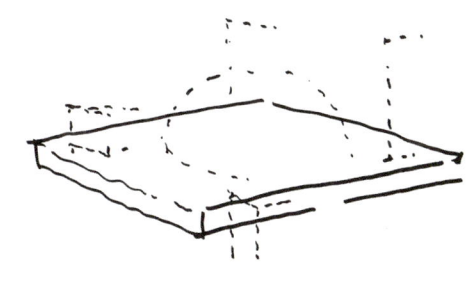

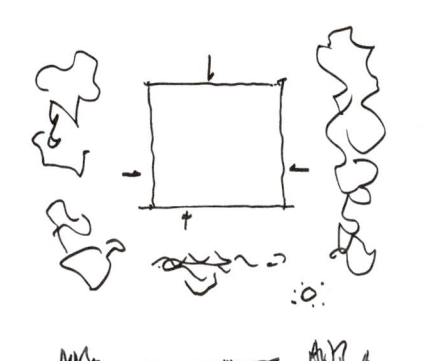

同じ場所にあった旧文化センターと武道館を建て替え、新しく建設されたこのセンターは三原市の中心から、それほど遠くない宮浦公園の一隅に建てられている。この公園はグラウンドも含めて地域の住民によく使われ、センターの近くには小さな子供の遊び場もある。どの中小都市にも見られる普通の公園である。

与えられたこうした環境とプログラムの中でまず第一にイメージしたのは、公園の中のパヴィリオン的な佇まいをもった建築の姿であった。三原市は人口10万の都市である。1200人の席がいっぱいになり、ホワイエが講演の前後、人であふれるといったことは年間を通じて常時あることではない。しかし一方で、市にはリハーサル、練習室、そして本舞台も常に市民に積極的に利用して貰いたいという意図があった。こうした状況の中から、従来どちらかというと観客席と一体となった壮大なホワイエを避け、大きなイベントがない時は、市民や公園に遊びに来た人達も気軽に休んだり、時折、予定されている展示も含めた様々なイベントに参加できるような、もっとヒューマンなスケールをもったホワイエのほうがいいのではないかと考えるようになった。当然そ

View from the second floor terrace

Site plan

Foyer

のコーナーには小さなカフェもある。そしてホワイエの独立性を高めるために中庭を設け、天気のよい時はここを開放し、大きなイベントにも対応できるようにした。

Main Hall

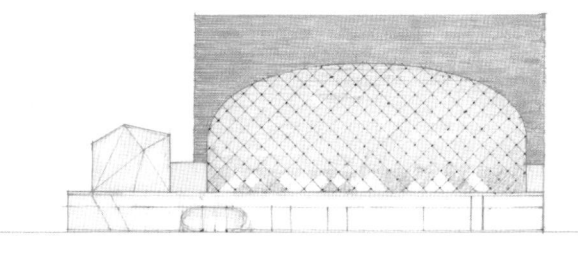

Shimane Museum of Ancient Izumo | 2006
島根県古代出雲歴史博物館

The Shimane Museum of Ancient Izumo was established to exhibit the artifacts and culture of the Izumo area, one of the cradles of culture and civilization on the Japan seaside and the source of valuable archaeological remains. Activity in this area can be traced back to ancient times when it functioned as a gateway to Japan from the Korean Peninsula and China, and was the site of the first Shinto shrine in Japan, the Izumo Grand Shrine, constructed during the 8th Century. The Shimane Museum is sited adjacent to the original location of

Izumo Grand Shrine

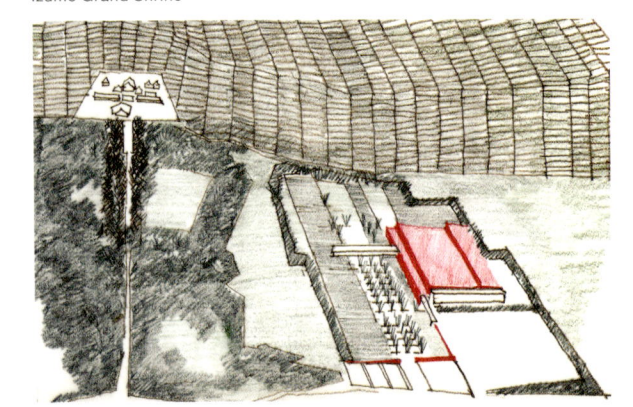

Exterior view from the south

the Izumo Grand Shrine where many of the important archaeological artifacts were discovered, which provides a unique opportunity to both view and experience the natural history of the region.

The site of the Shimane Museum consists of 6 hectares nestled at the base of the Kitayama mountain range. Given this natural setting, the building has been designed to complement the mountainous landscape and to produce a building form with a gentle silhouette that mimics the undulating terrain. Also, to pay homage to the historic use of metal in the region, a Cor-ten steel wall has been incorporated into the entrance facade of the building. Cor-ten steel in particular was chosen for its dual impression of an aged material with a distinctly modern appearance. In this way, the building acts as a mediator between the ancient and the modern as well as the constructed and the natural landscape.

Visitors to the Shimane Museum enter via the glazed entrance hall, which extends from the main building as a transparent glass pavilion. After purchasing tickets within the entrance hall, visitors then pass through the Cor-ten steel wall into the exhibition lobby and then into the four galleries. Surrounding the exhibition zone is a support zone, which consists of storage and preparation rooms, research facilities, and administrative offices. This clear spatial distribution allows ease of movement for museum visitors, as well as efficient museum management, maintenance, and security.

After touring the museum, visitors can return to the glazed entrance hall and relax in the second floor tearoom and third floor observation deck. Panoramic views of the surrounding landscape and the adjacent Izumo Shrine unfold and visitors can contemplate the exhibition artifacts once used on this site over 1200 years ago.

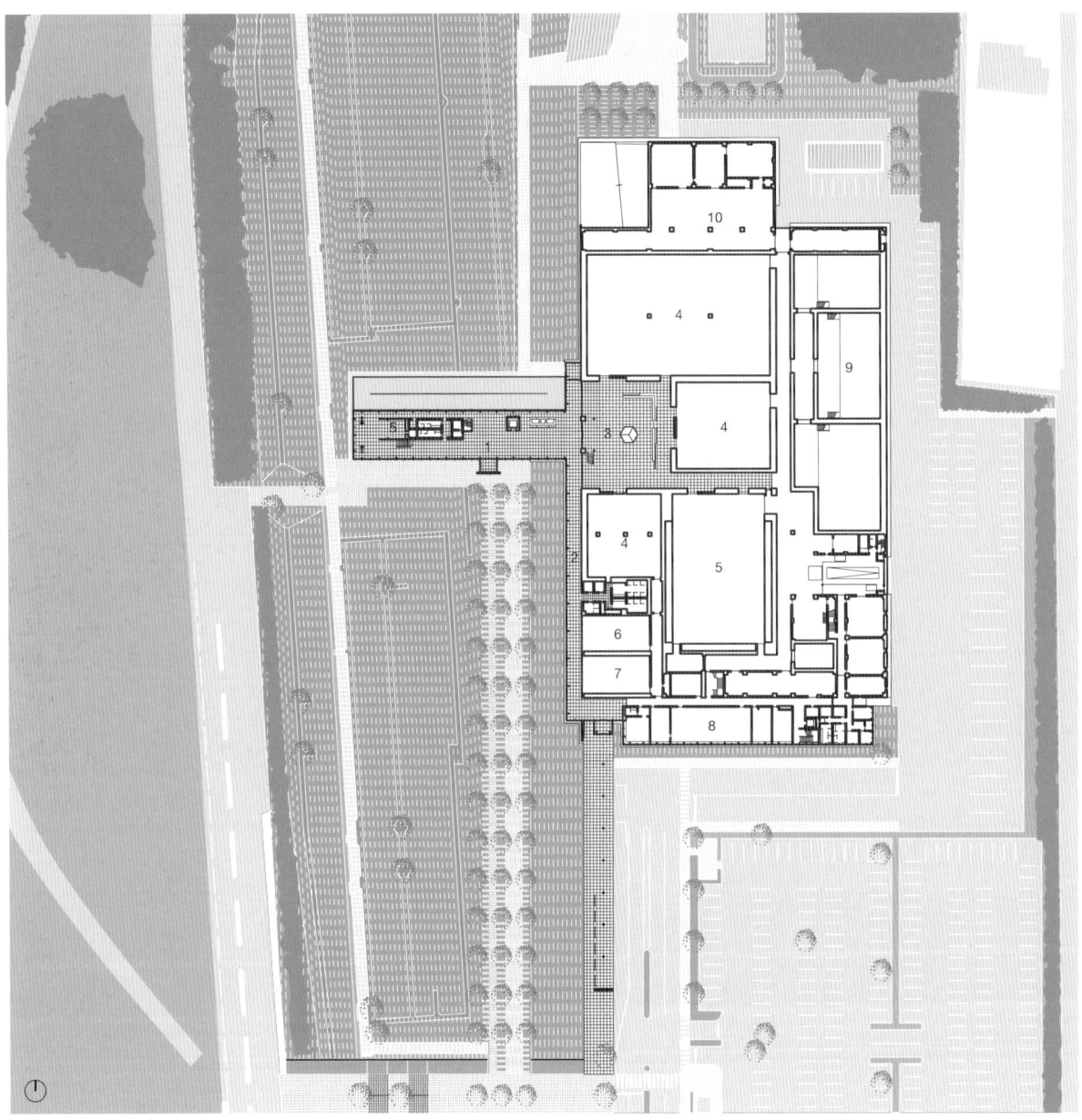

First floor plan (scale 1/1500)

1 Entrance hall
2 Gallery
3 Lobby
4 Permanent Exhibition
5 Temporary Exhibition
6 Lecture room
7 Library
8 Office
9 Storage
10 Mechanical

出雲は、宍道湖の水辺から出雲平野の穏やかな風景の広がりに、古代文化を育んだ悠久の歴史が今も感じられる地である。近年発掘が相次ぐ出雲の古代遺跡では、1984年に神庭荒神谷遺跡から356本の銅剣、1996年に加茂岩倉遺跡から39個の銅鐸が出土した。2000年には出雲大社の境内から巨大な柱跡が発掘され、古代すでに大規模な木造建築であったことも明らかになった。これらの貴重な文化遺産の多くが、この博物館に収蔵、展示されている。

敷地は出雲大社の東に隣接し、古代の風景が継承された場所性を強く感じさせるところである。設計では、この北山山系を背景とする緑の多い景観構成に参加しながら、庭園博物館という構図の中で、いかに歴史の重層性を演出するかを課題とした。配置においてまず、出雲平野のような伸びやかに大地の広がる庭園を設定し、その外周を連続する松林で囲うことにより、北山の山並みを借景として浮かび上がらせた。さらに、出雲大社の歴史的な佇まいを尊重し、この庭園が大社境内の豊かな自然に囲まれた環境とつながりのある静寂な場所となるよう、博物館の建築を庭園の南東脇の位置

Entrance pathway [M.Y.]

View from entrance hall [T.K.]

に集約した。

景観の構成要素として建築は、ガラスと鉄による極めて抽象的な図象による構成を取った。庭園中央のガラスの直方体はエントランスロビー空間で、その東端部がコールテン鋼の壁に貫入している。建築表現において、文化財を保護するための閉鎖性を重厚なコールテン鋼により、また、人のいる場所の開放性を透明なガラスによって表象し、空間と素材感の対比を強調しながら簡潔で力強い構成とした。

人々は展示された文化遺産にいにしえを偲び、歴史を巡る様々な体験の後に、ガラスのロビーにおいて再び北山に迎えられる。さらに階段を上昇するにつれて、庭園に浮かぶ空中園路を回遊するように、取り巻く庭園と背景の山影が変化する。最後に出雲大社の屋根が遠く木々の間に見えてくる。このような古代から継承されてきた歴史の舞台のリアルな体験を通して、人々にとってこの博物館が、過去から現在そして未来へと想いを巡らせながら、静かに思索する場となっている。

Entrance hall [M.Y.]

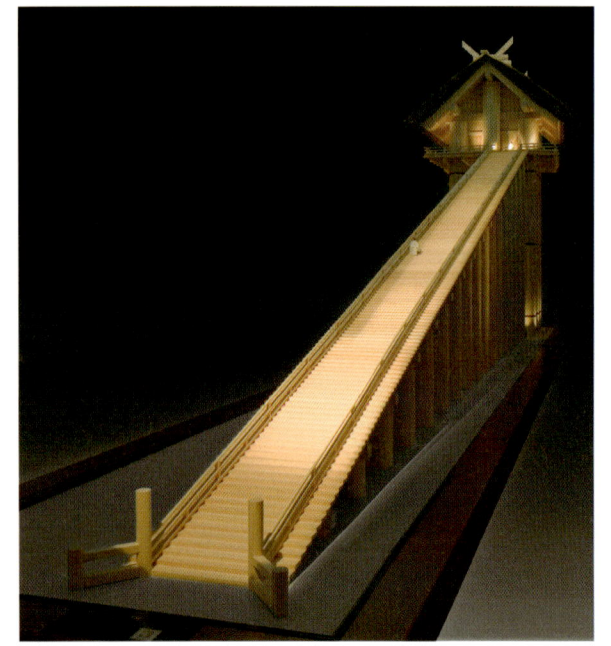

Model of Izumo Grand Shrine

Bronze implements exhibition space [T.K.]

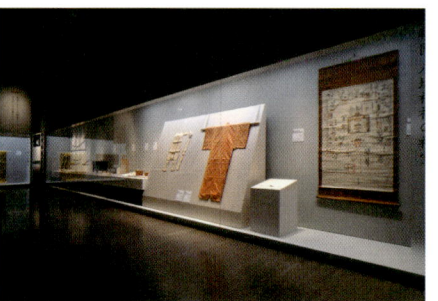

Special exhibition space [T.K.]

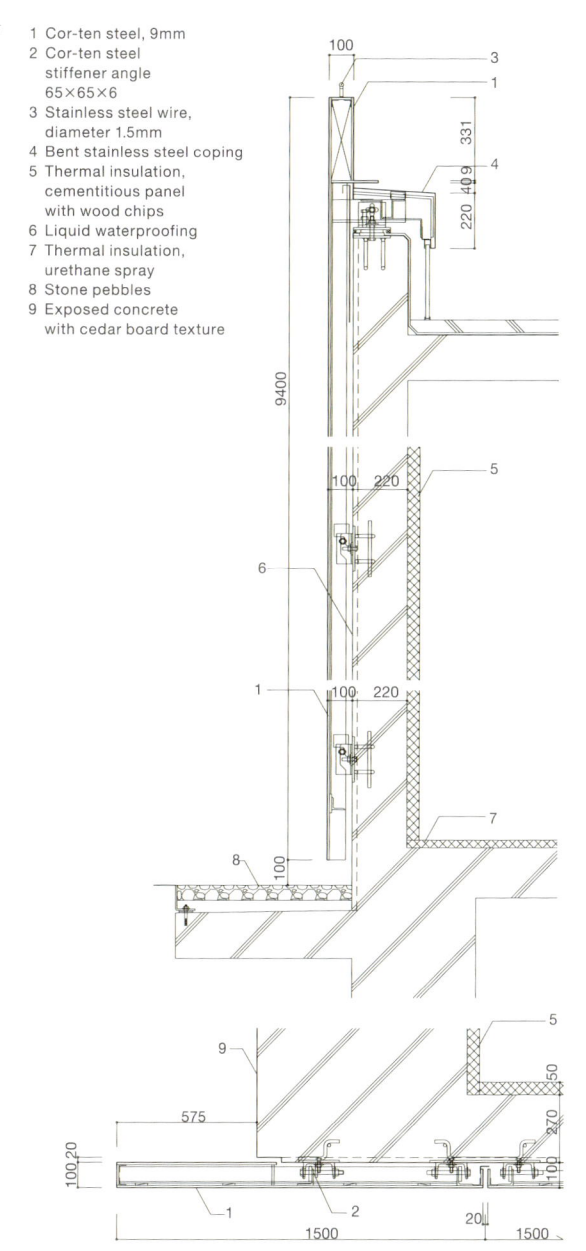

1. Cor-ten steel, 9mm
2. Cor-ten steel stiffener angle 65×65×6
3. Stainless steel wire, diameter 1.5mm
4. Bent stainless steel coping
5. Thermal insulation, cementitious panel with wood chips
6. Liquid waterproofing
7. Thermal insulation, urethane spray
8. Stone pebbles
9. Exposed concrete with cedar board texture

Detail section of Cor-ten steel wall (scale:1/30)

View of entrance hall and Cor-ten steel wall [T.K.]

Cor-ten steel wall [T.K.]

Haus der Hoffnung | 2012
希望の家　名取市文化会館多目的ホール

On March 11th, 2011, one hour after the Great East Japan Earthquake, a tsunami covered the port of Yuriage and reached near the Natori Performing Arts Center designed by Maki and Associates in 1997. That night, over 1,300 refugees headed to the Performing Arts Center, still lit by its emergency generator. Approximately 400 refugees were housed at the Arts Center until April, when they moved to their respective homes and temporary shelters. In June, a memorial was held in the Arts Center's main hall for the victims.

View from the south [S.O.]

Immediately after the earthquake, Maki was approached by the Sonja and Reinhard Ernst Foundation in Germany with a generous offer to help the affected areas. The result was a community facility for the children and the elderly named Haus der Hoffnung, donated to Natori City by the Foundation. As the Arts Center stood in a central location for over 1,000 temporary homes in the area, the Center's south garden was selected as the project site, and Maki and Associates accepted the pro bono commission. The facility was donated to Natori on Culture Day in November 2011, with elderly visitors from temporary shelters and local children (who had contributed mural designs for the building walls) in attendance.

Haus der Hoffnung is a single-story wooden structure consisting of small walled volumes nested under circular and crescent-shaped roofs. On the exterior walls of the small volumes are three mosaic-tiled murals replicating drawings

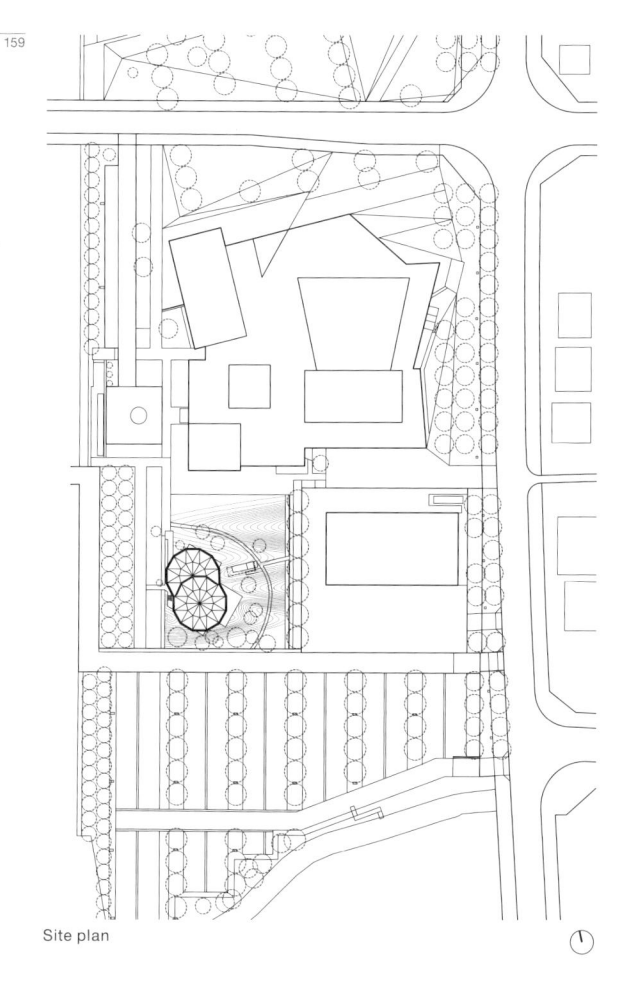

Site plan

Natori Performing Arts Center -1997

Foyer housing local refugees -2011

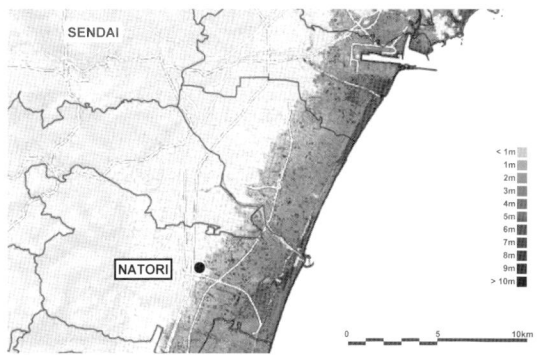

Map showing tsunami levels along the coast near Sendai and Natori. Darker areas indicate more damage.

created by children in Germany and students of a local elementary school in Yuriage. Under the circular roof is an enclosed multi-purpose room intended to house functions such as gatherings, concerts, and skits and, together with the play room and tatami room, may be used as one large space.

2011年3月11日、東日本大震災の地震発生の1時間後、津波が閖上港を襲い、文化会館(当社設計1997年竣工)の近くまで浸水してきた。夜には文化会館の自家発電による明かりを頼りに1300人余の方が避難して来たということだ。その後4月に文化会館で避難生活をされていた400人ほどの方が、仮設住宅や自宅に移られた後、6月に文化会館大ホールで犠牲者の方々の慰霊祭が行われた。

希望の家は震災直後に、以前我々が設計した長野のTRIADで縁のあっ

Aerial view

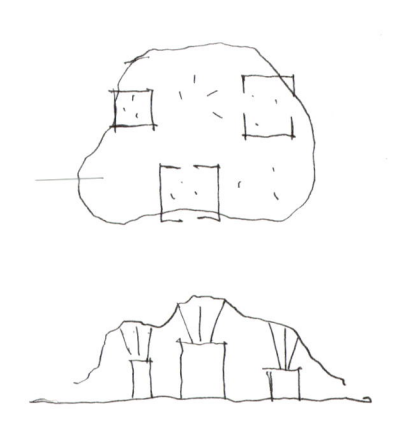

Model

たドイツのラインハルト・アンド・ソンヤ・エルンスト財団から被災地への支援の相談があり、子供からお年寄りのためのコミュニティー施設を名取市に寄贈することになったものである。1000戸余の仮設住宅地の中央に位置する文化会館の南庭を敷地として、我々はその設計をボランティアで引き受けた。2012年11月の秋祭りの日、名取市に寄贈され、仮設住宅のお年寄りや壁画を制作した小学生など市民の方をお迎えすることができた。

希望の家は木造平屋建てで、水平方向の圧力を担う壁に囲まれた小さなヴォリュームと、円形と三日月状の二つの屋根から構成されている。小さなヴォリュームの外壁のうち3枚は、ドイツの子供と地元閖上の小学生が描いた壁画をモザイクタイルで再現し、2国の友好のシンボルとなっている。円状の屋根の下には、小さな集会やコンサート、劇などに使用される多目的室を設け、隣接する遊戯コーナーと畳コーナーと一体的に使用することが可能である。

Multi-purpose room

Mosaic tile murals

Natori Mayor Isoo Sasaki and Reinhard Ernst at one-year anniversary

Aga Khan Museum | 2014
アガ・カーン ミュージアム

The Aga Khan Museum is one of two buildings developed in a 6.8 hectare (16.8 acre) site together with the Ismaili Center designed by Charles Correa and Formal Gardens by Valdimir Djurovic. From the site itself, panoramic distant views of the Toronto skyline unfold.

The Museum, a cultural civic facility open to the general public establishes a strong dialogue with the Ismaili Center on a central axis across the Formal Gardens. The two buildings, sacred and secular,

View from the west

are unified through the gardens and landscape aimed at achieving a sense of harmony in a park setting throughout the entire site.

The Aga Khan Museum, the first museum in North America devoted to Islamic art and culture, is an initiative of His Highness the Aga Khan, the 49th hereditary Imam of the Ismaili Muslims. Dedicated to presenting an overview of the artistic, intellectual and scientific contributions that Islamic civilizations have made to world heritage, the Museum is home to galleries, exhibition spaces, classrooms, a reference library, auditorium and restaurant.

The design of the Museum is inspired by a vision statement of "Light" by His Highness the Aga Khan. The notion of "Light" has been an inspiration for numerous human faiths and decades of history are referred to as the enlightenment.

[J.A.]

The rectilinear building is oriented forty-five degrees to solar north where all its sides are exposed to the sun. The form has been chiseled to create a concaved angular profile that is also a natural expression of the two level building. Clad in sandblasted white Brazilian granite, the surfaces of the building are set in motion in a constant interplay with the sun in light and deep shadows. The effect is similar to a sun dial.

Within the building, a fully glazed courtyard encircled by a layer of free flowing public space in the form of a grand cloister establishes the hub of the Museum. The galleries, exhibition spaces, classrooms, library, auditorium foyer and restaurant/shop, are all equally, non-hierarchically, accessible from the hub. This central public space paired with the courtyard is non-proscriptive enabling a wide range of activities to unfold such as performances, installations, public gathering and receptions.

Aerial view from the east

The courtyard is intended as a permanent peaceful sanctuary creating its own internal world secluded from the outside environment. Its glass walls are imprinted with a double layered pattern in line and void to create a three dimensional effect recalling the traditional Islamic *Jali* screens. The light from the courtyard constantly cast moving patterned shadows on the soffits, walls and floor of the grand cloister animating the interior spaces.

The Museum will live on to represent the living traditions of Muslim societies and to teach the artistic and cultural practices across Islam and its civilizations, past and present. The Buildings, the Gardens and Park, reflect the Aga Khan's long standing relationship with Canada and his appreciation for the country's commitment to pluralism and cultural diversity.

[M.V.]

View from formal garden [J.A.]

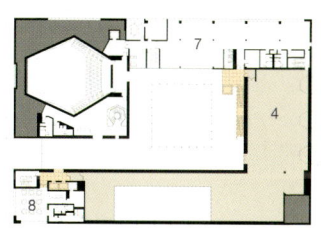

Second floor plan

1 Lobby
2 Reception & Exhibition
3 Courtyard
4 Exhibition
5 Restaurant
6 Auditorium
7 Office
8 Lounge

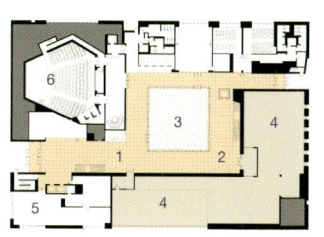

Ground floor plan

アガ・カーン ミュージアムは、6.8haの敷地の中に計画された二つの建物のうちの一つである。もう一つの建物はチャールズ・コレア設計のイズマイリ・センター（礼拝堂）であり、庭園はヴラディミール・ジュルヴィッチの設計による。敷地からはトロントのスカイラインを遠くに望むことができる。

一般市民に開かれた文化施設として、このミュージアムは幾何学的にデザインされた庭園をはさんでイズマイリ・センターと対峙して建っている。一つの公園としての敷地の中でイスラム世界の聖と俗を表現する二つの建物を庭園やランドスケープによって結び付けることで、敷地全体に調和した関係を感じさせるようにした。

北米で初のイスラム芸術文化のための博物館であるアガ・カーン ミュージアムは、イズマイル派第49代イマーム（最高指導者）であるアガ・カーン氏の主導のもと建設された。イスラム文明がこれまで世界に寄与してきた芸術的、知的、科学的に継承されてきたものを概観できるようにするために、このミュージアムにはギャラリー、展示スペース、教室、図書室、オーディトリアム、レストランが備えられている。ミュージアムのデザインは、アガ・カーン氏が提示した「光」というテーマから

Multi-purpose auditorium

[J.A.]

始まった。光は宗教の違いを越えて多くの人々の信仰にインスピレーションを与えてきたし、歴史上多くの場面で悟りを意味してきた。建物の配置と形状は、光がもつ神秘性を表現するように決定されている。

矩形の建物を南北軸に対して45度の角度で配置することで、建物のすべての面が1日に1回は陽の光を受けるようにした。建物の垂直方向のシルエットは中央部をくびれた形態とすることで、夏は上面が深い影を落とし、冬には陽がすべて壁に当たる。サンドブラスト仕上げのブラジル産白花崗岩で覆われた外壁は、まるで日時計のように光と影の戯れが織りなす移ろいを写し出す。

床から天井までをすべてガラス張りとした中庭を囲む空間は、大回廊として自由に回遊できる共用空間であり、同時にミュージアム内部の動線のハブとしている。ギャラリー、展示スペース、教室、図書室、オーディトリアムの前室、レストランと店舗、これらすべてが対等に、ヒエラルキーをもたずに中心からアクセスできる。中庭と対になったこの中央の公共スペースでは、制約なく

East elevation

Mock-up of exterior corner

1. 50mm stone cladding
   Air space
   100mm rigid insulation
   Air barrier membrane
   Concrete
2. Stone pavers & setting bed
   Snow melting tubes
   Protection board
   5mm thick waterproofing membrane
   Concrete slab
3. Sealant in 8mm joint
4. Extruded aluminum coping
5. Air terminal
6. Stone ballast
   Filter fabric
   100mm rigid insulation
   2 ply roof membrane
   Concrete topping on steel deck
7. Insulated glass in aluminum curtainwall frame
8. Stainless steel floor grille and frame

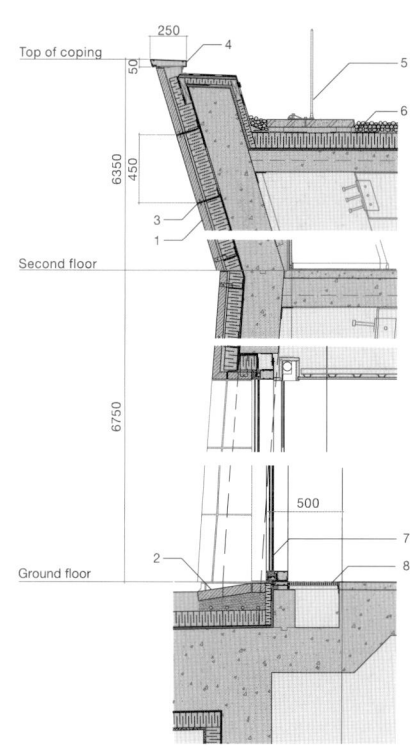

Detailed wall section (scale:1/50)

パフォーマンスやインスタレーション、集会やレセプション・パーティーといった多様な活動が可能である。

中庭は、変わることなく外界から切り離された独自の内部世界を生み出すための、穏やかで心安らぐ聖域として計画されている。中庭を囲むガラス面は、線と面のパターンがネガ・ポジの関係になるようにプリントした二重ガラスによって構成され、イスラムの伝統的なスクリーンであるジャリを想起させるよう立体的な効果を生み出している。中庭から建物内に射し込む光はこのスクリーンを通過することで大回廊の軒、壁面、床面に常に動き続ける影を落とし、刻々と変化する内部空間をつくりだしている。

このミュージアムはイスラム教徒の社会が現代でも保ち続けている伝統を象徴し、イスラム教とその文明がこれまで生み出してきた、そして現在も進行させている芸術的、文化的活動について学ぶことのできる場として生き続けていくだろう。建築群、庭園、

Entrance lobby [J.A.]

Entrance reception

そして公園は、アガ・カーン氏とカナダとの長年にわたって培ってきた関係を反映したものであり、カナダという国が多民族の共存と文化の多様性に対して寛容であることへのアガ・カーン氏からの感謝の気持ちを表現している。

Double-height exhibition space and skylights [J.A.]

Isramic art exhibit with ceramic frit screen beyond [J.A.]

Double-height exhibition space

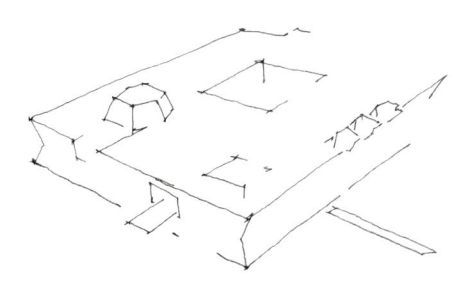

The Japanese Sword Museum | 2017
新刀剣博物館

South elevation

Site plan

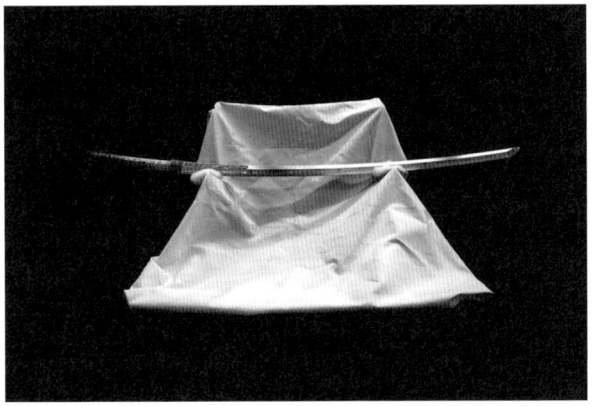

Concept (Japanese sword, Katana)

Site model

Perspective of exhibition space

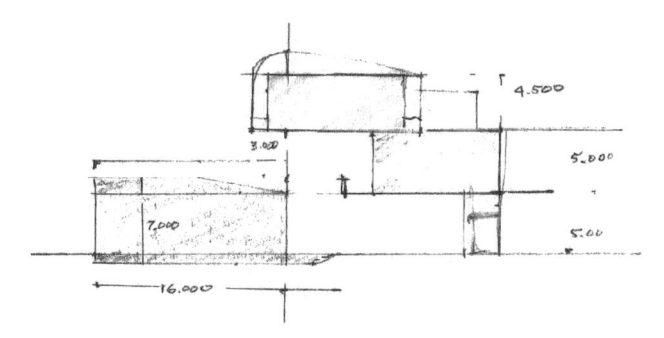

The Ryogoku area of Sumida Ward has housed numerous samurai residences since the Edo period. Today, the area is still a center of Japanese history and culture, evidenced by an abundance of cultural facilities— including the Edo-Tokyo Museum, Sumida Hokusai Museum, Sumo Hall, and numerous small craft galleries. The project site is located within the Former Yasuda Garden, which echoes a traditional Japanese strolling landscape characterized by a meandering path around a central pond. To enhance the unique characteristics of this site, the project will not only exhibit Japanese Sword culture, but also will promote local culture and create linkages to the garden itself and to other sightseeing spots. The design of the museum— a cylinder protruding to the pond and two wings— reflects the former Ryogoku Auditorium, but updates the dome structure with a vaulted roof, reducing its height and better integrating with the Former Yasuda Garden.

The first floor of the museum houses casual public functions such as a museum shop, exhibit/information lounge, auditorium, and café, and maintains a strong connection to the Garden. These spaces are designed as a break area for garden visitors, or a meeting point for neighborhood explorers. The second floor houses the museum administration areas, spaces for Japanese sword maintenance, and exhibit planning. The top floor houses a Japanese sword exhibit space and a roof terrace overlooking the garden. It is hoped that the museum will display the arts and crafts aspects of Japanese swords, and disseminate a comprehensive picture of Japanese samurai culture in conjunction with the adjacent garden.

墨田区の両国地区は江戸の中期から武家屋敷が整備され、現在は江戸東京博物館、北斎美術館、国技館、それに職人技を伝える街角のミュージアムなどが点在し、日本固有の歴史と文化を今に伝える地域となっている。敷地は池泉回遊式の庭園が残る旧安田庭園の一角であり、このような立地を活かし、庭園散策や地域の展示館、名所旧跡と連携する庭園博物館として計画された。博物館はこれまで建っていた旧両国公会堂の佇まいを継承し、池に向かって張り出した円筒部とその両側の翼部から構成される。また公会堂のドームに変わり、頂部にはヴォールト屋根が架けられ、高さを抑えて庭園との調和を図っている。

庭園との連続性の高い1階は、ミュージアムショップ、展示・情報ラウンジ、研修室やカフェなど、気軽に立ち寄り、利用できるパブリックなスペースを配置し、庭園散策の休憩所や街歩きの拠点としても使える計画である。2階には博物館の運営および日本刀の審査や展示の企画を行う管理、学芸の諸室を、そして最上階には日本刀の展示室と、新しい視点から庭園を楽しめる屋上庭園を配している。美術、工芸としての日本刀に加え、大名屋敷の庭園とともに、日本古来の武家文化を広く発信していくことを目指している。

◎Toward Campus   Keio University Mita Campus | 1981
◎キャンパスへ   慶應義塾図書館・新館

View of the new library through the old library arch   [S.K.]

Keio University, the oldest university in Japan, celebrated its 155th anniversary in 2014. The Mita campus—where Keio was first founded—houses the central facilities of the institution. The buildings date from all periods of the university's long history. The most symbolic structures are the old library, built 106 years ago, and the later constructed administration. The design intention of the new library was to give the new buildings their own expression while echoing the surrounding context.

The new library is planned across the old library and the administration building, and a quiet open space was created in the middle, intended to recapitulate the university's history. The fourth-floor cornice of the new library is 16 meters high, similar to the heights of the other two buildings. The two libraries are both 13 meters from the administration building and are arranged symmetrically. Half of the new library volume is built underground to reduce scale and accommodate for the high-density campus.

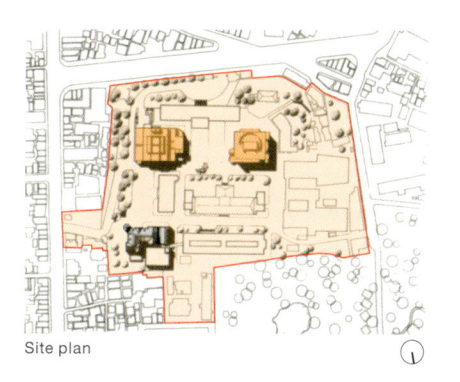

West elevation [K.M.]

Site plan

Site model

日本でもっとも古い大学である慶應義塾は、2014年に155周年を迎えた。三田のキャンパスはその慶應義塾の発祥の地であると同時に、現在も大学の中核をなしている施設群が存在する。そして、三田のキャンパスはこの長い歴史で、一つ一つ時代の刻印を押しながら集積された建物群によって形成されている。その中でも一番象徴的な存在が、もっとも古い演説館、106年前に建てられた旧図書館と少し遅れて建てられた本部棟等である。したがって、新図書館・大学院棟を建てるにあたって、こうしたコンテクストの中で、各々が独自の表現をもちながら、しかし微妙に反応し合うことが当初から意図されていた。

特に新図書館は旧図書館と本部棟を介して相対し、この三つの建物の間に、塾の歴史を象徴する静かな広場を形成する。そのために、この新図書館の4階の軒線は、他の二つの建物とほぼ同じく16mであり、また新・旧図書館とも、本部棟の間に13mの距離を保ち対称形を形成している。このキャンパスはすでに狭隘な敷地にかなり高い密度で建築の群が建設されている。そのためにも、かなりの容積をもつ新図書館はその半分を地下に沈め書庫とした。

Washington University in St. Louis
Sam Fox School of Design & Visual Arts | 2006
セントルイス・ワシントン大学
サム・フォックス視覚芸術学部

The Sam Fox School of Design & Visual Arts at Washington University in St. Louis consolidates and expands the facilities and programs related to the study of art, art history and archaeology and architecture. The two new buildings (the Mildred Lane Kemper Art Museum and the Earl E. and Myrtle E. Walker Hall) together with the three existing buildings (Bixby Hall 1926, Givens Hall 1931, Steinberg Hall 1961— designed by Fumihiko Maki) have become an ensemble of spaces that function as a mini-campus within the larger university. A

Aerial view

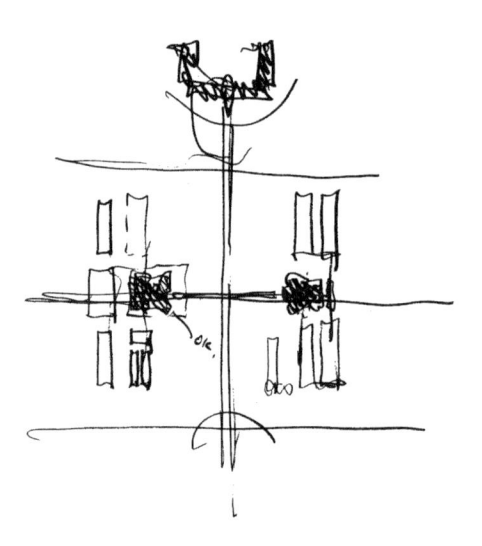

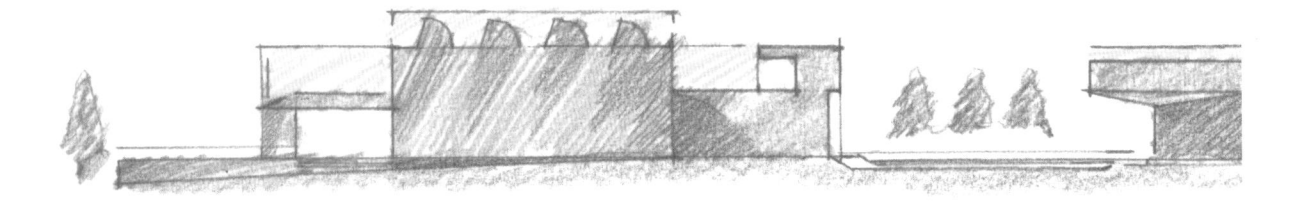

Sculpture Garden

network of courtyards and terraces has been designed to unite five buildings and five departments to establish a new Center— the Sam Fox School. The planning strategy ties into the long tradition of campus planning at Washington University.

The Mildred Lane Kemper Art Museum functions as a gateway building to the Campus as well as the center piece of the Sam Fox School serving as the academic symbol for the visual arts at Washington University. The facility has also become an important cultural institution for the larger St. Louis community. The new art museum houses and exhibits Washington University's collection of art, which ranges from ancient artifacts to modern art. The museum drew approximately 20,000 visitors in its opening year and has proven to be one of the finest university museums in the country.

[R.P.]

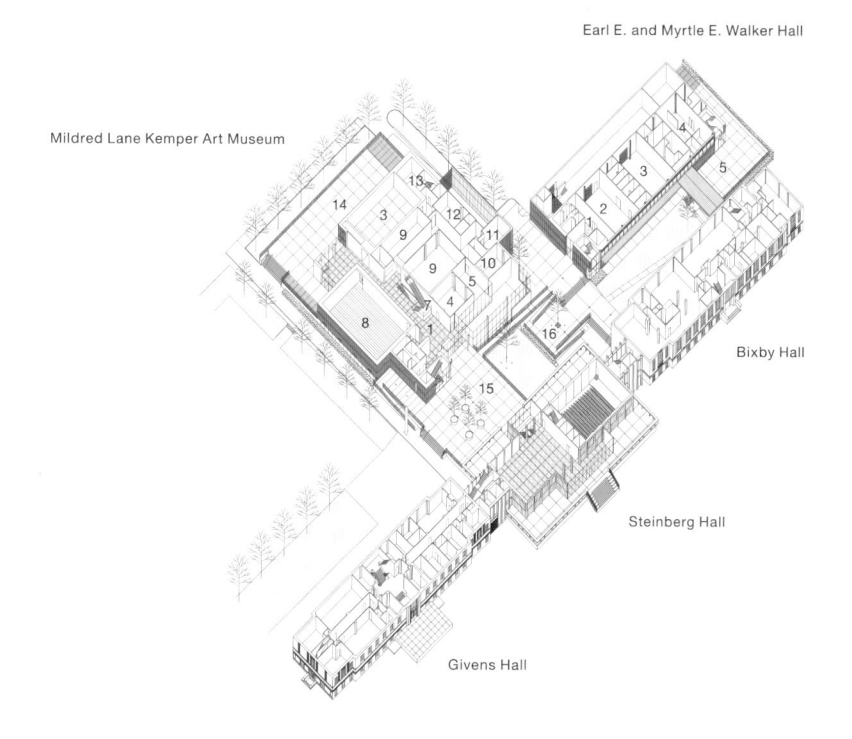

Mildred Lane Kemper Art Museum

Earl E. and Myrtle E. Walker Hall

Bixby Hall

Steinberg Hall

Givens Hall

Axonometric

Earl E. And Myrtle E. Walker Hall

1 Martin Foyer
2 Metal Sculpture Studio
3 Wood Sculpture Studio
4 Sculpture Graduate Studio
5 Shapleigh Courtyard and Terrace

Mildred Lane Kemper Art Museum

1 Saligman Family Atrium
2 May Department Stores Foundation Foyer
3 College of Art Gallery
4 Lopata Art History Classroom
5 Lehmann Museum Classroom
6 Baizer Family Elevator
7 Freund Family Grand Staircase
8 Temporary Display
9 Painting Storage
10 Receiving Room
11 Workshop
12 Sculpture Storage
13 Display Storage
13 Florence Steinberg Weil Sculpture Garden
15 Jordan Foundation Central Plaza
16 Dula Foundation Central Courtyard

The two new buildings of the Sam Fox School have been designed to harmonize with the two existing historical buildings in Neoclassic style with a strong horizontal composition. The facades of the new buildings are primarily cladded in Bedford Limestone, 8 inches high by 30 inches wide units to match the materiality and texture of the surrounding buildings.

このプロジェクトは、新たな増築により、分散した建築・芸術学部をサム・フォックス・アートセンターという一つのコンプレックスとしてインターアクティブに連携させ、建築や視覚芸術に関わる施設やプログラムの充実を図るものである。敷地は大学のメイン・キャンパスの表玄関にあたり、そこにミルドレッド・レーン・ケンパー・アートミュージアムおよびアール・EアンドマートルE・ウォーカー・ホールの2棟が計画された。それらはワシントン大学の伝統的なキャンパス・プランニングの手法に則り、連続するオープン・スペースを既存の建物との間に構成し、ミニ・キャンパスをつくりだすよう配置されている。

The atrium of the Kemper Art Museum

School of Art Gallery

ミルドレッド・レーン・ケンパー・アートミュージアムはこのコンプレックスにおけるアカデミックなシンボルとして、さらにはセントルイス地域における文化施設の拠点の一つとして計画された。この美術館は、ワシントン大学が所持する古代の工芸品から近代アートまでといった幅広いコレクションを収蔵し、展示している。2006年10月の開館から、1年で約2万人の訪問客が記録され、全米でも名だたる大学美術館といえる。

コンプレックス内の既存の建物はライムストーンを主要な外装材とし、水平方向が強調されたコンポジションをもつので、計画された二つの建物もそれらに調和するようデザインされた。外壁のデザインは小さなライムストーンのモジュール（750mm x 200mm）を基調とし、既存のコンテクストとの調和を図りつつ、かつ新鮮な印象をキャンパスにつくり出している。

The southwest corner of the Kemper Art Museum [R.P.]

Lighting fixture detail

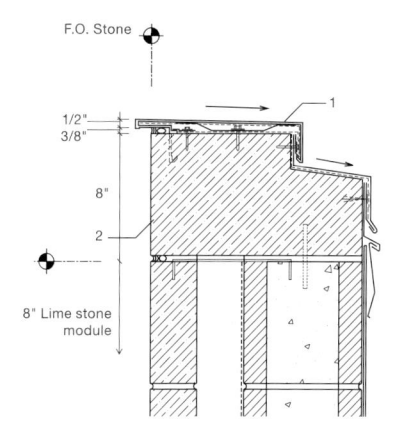

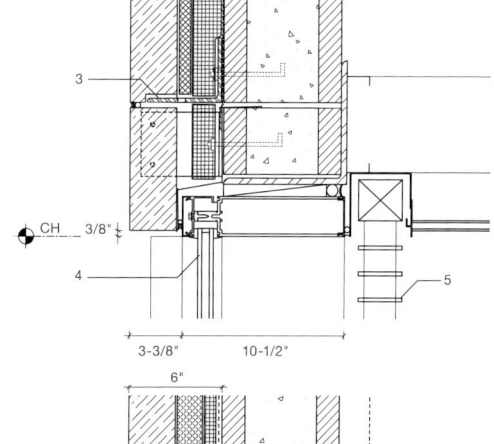

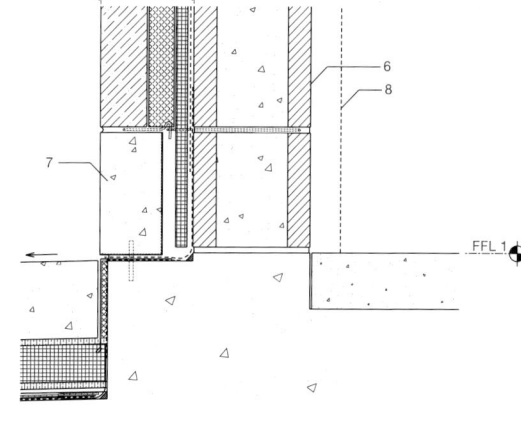

1 Aluminum coping
2 Stone coping
3 4"X 5" Continuous stainless steel shelf angle
4 Curtain wall system
5 Wood blinds
6 Concrete masonry unit
7 Precast concrete panel
8 Interior furring

Detailed section of limestone wall (scale:1"=1'-0")

University of Pennsylvania
Annenberg Public Policy Center | 2009
ペンシルバニア大学
アネンバーグ・パブリックポリシーセンター

The Annenberg Public Policy Center (APPC) is an independent policy think tank established at the University of Pennsylvania in 1994. Sited along a pedestrian thoroughfare dotted with red brick structures, the APPC's exterior palette of layered glass and wood creates a "warm transparency" that complements its masonry context while still presenting an open, modern image befitting a program dedicated to public policy. Deference to

View from the north

adjacent volumes and eave lines further integrate it with the scale and spirit of the Penn campus.

The exterior skin of the APPC is an aluminum and glass curtain wall with operable awning units. This layered wood and glass system is the primary aesthetic motif of the project, and is engineered to optimize comfort and flexibility. Operable exterior windows, sliding wood panels, and roll shades allows each user to individually tailor lighting, ventilation, shading, and thermal insulation throughout the year. The result is an ever-changing facade that responds to individual preferences, lighting needs, and interior use patterns.

East facade [J.T.]

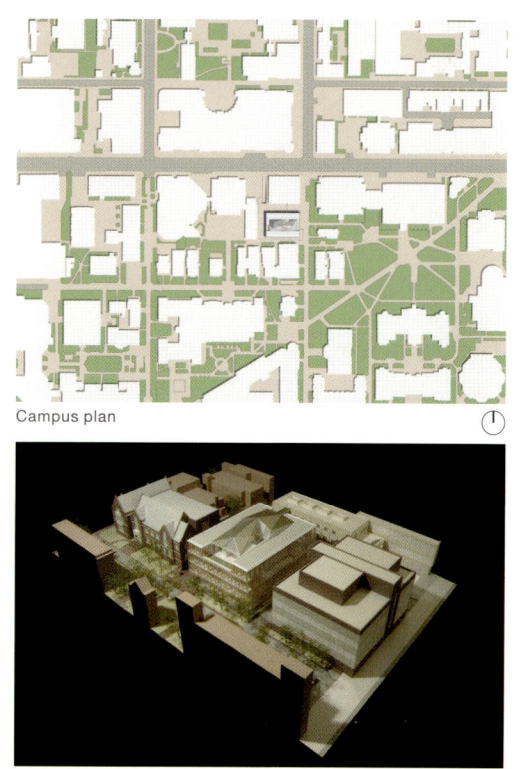

Campus plan

Site model

ペンシルバニア大学のアネンバーグ・パブリックポリシーセンターは、1994年に創立され、これまでに報道の内容や公共政策、それに広く情報に関する研究を行ってきた。敷地はキャンパスのほぼ中央部にあり、勾配屋根の旧い煉瓦造やライムストーン仕上げの建物など、時代の変遷を感じさせる建築群に隣接している。アイビーリーグの長い歴史をもつこのようなコンテクストを考慮し、新しいセンターは軒の高さを既存の建築と調停すると同時に、現代的で透明感をもちながら周囲の素材感とも調和する暖かい色調の外装がふさわしいと考えていた。

アネンバーグ・パブリックポリシーセンターの質感と建築の表情をつくるのが全周を覆うダブルスキンの表層である。内部の空間は研究者間の交流を促進し、また多様な研究体制に対応するよう、フレキシブルで流動的につくられている。1階のアゴラからスカイライトの光あふれる最上階のラウンジまでがアトリウムの吹抜けを通じてつながり、これが中心となって周辺の空間を結びつける。そしてアトリウム周りの研究スペースはパーティションによって軽く仕切られ、階をまたいで連携しながら相互に研究活動の様子が感じられる構成となっている。

Corner office [B.H.]

Glass curtain wall and sliding wooden screens [B.H.]

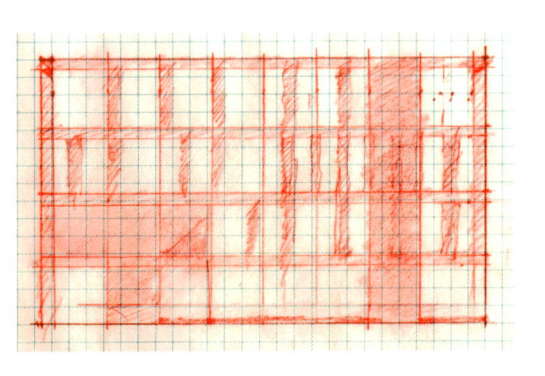

Atrium [B.H.]

Main entrance

Massachusetts Institute of Technology
The Media Lab Complex | 2009
マサチューセッツ工科大学
メディア研究所

The idea for the Media Lab came into being in 1980 from Professor Nicholas Negroponte and former MIT President and Science Advisor to President John F. Kennedy, Jerome Wiesner. The Lab grew out of the work of MIT's Architecture Machine Group and was built upon the seminal work of the faculty, which included a variety of research disciplines such as cognition, learning, music, graphic design, video and holography. The lab has pioneered a research environment where academia and industry collaborate and has cultivated

View from the Charles River [A.G.]

Conceptual model

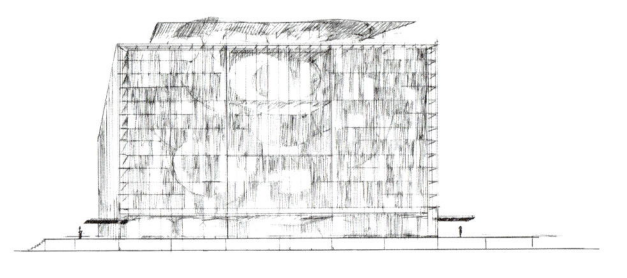

a culture built around cross disciplinary research groups much in the spirit and vitality of architectural "ateliers."

The Media Lab expansion developed by Maki and Associates is founded upon a concept of double height labs that step in section to afford visual connectivity amongst research groups with maximum transparency. Each lab faces onto a multi-tiered atrium that acts as the central hub of the complex and links to the original Media Lab building built in 1985 by I.M.Pei. The Atria serve to provide space for research/sponsor presentations, exhibition, and gatherings amongst a variety of research disciplines.

The two Atria centered within the building enable extended and elongated lines of sight to the various activities occurring throughout the building. This strategy offers a high level of transparency and interconnection between the lab spaces. The Atria terminate with the "winter garden" on the top floor,

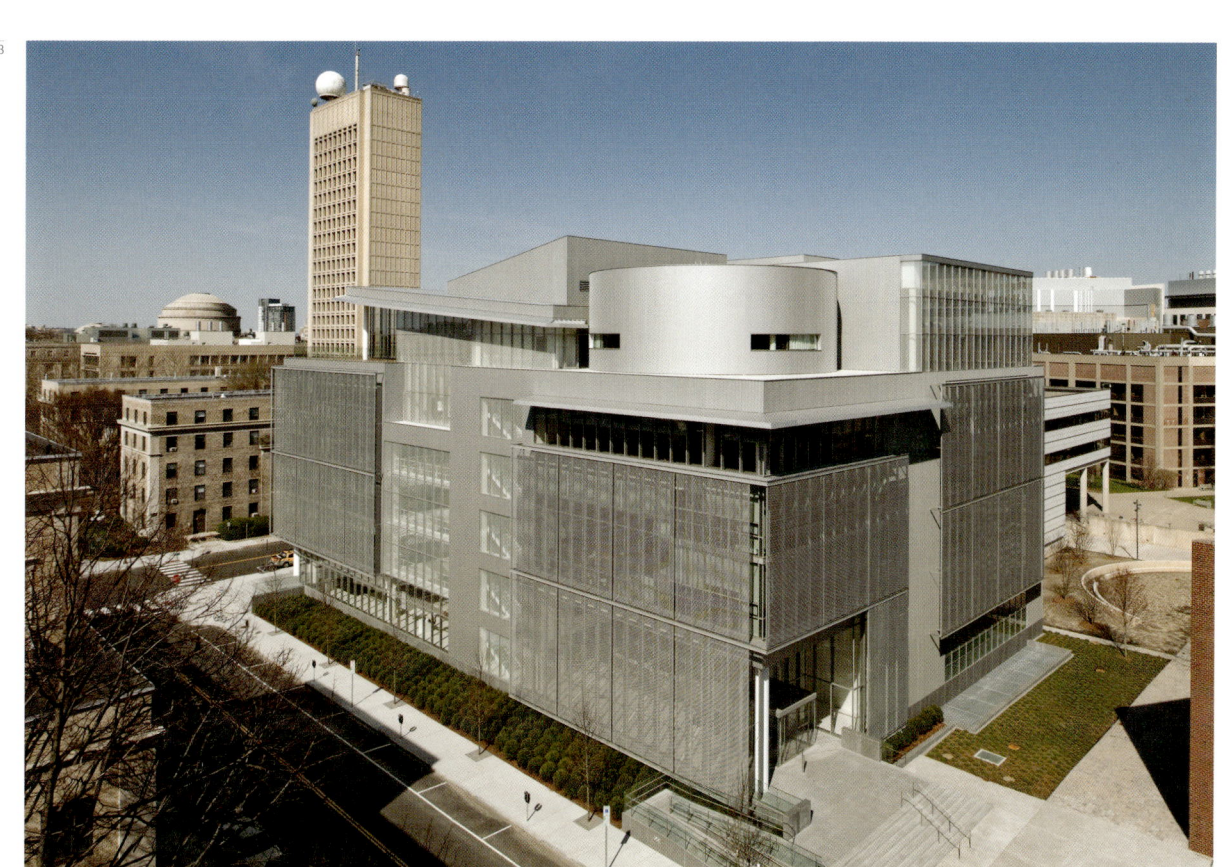

View from the southeast

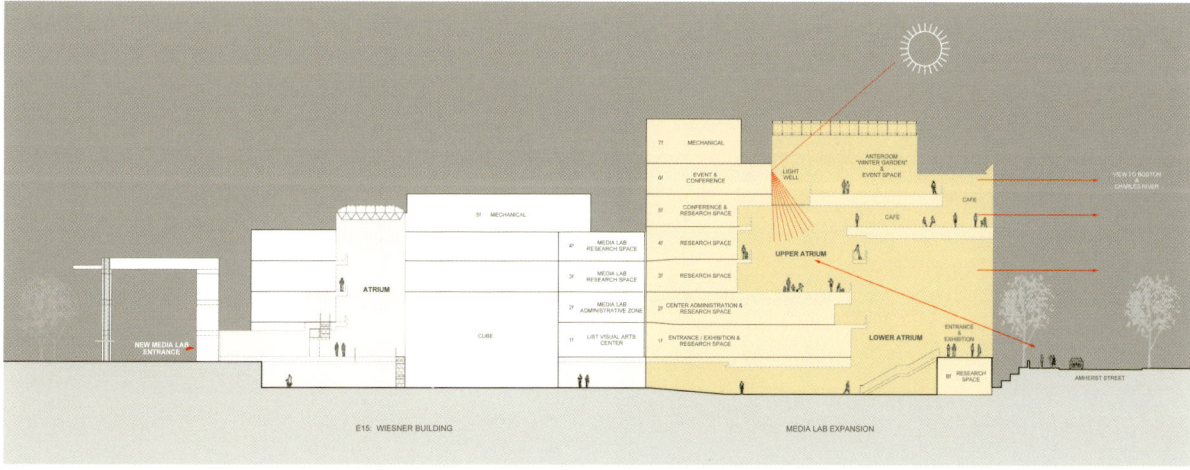

Section diagram

consisting of an event space, a large conference room, and a lecture hall surrounding the central reception area.

The Media Lab's sponsorship program allows open access to the research projects; therefore, the building has been designed to showcase the work within. The building is clad in aluminum and glass with a second layer of louvered screens that overlays the glazing providing the necessary environmental shading. The laboratories have an abundance of natural light and a variety of views to the exterior, in stark contrast to ordinary laboratory facilities that are often highly concealed. The exterior image of the building transforms throughout the day with the changing sunlight conditions illuminating the varying levels of transparency and spatial depth occurring within the building.

Laboratory

View upon entering the Lower Atrium [A.G.]

Laboratory [A.G.]

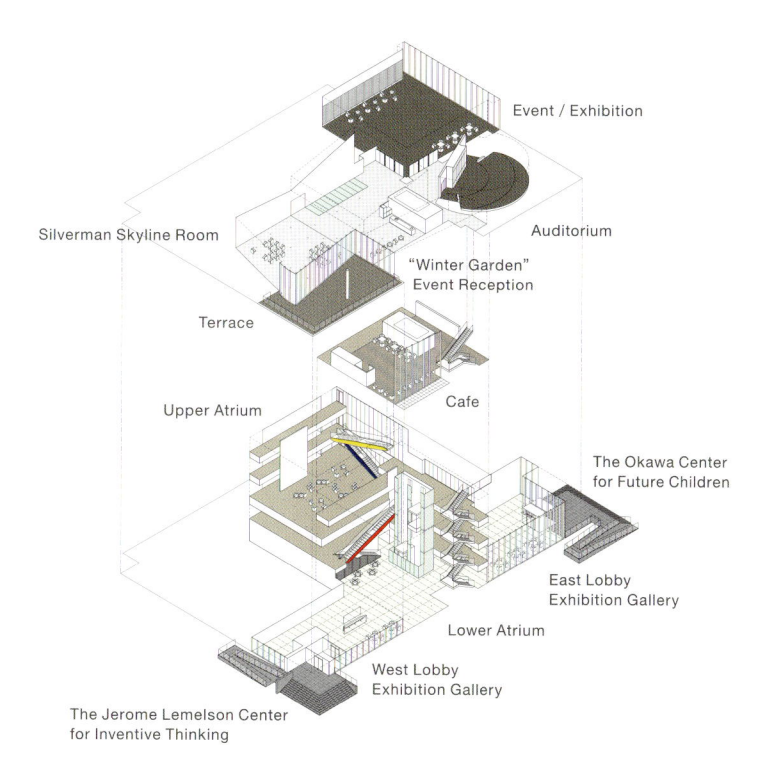

Event / Exhibition
Silverman Skyline Room
Auditorium
"Winter Garden" Event Reception
Terrace
Cafe
Upper Atrium
The Okawa Center for Future Children
East Lobby Exhibition Gallery
Lower Atrium
West Lobby Exhibition Gallery
The Jerome Lemelson Center for Inventive Thinking

Axonometric

MITのメディア研究所は、認知科学、学習科学、音楽、グラフィック・デザイン、ビデオ、ホログラフィー等の研究活動を行う機関として、1980年に大学のアーキテクチュラル・マシーングループから分離して設立された。ここでは建築のアトリエのような環境の中、企業と大学が協力し、自由な発想で様々な領域・分野を横断しながら、常に新しい研究を開拓し続けてきた。そのような研究活動の拡大と、グループ間の交流をサポートするようなスペースの必要性から、大規模な増築が計画された。

このような要求に対して、我々は、1985年にI.M.ペイによって設計された既存建物との結節点ともなるアトリウムを核とする空間構成を提案している。このアトリウムは、建物中央を6層にわたって展開する主要動線空間であり、またその中に展示、パフォーマンス、集いの場を設けることによって、一般の人々がメディア研究所の活動や研究内容に触れる機会を提供している。

中央の連続した二つのアトリウムでは、建物内で起こる様々なアクティビティーを眺めることができ、従来の配置計画では希薄であった研究室間の

Evening view of the roof terrace

Cafe   [A.G.]

透明性や相関性を強めている。最上階には、アトリウム上部のクライマックス空間として「ウィンターガーデン」があり、これを中心にイベント・スペース、大会議室、講堂が設けられている。

メディア研究所には、世界中から多数の学者やスポンサー、企業の社員などが訪れ、新しい研究プロジェクトの見学や研究者との会議が日常的に行われている。建物はアルミとガラスのカーテンウォールで包まれ、環境制御のためのアルミルーバーのスクリーンが2層の単位で研究室を覆っている。通常は閉ざされがちな研究室だが、ここでは自然光に満ちた空間が生み出されている。様々な透過性と奥行きをもつこの建物の姿は、日の光に応じて、常に変化し続けるものとなる。

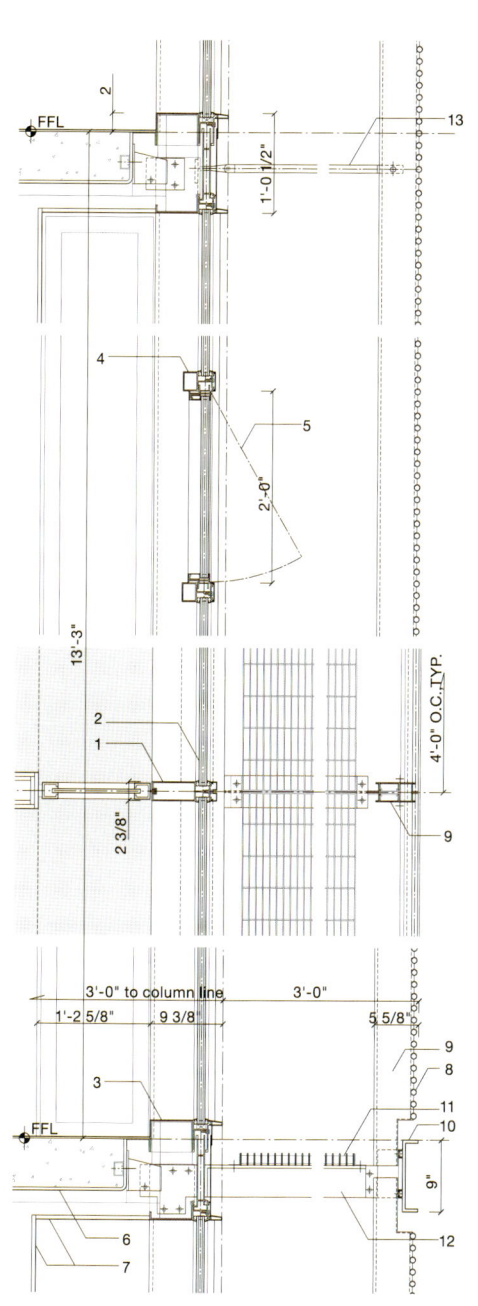

South elevation at dusk [A.G.]

Detail of pipe louvers [A.G.]

1 Extruded aluminum mullion, pvdf coated
2 1" Insulated tempered glass (1/4"+1/2" argon gas+1/4") with Low-e coating
3 Extruded aluminum sill, pvdf coated
4 Extruded aluminum transom, pvdf coated
5 Operable window
6 Concrete slab with 3/8" bent steel plate
7 Painted gypsum board
8 Extruded aluminum pipe louver, pvdf coated. 3/4" dia. at 1 1/2" on center, typical
9 Extruded aluminum louver mullion, pvdf coated
10 Extruded aluminum channel, pvdf coated
11 Aluminum grating, pvdf coated
12 Galvanized steel outrigger
13 1" Dia. stainless steel strut

Facade detail (scale:1/2"=1'-0")

Tsuda College Sendagaya Campus | 2017
津田塾大学千駄ヶ谷キャンパス

The site is located in front of Sendagaya station, anchored on the corner by Tsuda Hall (designed by Maki and Associates thirty years ago). Envisioning the site as the center of its urban campus, Tsuda College is starting a new fine arts department here. Protecting the cultured atmosphere of the Sendagaya area, the height of the new complex is kept between three and five stories, even though it fronts the station and could be developed higher. An existing row of cherry trees along the sidewalk is maintained and serves

View from the northeast

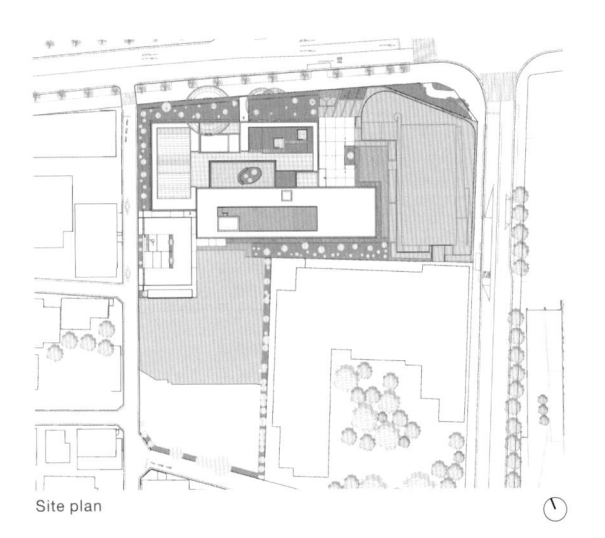

Site plan

Tsuda Hall -1988

[T.K.]

as a green buffer zone for the building and streetscape. The site planning centers on intimate open spaces surrounded by mid- to low-rise towers, while also considering area for a planned second phase expansion.

On the interior, the first three floors of the low-rise volumes consist of public spaces used frequently by students—conference rooms, library, study labs, and a cafeteria. These spaces are open to the university community and designed to promote interaction. The fourth and fifth research floors have a quieter atmosphere, consisting of research rooms, instructor break rooms, and seminar rooms. Multi-story lounges on each floor connect different programs and serve as central gathering spaces for the university community.

Aerial view from the northwest

Interior perspective

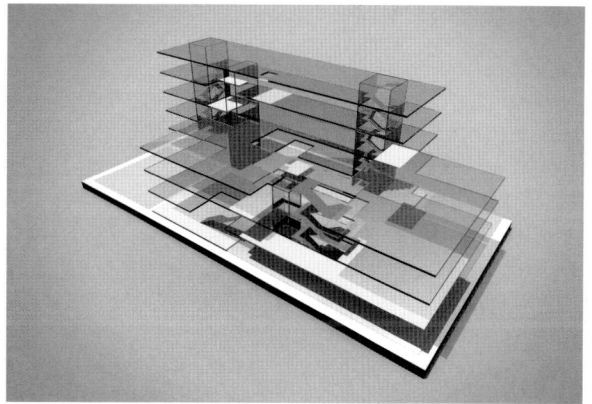

Conceptual model

敷地は千駄ヶ谷の駅前にあり、その駅側のコーナーには30年ほど前に我々が設計を行った津田ホールが建っている。この計画は、その津田ホールに隣接して、津田塾大学が都心部の拠点として新たにキャンパスの整備を行うものであり、文系の新学部が創設される予定である。千駄ヶ谷特有の文教的な景観に配慮し、新学部の校舎は3層と5層のコンプレックスで構成され、駅前でありながら高さを抑えたヒューマンスケールのキャンパスがつくられる。そして歩道に沿っては、桜の古木を残しながら厚みのある緑地帯を整備し、緑豊かな街路沿いの風景が展開する。キャンパスの構成は小さなオープンスペースを囲みながら中低層の校舎群が連なり、将来の2期計画へと伸展していく計画である。

内部の構成は3階までの低層部には学生がよく利用する講義室群と図書室、ラーニングコモン、カフェテリアなど、共用のスペースを集約して設けている。これらのスペースには気軽に立ち寄ることのできる開放性をもたせ、学生間の活発なコミュニケーションを引き出そうとするものである。一方、上層の4、5階には研究室、講師室、セミナー室などが置かれ、少し落ち着きのある研究者フロアーが形成される。そして各階に吹抜けの小ラウンジを設け、層をつなぐパブリックスペースの核としている。

◎Toward Ocean

◎海へ

Zeebrugge Ferry Terminal Competition | 1989
ゼーブルージェ・フェリーターミナル　コンペ案

Our proposal for Zeebrugge Ferry Terminal is situated in the outer port of Zeebrugge in Northern Belgium. The site is on an exposed strip of land jutting out into the sea and is covered by a dense forest. A circular deck provides a plateau on to which four quasi-sculptural elements are placed. These four elements, each different in form and function, consist of the Terminal Office Tower, Fitness Center, and Cafe Wheel and Restaurant.

The simplicity of the circular form represents the celestial vault containing a variety of constellations, a world governed by polar coordinates. The four elements on the plateau reflect elements associated with the water (the Terminal could be a compass arrow, the Office tower an iceberg, the Fitness Center and Cafe the wings of a seabird in flight). Viewed from an approaching ship, the plateau provides a stable, unchanging base upon which these sculptural elements form ever-changing silhouettes.

ゼーブルージェ港の一隅に予定されたこの新フェリーターミナルは、英国、スカンジナヴィアとの海路を結ぶ重要な拠点として、さらに近い将来、実現が予定されているドーヴァー海峡のトンネル完成時には、これまでのフェリーサービスに対する需要の減少という懸念に対して、その存在をアピールしようという狙いが含まれている。

フェリーターミナルは、こうした要望に応えて、円盤状のプラットフォームの上に、様々な形態の施設が展開するという構想のもとに生まれた。プラットフォームからはゼーブルージェの港と北海を一望にでき、その上に四つの棟が計画された。羅針盤のような機構の中央に向かって突出した部分は、税関、ウェイティング、カフェ、展望台が含まれる。各々が特異な形態をもった円盤状の集合体は、都市の建築と全く異なる新しい様相をたたえている。

Model [T.K.]

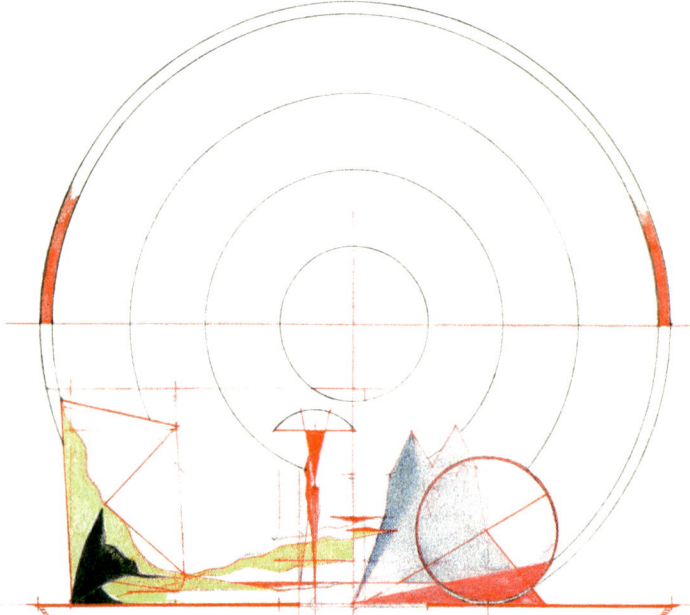

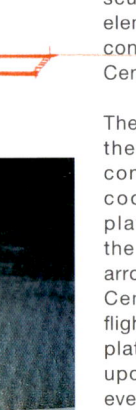

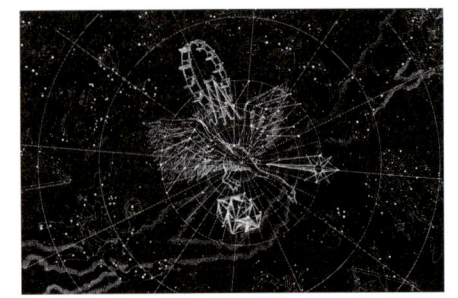

Concept image

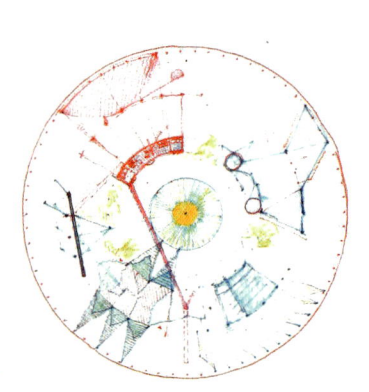

Palazzo del Cinema Competition | 1990
シネマパレス　コンペ案

View from the canal

Site photo

Model　[J.A.]

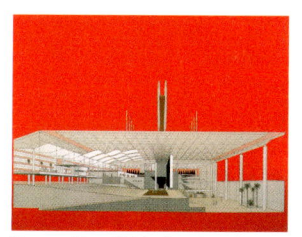

Perspective of Lido Beach entrance

Outdoor theater

Our proposal for the Palazzo del Cinema attempts to express the spirit of Venice, both eternal and temporal, in one striking entity: a glass palace on the water. Changing from day to night, its solid mass is gradually transformed and dissolves into a glowing, festive illusion.

Poised on the island of Lido in Venice's lagoon, the Palazzo del Cinema is a meeting place of two worlds. One of which is the sandy and expansive beaches of the Adriatic Sea, and the other, the gentle neighborhood of Venice's canals. The glass palace faces the plaza with an open-air space sheltered beneath a vast canopy. Underneath this roof lie a 1500-seat outdoor cinema, a café, and shops intended to generate new activity in this part of the Lido.

This Palazzo del Cinema was intended at first as a home for the Venice Film Festival, but it has been conceived as a public gathering place for other events all year long. The formal spatial organization is reminiscent of a hilltown, where the seven cinema rooms of different sizes and shapes have been interlocked three-dimensionally on different levels.

The roof provides two outdoor terraces: the lower rooftop is a garden terrace that faces the canal; and the higher rooftop is a reception terrace that offers a panoramic view of the Adriatic Sea and Venice.

ベネチアのリドは19世紀に開発されたまちで、シネマパレスのある付近はカジノ、ホテルなどがあり、観光地を形成し、夏は特に海水浴などで賑わう。敷地の南面に白砂の海浜が広がり、新しいプログラムは中劇場、オフィス、カフェ、ショップなどの施設を一段と拡充して、映画祭のみならず国際会議にも利用しえること、また野外劇場は大屋根をもつことが要求された。

我々の提案は、これらの施設を一つのクリスタルなパレスとして統合し、かつ演出することにあった。透明であることによって、パフォーマンスすなわち空間とその中における人間の動きを視覚的に演出しようという試みなのである。まるでヒルタウンのような形状をもつこのクリスタルパレスは、大小異なる七つのシネマルームを立体的に組み込むような空間構成としている。

屋上にはレセプションの場が設けられ、人々は改めて、ベネチアあるいはアドリア海へと広がる眺望を享受するであろう。

Vousaari Tower Competition | 1999
ヴォサーリ・ニュータウン高層住居　コンペ案

Vuosaari is a satellite city located ten kilometers east of Helsinki. The tower includes five housing unit types, ranging in size from 55 to 160 square meters, each with an ocean view. Comprised of two parallelogram floor plates and a triangular core, the tower's acute angles enable most rooms within each unit to have ocean views. Because of its unique, irregular shape, the tower's silhouette varies according to lighting conditions, direction and distance.

Aerial view form the southeast [T.K.]

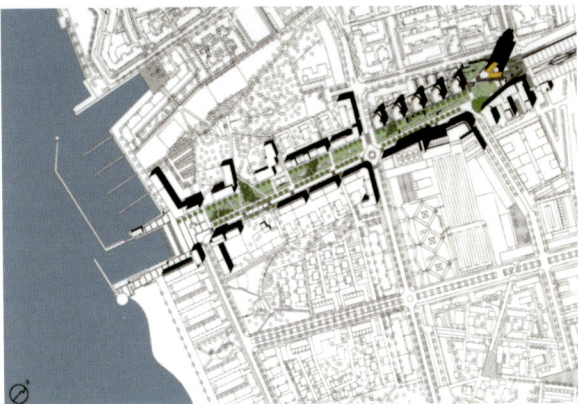

Location plan

ヴォサーリは、ヘルシンキの衛星都市群の一つとして、その東、約10kmのところに位置し、高速道路、鉄道でヘルシンキと結ばれている。このプロジェクトの規模は、55㎡から160㎡まで五つのタイプを含む集合住宅で、特に各住居から海への眺望が開けている。タワーは二つの平行四辺形のプレートとコア部分が形成する三角形の形状からなっている。鋭角的なシルエットを有するタワーは、光の状態に応じて、また見る方向、距離によって様々なシルエットを与えるとともに、各ユニットのほぼすべての居室から海への眺望を可能としている。

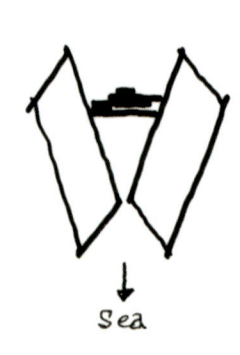

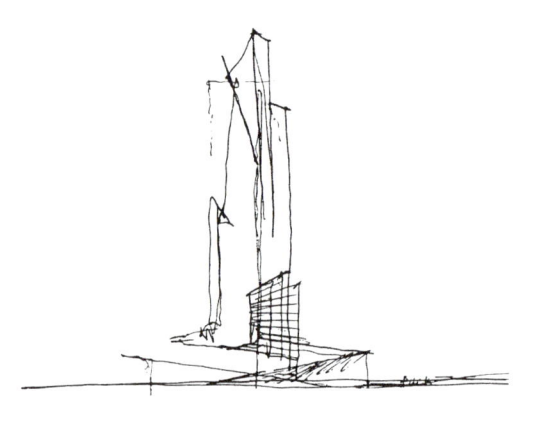

Hong Kong Ocean Terminal Extension | 2003
香港オーシャンターミナル

Overview from Hong Kong's peak

Perspective of atrium

The Ocean Terminal Extension was the winning competition entry in an International Competition held in early 2003. The program includes immigration and boarding facilities for an International Ferry Terminal, generous retail spaces, and the boarding deck for a 75 meter observation wheel located on the roof.

Visitors can experience panoramic views of Hong Kong Island and Bay through its fully transparent curtain wall, while a cascading atrium gestures towards the open sea. The design thus acknowledges the singular beauty of its location, while also providing a sense of internal connectivity to draw visitors through the complex.

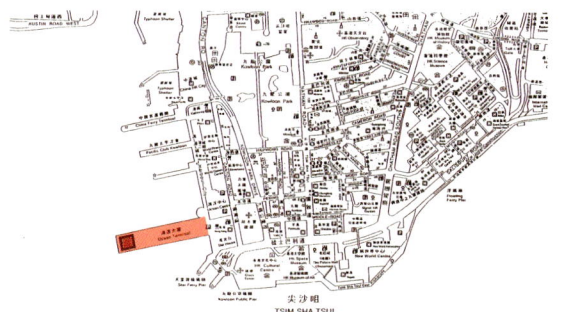

Location map

この計画は、2003年に開催された国際コンペティションの一等案であり、国際線のフェリーターミナルと商業施設、そして高さ75mの屋上観覧車の複合施設である。

来訪者は、階段状に連なるアトリウムを通してその先に広がる海へと導かれ、透明なカーテンウォール越しに香港島と湾を一望することができる。施設内に魅力的な連続性のある空間をつくり出し、周りの美しい景観をさらに引き立たせるよう構成されている。

GROUP FORM & COLLECTIVE FORM

群造形&集合体

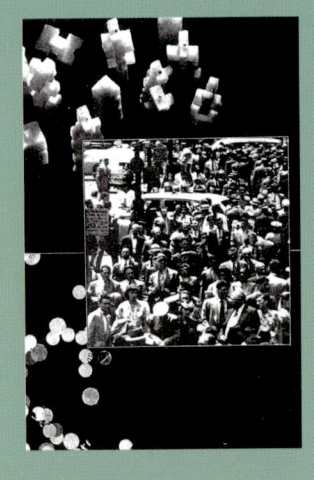

Shinjuku Terminal Redevelopment Project (1960)

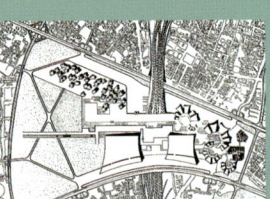

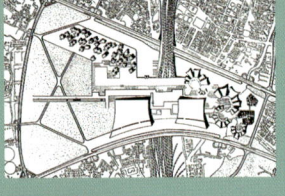

Shinjuku Terminal Redevelopment Project (1960)

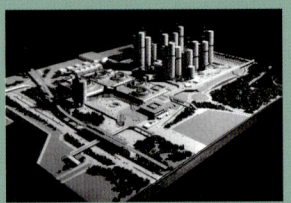

International Competition for UNIDO & IAEA (1969) [O.M.]

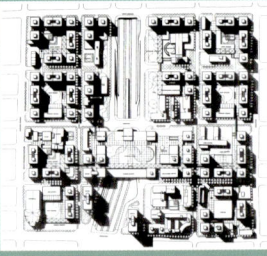

Shinjuku Project (1960)

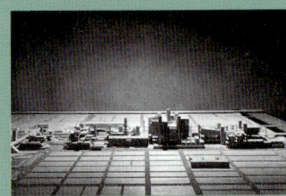

K Project (1964) [O.M.]

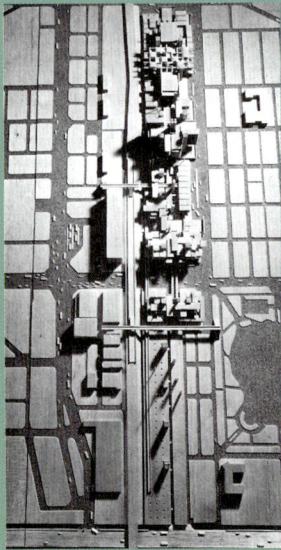

K Project (1964) [O.M.]

COMPOSITIONAL FORM

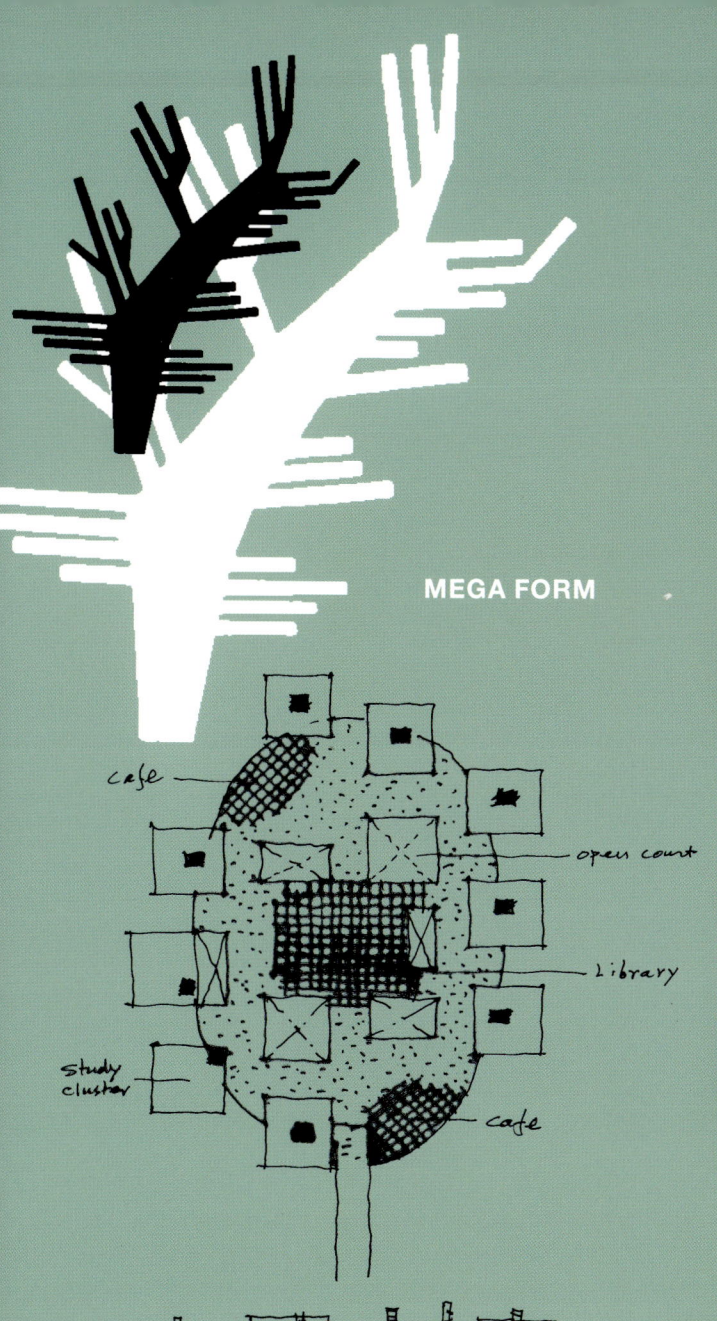

群造形は、1960年、東京で開催された世界デザイン会議において、新宿計画に託して、「メタボリズム1960年」の中で大高正人とともに発表したものである。その後、ワシントン大学から、グループ・フォーム、メガ・フォーム、コンポジショナル・フォームの三つのパラダイムを比較検討した"Investigations in Collective Form"という冊子が出版された。

MEGA FORM

Tokyo Plan 1960
(Kenzo Tange, 1960)

Plan Obus for Algiers
(Le Corbusier, 1933)

Republic Polytechnic Campus (2006) [D.P.]

Hydra Island

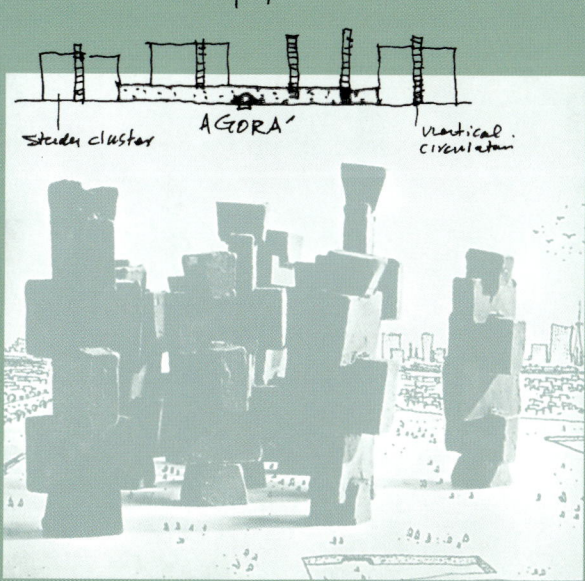

GROUP FORM

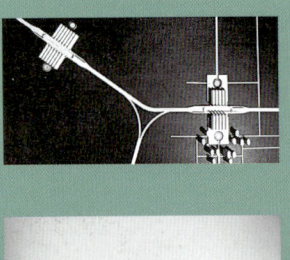

Boston Transportation Exchange (1965)

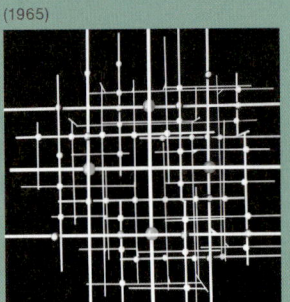

Open end system

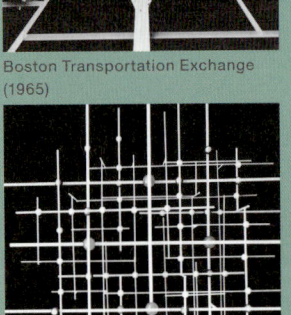

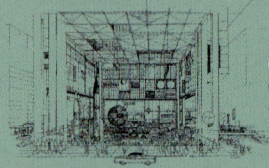

City Room

City Corridor

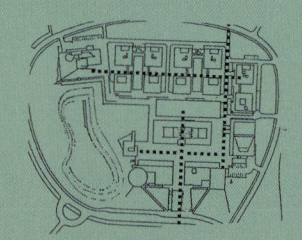

Keio University Shonan Fujisawa Campus (1992)

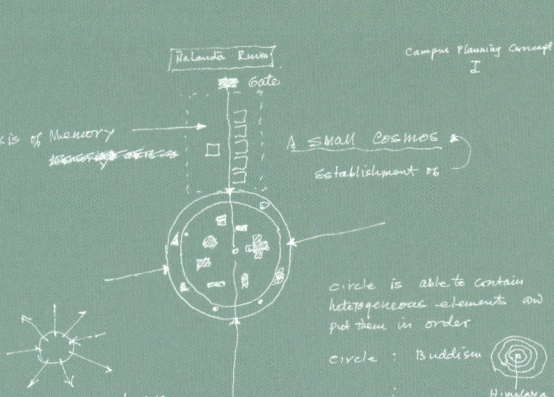

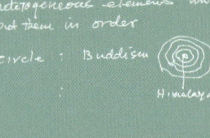

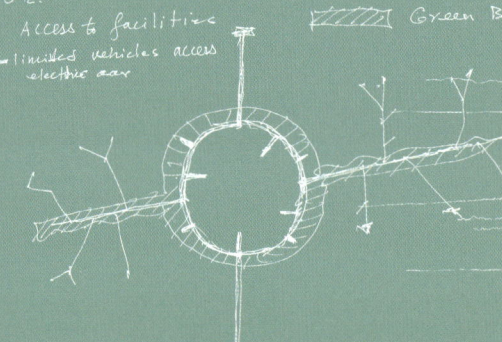

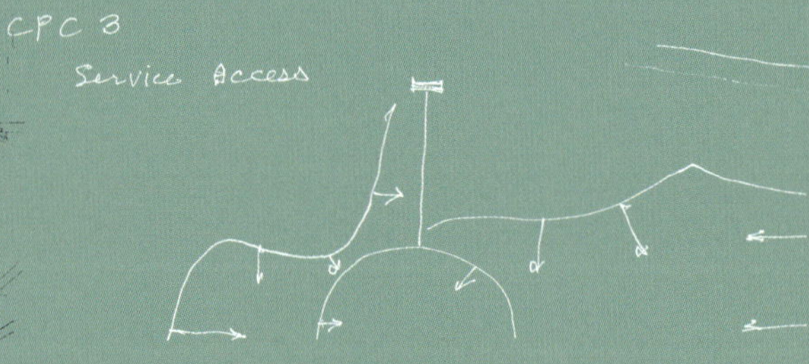

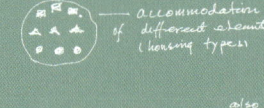

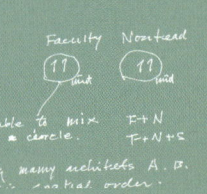

Hillside Terrace Complex

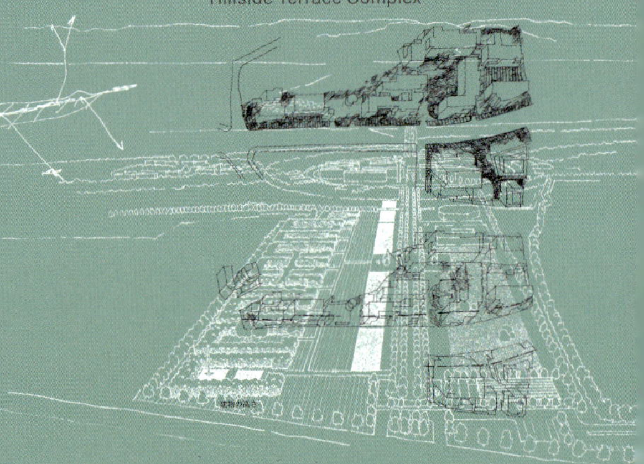

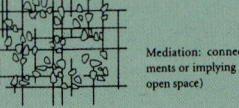

Campus Planning Concept I

Nalanda Ruin — Gate
Axis of Memory

A SMALL COSMOS
Establishment of

circle is able to contain heterogeneous elements and put them in order

circle : Buddism
Himalaya

receiver & projector of
Gate
mountain

CPC 2. Access to facilities
— limited vehicles access
electric car

Green Belt

CPC 3 Service Access

Residential Circle
60 M
communal facility
optimum size for forming a community.

separation & Linking

accommodation of different element (housing types)
Faculty Nontead
11   11

also able to mix within a circle.   F+N
easier phasing   F+N+S
possibility for assigning many architects A. B.
central order

Mediation: connection with intermediate elements or implying medium (including composed open space)

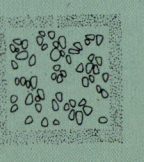

Definition: enclosing disparate structures with a sensible barrier; producing unity within the barrier and separating from what is outside

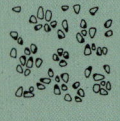

Repetition: giving each element a feature that is common to all in the group so that each is identifiable as a part of the same order

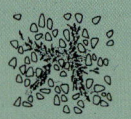

Sequential Path: placing activities that are performed in sequence in identifiable spatial relation to one another

Golgi Structure— a model of vertical Figure & Ground [T.O.]

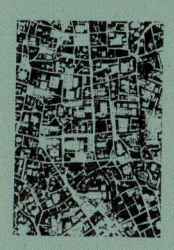

figure and ground | grid | natural form
Three paradigms of a city

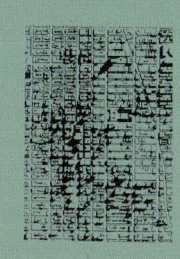

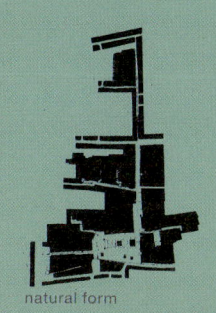

× slab as generator of new urban form for offices

○ Use new modern technology. Cantilever.

Bubble

○ Urban facilities (commerce, culture, entertainment) mixed development

Competition for Frankfurt am Main Center (1993)

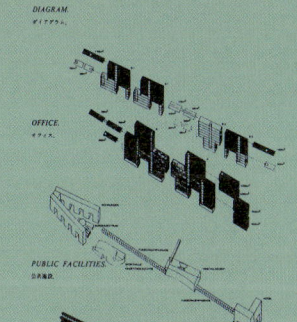

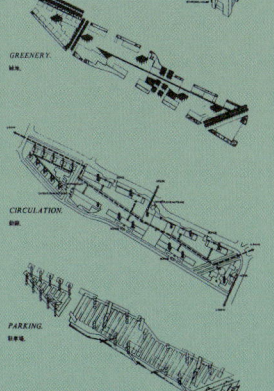

DIAGRAM
OFFICE
PUBLIC FACILITIES
GREENERY
CIRCULATION
PARKING

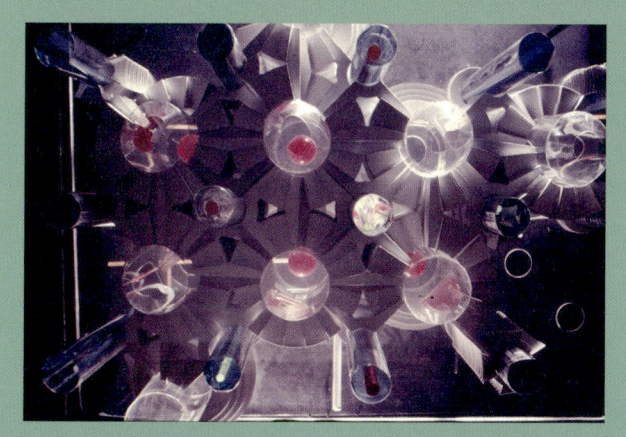

4 | Group Form & Collective Form

群造形&集合体

Through my two journeys to the West—Asia, Middle East, and the Mediterranean coast—in 1959 and 1960, I have learned many things. Within village groups made from plastered sundried bricks and shingled roofs, there always existed a certain "model", and I was often deeply moved by their overall form. This observation served as the backbone of the proposal of "group form" in *Metabolism 1960*, done in collaboration with Masato Otaka. It was around the time when investigations of villages had just started to catch on with architects and historians in Japan. The idea of groups formed by individual entities has been consistently put into our practice over the next half century.

Investigations in Collective Form published by Washington University in St. Louis in 1964 provides an objective examination of benefits and disadvantages of mega structures (which often included urban infrastructure) proposed by popular architects at the time, such as Yona Friedman and Le Corbusier, and "Tokyo Project 1960" by Kenzo Tange. Perhaps because of this objective nature, this publication has been widely read in universities in the United States even today.

Since the end of 1960s, I have been fortunate to realize numerous examples of group form, such as the Hillside Terrace development and Rissho University Campus project. I was also blessed with the opportunities to make interventions in existing group forms, such as TV Asahi, 4 World Trade Center, and university projects both inside and outside of Japan.

The Golgi Structure is another proposal investigating similar concepts. In the formation of collective forms in dense urban cities, solid architectural groups regulate the exterior spaces, such as streets and plazas. This composition of figure and ground has existed as early as ancient cities in Europe. The Golgi Structure is a model of high-density urban space that conveys the dynamism between three-dimensional architectural groups and exterior spaces.

As shown in our university campus projects, many of our experiences focus on the creation of optimal collective forms with individual entities that serve different functions from each other, rather than group forms created by similar entities. In these projects, we have often found ourselves questioning the exterior spaces that link the heterogeneous entities and the architectural spaces that face them.

"Collective Form of Open Spaces", introduced in the final chapter, challenges the conventional notion of "architecture first" by introducing a new paradigm—"exterior spaces first".

1959年と1960年の2回にわたる西方への旅—アジア・中近東、地中海沿岸—から、私は多くのことを学んだ。日干し煉瓦を下地にした塗壁と瓦屋根で構成された民衆群が構成する集落・都市の中に常にその民衆一個体には、ある〈かた〉が存在し、その集合がつくりだす全体に感動させられるものが多かった。その時の発見が「メタボリズム1960年」の宣言の中で大高正人との群造形の提案の骨子をなしている。これは日本でもようやく建築家・歴史家の人々の中でも集落調査が始まった頃である。個から全体へという思想はその後、半世紀の私達の様々な集合の試みの中で一貫して守り続けられてきた。

1964年にセントルイス・ワシントン大学から出版された『集合体の研究』では、群造形とともに当時流行したヨナ・フリードマンあるいはル・コルビュジエ、そして丹下健三の東京計画1960に、都市インフラも含めた土木的スケールのメガ・ストラクチャーなどをより客観的にそのメリット・デメリットを解析している。

その客観性のゆえか、このテキストは現在米国の大学でも広く使われている。

私は1960年代の終わりから、ヒルサイドテラスあるいは、立正大学キャンパスにおいて、深く集合体の実験に携わる幸運に恵まれた。さらにその後も多くの国内外のキャンパスあるいはテレビ朝日、4 ワールド・トレード・センターを始め集合体の一端に参加する機会も得てきた。

一方、提案面ではゴルジ体の提言がある。周知のように集合体においては、密集した都市の形成において、Solidな建築群が、通り、広場等の外部空間を規定し、逆に外部空間が建築群のあり方を規定していくことは、たとえばヨーロッパの古典的都市に見られる、いわゆるFigure and Ground の構図として存在してきた。ゴルジ体は高密度都市空間における、より立体的な建築群と外部空間のダイナミズムのモデルであると解釈してよい。

我々がこれまで遭遇してきた集合体の体験の多くは、群造形の前提にある相似性の強い個の集合ではなく、たとえば大学のキャンパスのように様々なヘテロな機能を有した個の集合から、いかに最適な集合体をつくりだすかということが主要課題であることが多かった。そのためにはヘテロな個をつなげる外部空間とそれに接するそれぞれの建築空間のあり方が常に問われることになっている場合が多い。

この項の最後に収められたCollective Form of Open Spacesでは、従来の〈まず建築ありき〉という思考形式を逆転させた〈まず外部空間ありき〉という発想に基づく提案をしている。

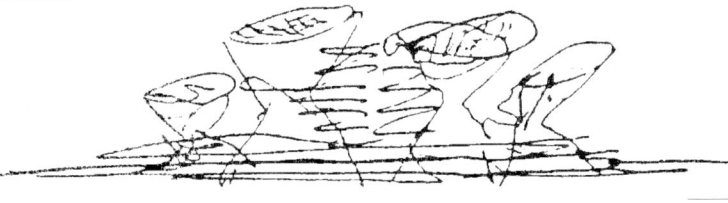

◎ Collective Form　　　　　　　　　　　　　　　　　　　　　　　　**Hillside Terrace** | 1969–1992
ヒルサイドテラス

◎ 集合体

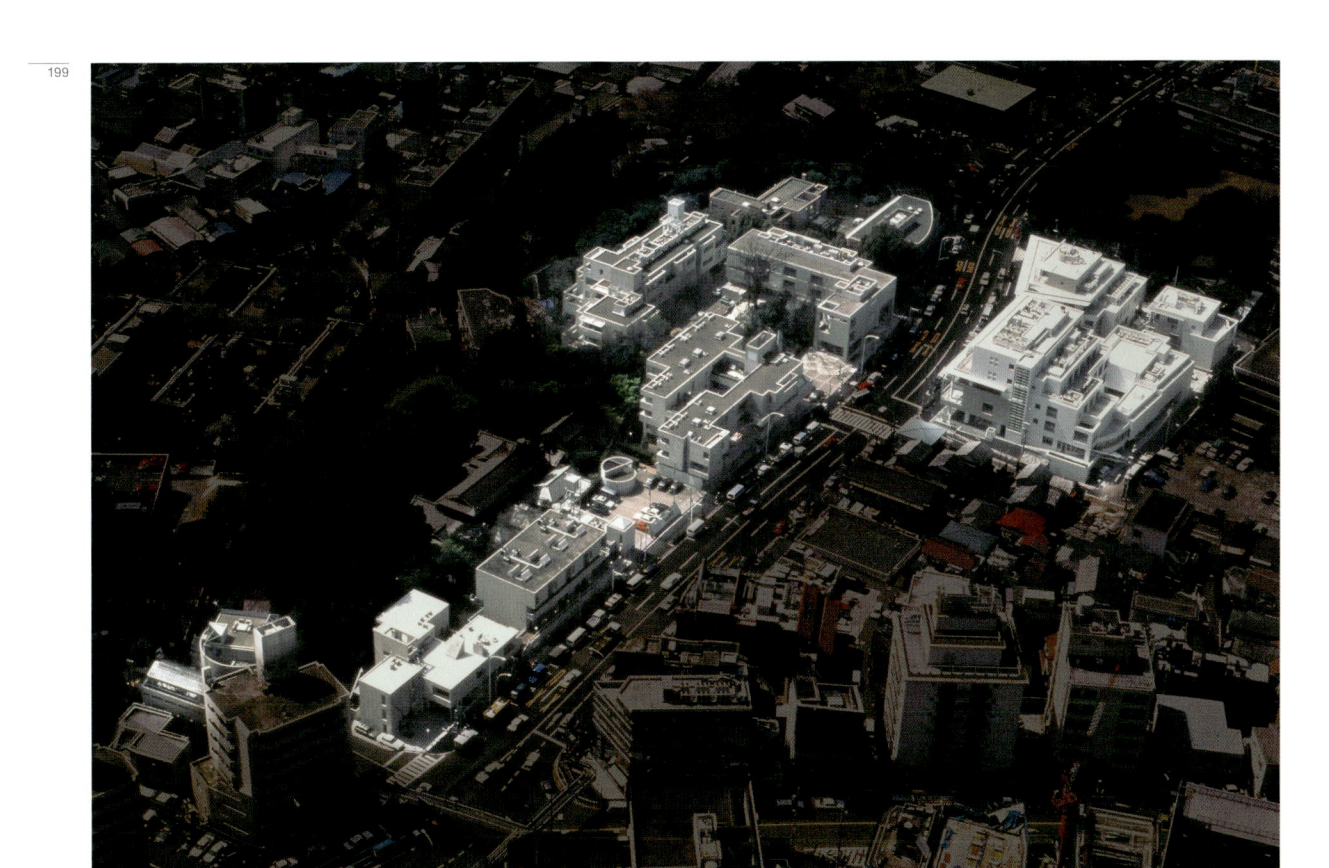

Aerial view -1992　　　　　　　　　　　　　　　　　　　　　　　　　　　　　　　　　　[ASPI]

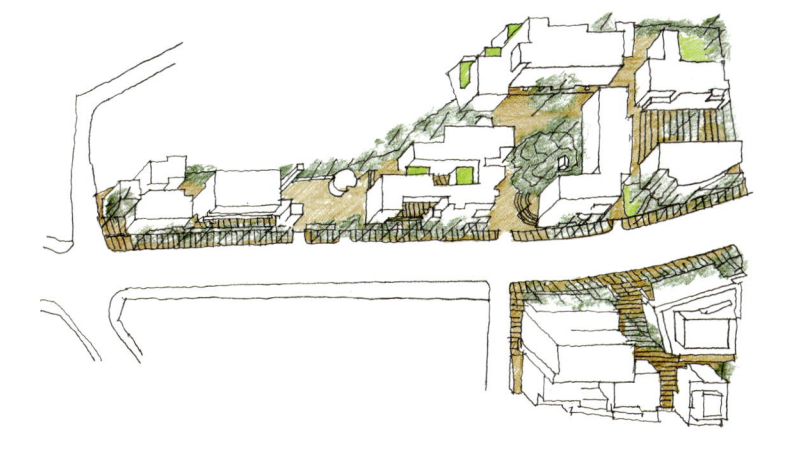

In the 1960s, the site of Hillside Terrace was merely a strip of sloping forested land in a fashionable suburban area of Tokyo known as Daikanyama; only a few wooden houses belonging to the Asakura family were located on the site. Though the site was designated as a restricted residential zone with a 10-meter height limit and floor-area ratio of 150%, it seemed destined to be a successful venture because of the location along a busy and vital thoroughfare connecting several important districts.

Despite the changes in planning and construction, several themes have remained consistent throughout the various phases of design of the Hillside Terrace complex. The first concern has been to maintain an intimate scale for the interior and exterior spaces. Second, much attention has been given to the interaction of the facade and street—understanding the sidewalk as a place of activity. Common pedestrian areas serve as transition spaces to the shops grouped around them.

Courtyard of Building B -1969

Exterior view of Building C -2015

The various phases of the complex are further unified by a consistent attempt to synthesize modern construction with a more traditional Japanese planning strategy; one that respects the specific character and boundaries of the site as given. In this case, the site is a rather historical piece of land— a small shrine perched on an ancient burial mound (kofun) gives evidence of human habitation as early as the seventh century, when Tokyo (then Edo) was no more than a small fishing village. Preserving this ancient spirit of the place is implicit in the notion of incremental development, which is difficult to achieve in a building without a sense of change over time.

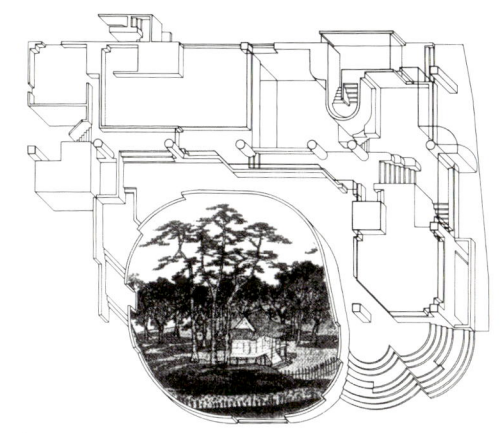

Sarugaku mound and Building D

Exterior view of Building D -2015

View from Building D to Building C -2015

1960年代、ヒルサイドテラスの敷地は代官山と呼ばれる東京のファッショナブルな郊外にある、緑が多く傾斜した細長い土地でしかなく、朝倉家は数軒の木造住宅を所有しているだけだった。敷地が住居専用地域に指定されていたために、建物規模は高さ10m、容積率150%に制限されていたのだが、交通量の多い幹線道路に面していたので、将来が有望な土地であることは明らかだった。

計画内容や建設方法は異なるものの、ヒルサイドテラスの建築群を様々なフェイズでデザインするうえでいくつかのテーマは一貫していた。もっとも重要視していたのは、内部空間と外部空間をともにいかに親密に感じることができるかというテーマである。次に重要なテーマは、ファサードと街路の間の相互作用であり、歩道を人々の活動の場としてとらえることであった。共用の歩行者エリアは、その周りに集められた商店への移行空間として位置づけられている。

この建築群の様々なフェイズは、それぞれの時代の建設方法と日本の伝統的な作法、すなわち与えられた敷地の性格や境界に敬意を払うという設計手法

Hillside Plaza -1987 [F.K.]

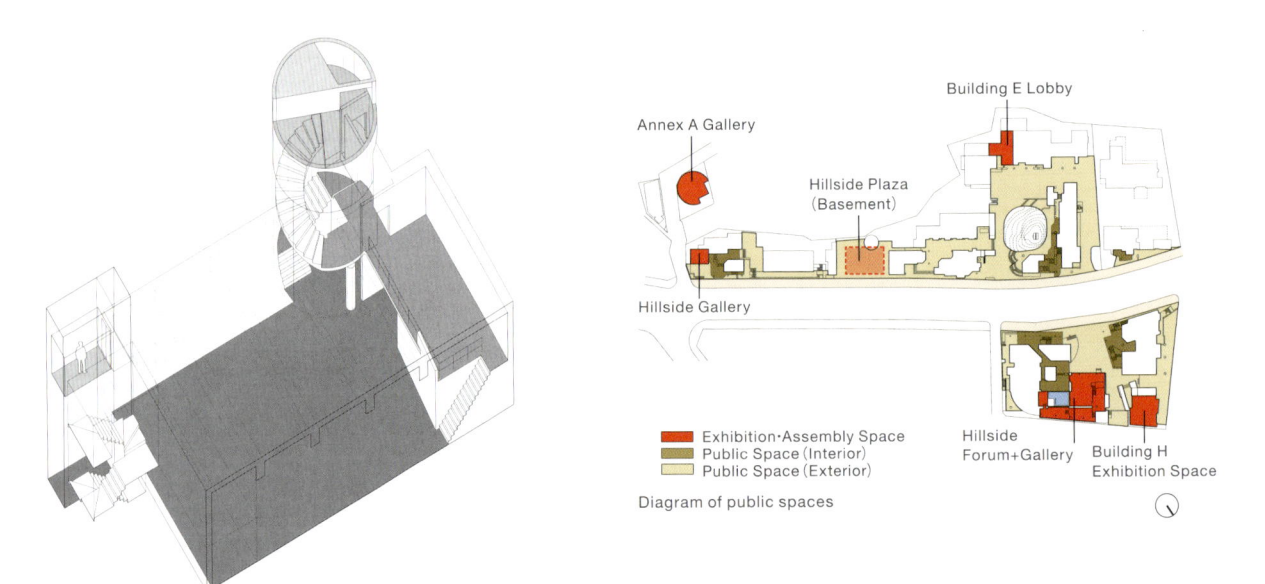

Axonometric of Hillside Plaza

Diagram of public spaces

とをどのように統合するかを常に検討していたという点で、さらに統一感をもったものとなっている。ヒルサイドテラスの場合は、敷地のもつ歴史的な背景が重要だった。小さな社が古墳の上に建てられており、東京（当時の江戸）が小さな漁村でしかなかった7世紀頃からこの土地は人々の住まいであったことがわかる。古代から続く場の精神を受け継ぐことがこの計画の重要なコンセプトを形成していたからこそ、多くのフェイズを経た後でも、単一の建物では実現できないような時を経た変化という感覚を表現できているのだと思う。

Courtyard -2015

Forum of Building F -2010

Cafe of Building F -1992

[J.A.]

HILLSIDE TERRACE 89-90

Keio University Shonan Fujisawa Campus | 1990–1994
慶應義塾湘南藤沢キャンパス

In the late 1980's, Keio University decided to establish a satellite campus centered around two new academic faculties: the schools of Policy Management and Environmental Information. The campus was constructed in four stages from 1990 to 1994, in the Shonan district of Fujisawa, 30 kilometers from central Tokyo. Manifesting a new spirit of education in the information age, the Shonan Fujisawa Campus has become the most celebrated institution of higher learning in post-war Japan.

Aerial view of campus

The site consists of four plateaus enveloped by a gentle swale, with a few interspersed evergreens and susuki (Japanese pampas grass) covering the land. On clear days Mount Fuji is visible beyond the woods on the top of the hill to the west.

In developing the campus plan, we took it upon ourselves to preserve the given conditions of the site and replenish the site's natural greenery. Using the existing site contours as a guideline for the basic layout of zones, we began by establishing two domains: a center and a periphery. This was a way of establishing distinct identity to each building cluster, while allowing the campus edge to merge gradually into the surrounding pastoral landscape. A loop road was constructed around a small rise in the middle of the site, defining the central domain within the loop and a peripheral domain outside.

The strategy to disperse the facilities corresponded to the university's desire to create the campus buildings as houses in

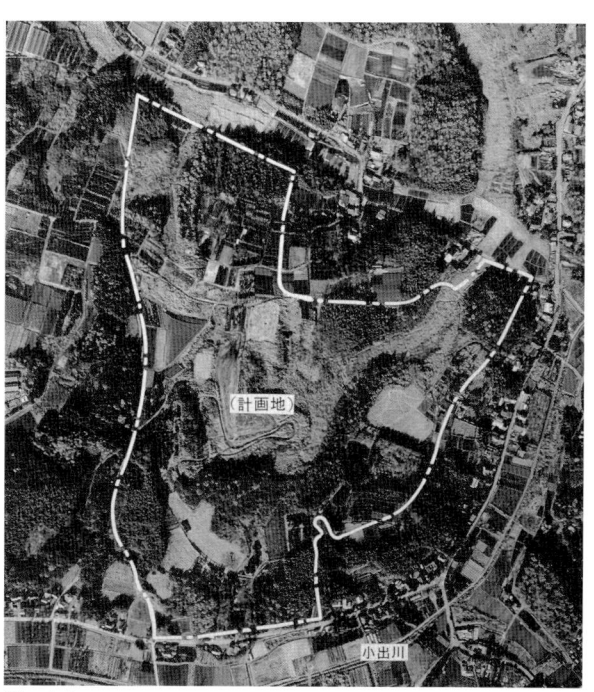

Site photo

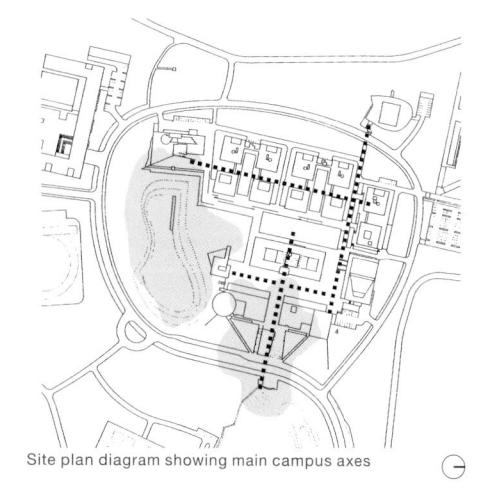

Site plan diagram showing main campus axes

a village. The positioning of vantage points and the framing of vistas were also crucial in developing the landscape planning. The public spaces of the various zones, ranging from outdoor plazas and courtyards to indoor malls and corridors, were placed along a Cartesian grid, forming a network of physical and visual connections between disparate parts of the campus.

1980年代終わりに慶應義塾は二つの新設学部、総合政策学部と環境情報学部を中心に郊外に新しいサテライトキャンパスを設置することを決めた。東京の都心から約30km離れた藤沢市の湘南地区に、1990年から94年にかけて四つのステージに分けてキャンパスが建設された。情報化時代の新しい教育方針を掲げた湘南藤沢キャンパスは、戦後日本の高等教育においてもっとも成功した施設の一つである。

Front view of the main gate

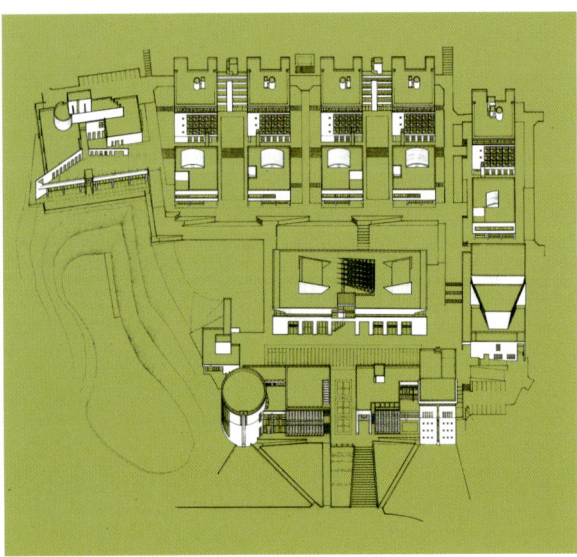

Axonometric of central campus

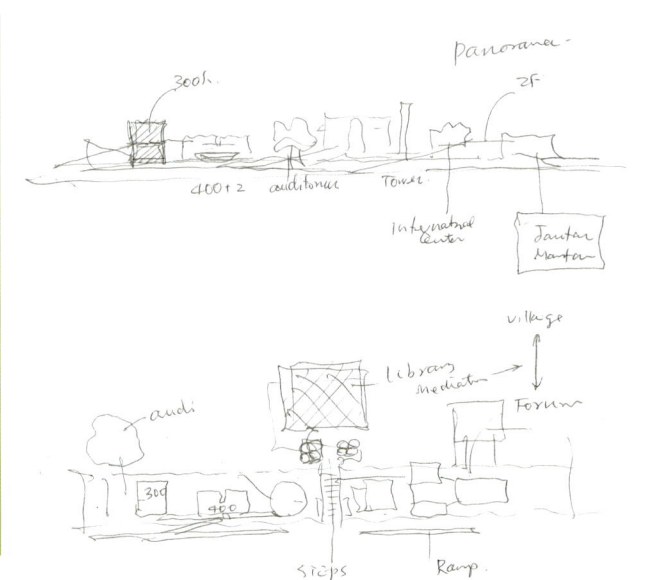

敷地には緩やかに傾斜した湿地帯を囲むように四つの台地があり、常緑樹がまばらに生えススキが一面を覆っていた。晴れた日には丘の上から西に富士山を望むことができた。

キャンパス計画を進めるにあたり、我々は敷地の現状をなるべく保存し、敷地の潜在自然植生に適した樹木を植えることとした。基本的なゾーニングのレイアウトを現状の等高線を尊重しながら考え、まず中心と周縁という二つの領域を設定した。このような設定で、それぞれの建物の集合体に独自の個性を与えながら、同時にキャンパスのエッジが周辺の田園風景に緩やかに溶け込んでいくという景観を生み出すことができる。ループ状の道路を敷地中央の小高い丘を中心に計画することで、ループ道路の内側の中心領域とその外側の周縁領域とを定義している。

施設を分散させて配置したのは、キャンパスを集落における住宅のように計画したいという大学の意向に沿ったものである。ランドスケープを計画するにあたっては、見晴らしのきく場所を特定し風景をどのように切り取るかが

Guardhouse at north campus entrance

Roof Terrace

Passage

重要な判断基準となった。屋外の広場や中庭から内部の回廊や廊下までも含めて、様々なゾーンの公共空間が直交座標の上に配置され、キャンパス内の異なる場所を直接、あるいは視覚的に結び付ける役割を果たしている。

Campus spine

View from the staircase in the Graduate Research Centre [J.A.]

Miraisozojuku
未来創造塾

Miraisozojuku proposes a dormitory-style research school aiming for a new educational experience for the coming generations. Its site plan echoes the existing campus and consists of mid to low-rise buildings organized in a village form. Public spaces—such as restaurants and lounges—are placed along a green pathway, while academic and research buildings are placed linearly around stepped plazas, creating a new plaza axis juxtaposed to the green axis.

Aerial view with extension shown in white (buildings designed by Maki at back, KMDW in front)

慶應義塾大学湘南藤沢キャンパスは開設以来、極めて先進的な教育研究の推進に取り組んできたが、未来創造塾の構想は、これに加えて滞在型の教育・研究拠点を新たに創設し、次世代の人材育成を目指すものである。未来創造塾の全体計画は、既存キャンパスのコンセプトを継承し、中低層の建築が分棟状に群立する集落型の構成である。木立ちの合間を抜ける緑道に沿ってレストランや交流ラウンジなど、まちに開かれた共用スペースを配する一方、レベルの異なる広場を囲んで、教育、研究施設群が並立し、緑道軸に対して広場軸を形成している。

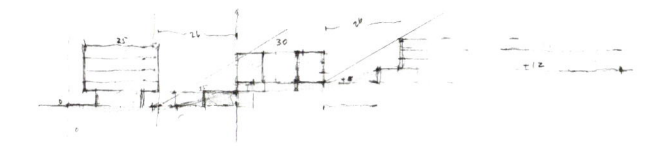

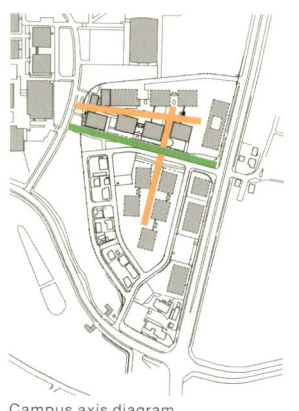

Exterior view

Campus axis diagram

Frankfurt am Main Center Competition | 1991
フランクフルト・マイン・センター　コンペ案

The design of a large urban complex in the very heart of Frankfurt represents a complex architectural challenge. For this project, we set out two primary goals: first, to maximize outdoor green space in the new development; and second, to provide a new identity for the district by consciously relating individual buildings to a larger whole.

Our architectural investigation began to ask how the high-rise buildings might achieve a figural, symbolic identity in the

South elevation

Model in urban context

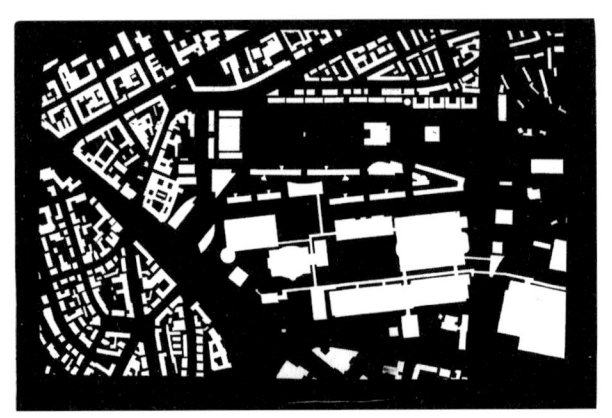

Site plan

city. Experiments in relating separate buildings, in staggering their heights, and in creating opening sand gateways with the block suggested the rich potential of figural silhouettes defining slab-type buildings. Individual buildings began to assume their own characters, the whole ensemble resembling a family or even a set of chess pieces. Thus, the two tallest buildings in the center became the father and mother of the group, and other buildings, the children.

The same cut-outs, gateways, and slit-like openings that give each building a figural silhouette also frame views throughout the complex, so that both solid buildings and void openings have complementary figural readings.

Aerial view

Concept

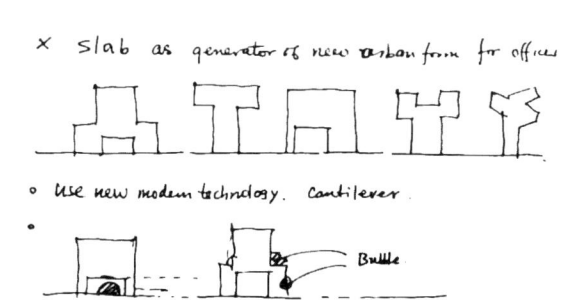

フランクフルトは経済活動の盛んな都市であり、都心部に多くの高層建築をもつ。我々の提案は、地上レベルに最大限の公共スペースを確保するために、スラブ上のユニットを高層化し、敷地のエッジに並立させることから出発している。それは、単なるオブジェ・タイプのスカイスクレイパーではなく、一つのスーパーブロックを形成する、新しい建築タイプとして提案されている。スラブ状のユニットに対し、大きな開口部を設けたり、凸型の要素を付加したりという建築的操作によって、この複合施設全体に〈形態〉(form)ではなく、〈形象〉(figure)としての独自性を与えることができる。二つの大きなオフィスには〈父〉と〈母〉、そのほかの小さなオフィス、ホテル、ハウジングには〈子供〉、といった連想を可能にする象徴性を与えることによって、この建築群を、一つの大きな家族のような集合体として認識させることができるのである。こうした門型の開口や〈図〉としての隙間は、内部の領域と外部の領域に敷居的な役割を果たしながら、両義的な空間を演出することができる。

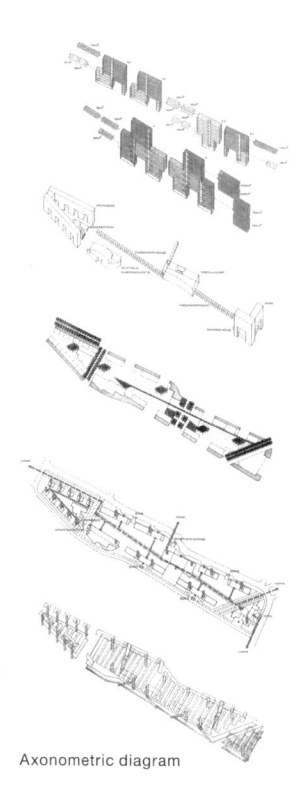

Axonometric diagram

Isar Büropark | 1995
イザール・ビューロパーク

Isar Büropark, our first project built in Europe, developed from a winning entry for an architecture and urban design competition for the development of a four-hectare office park district near Munich's new international airport. The design concept arose from a study of the landscape of the local area known as Hallbergmoos. By preserving and using to the fullest advantage the surrounding forests and meadows, a new type of working environment was created for high-technology industries, combining the exciting, urbane atmosphere of high-tech offices with more contemplative,

Eye-level view through the landscape [J.A.]

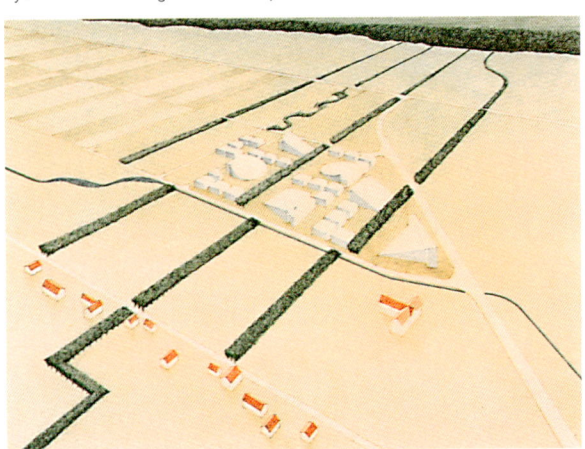

Perspective

leisurely, and rural qualities already in the site.

The site strategy was based on a study of relationships between land patterns and natural forces—whether this means the age-old layout of farming fields according to the slope of land and direction of watercourses or the inscription of airport runways according to the predominant winds. The grounds of the office park recollect the meadow ecology into which new interventions are introduced in juxtaposition—paving blocks, wooden boardwalks, crystalline office buildings whose roofs mirror the sky. Nearby Isar Forest is echoed in the site by means of dense *allees* of maple trees crossing the complex. All of the office buildings are oriented toward these *allees*, and numerous footpaths offer alternative routes among offices, the town of Hallbergmoos, and the forest. The public areas of each building are oriented to face one another so as to increase visual communication and activate the park setting of the inner blocks.

Site model

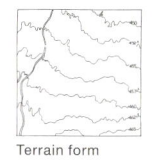

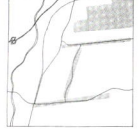

Terrain form | New airport | Population | Green zone network | Car ports and parking ramps | Public spaces and vertical circulation

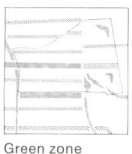

Old settlement | New development | Land use and infrastructure | Public facilities | Entrances and public spaces | Office spaces

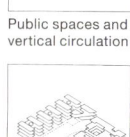

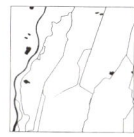

Water feature | Land pattern | Pedestrian network | Atria and glass corridors | Working spaces | Atrium and glass roofs

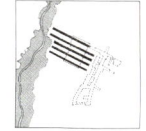

Existing vegetation | 'Arms of Isar' | Vehicular network | Street scape | Construction phase | Trees and building plate

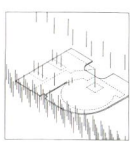

Analysis diagrams

ヨーロッパで建設した最初のプロジェクトであるイザール・ビューロパークは、ミュンヘンの新しい国際空港の近くにある4haのオフィス・パーク全体の建築およびアーバンデザインを対象としたコンペで最優秀案として選ばれたことから始まった。デザイン・コンセプトは、ハルベルクモースと呼ばれるこの地域特有の景観をスタディーすることから生まれた。周辺の森や牧草地を保存すると同時に最大限に活用することによって、ハイテク産業のための新しいタイプのオフィス環境を生み出している。都市的雰囲気をもった刺激的なハイテク・オフィスを、敷地がもともともっている穏やかでゆったりとした田園の雰囲気に結び付けている。

配置計画は土地形状のパターンと自然の中の様々な力学との関係、すなわち土地の傾斜や水路の向きに沿った大昔からある農地のレイアウト、そして卓越風に対応した滑走路の向きなどを詳細に検討することから生まれた。オフィス・パークという場所に牧草地という生態系を感じさせるようにしながら、舗装ブロックや木製のボードウォーク、そして屋根が空を反射して写しだすようなクリスタルなオフィス棟を並置させている。楓を何層にも並べた並木

Open office space

The atrium in Haus 5

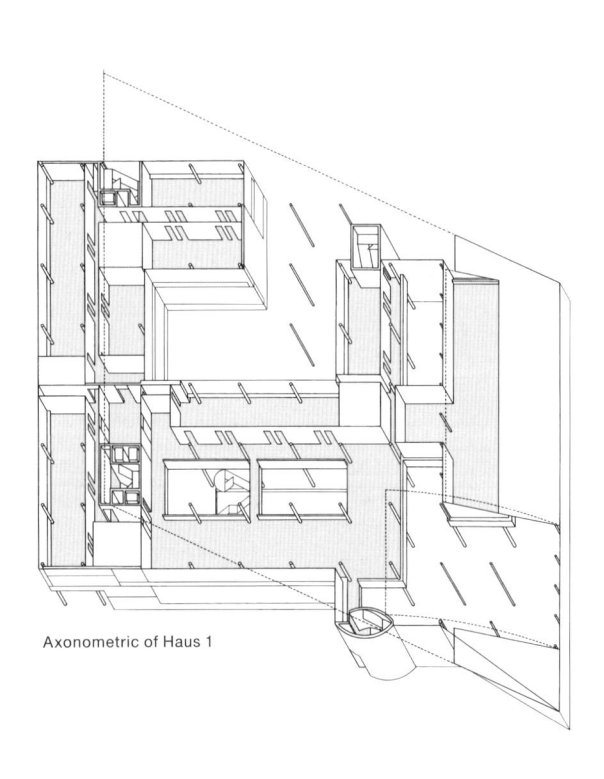

Axonometric of Haus 1

道を敷地内のメインストリートとして横断させることで、近くにあるイザールと呼ばれる森を連想させている。すべてのオフィス棟はこの並木道に向いて配置されており、オフィスとオフィスの間を結んだり、ハルベルクモースの街へ向かったり、あるいは森へ向かったりといった小道が無数に重ねあわされている。それぞれの建物の公共部分は互いに向き合うように配置され、視覚的なコミュニケーションを促し、この公園的な環境を建物内部でも感じられるようにしている。

Exterior view of Haus 5 [M.P.]

Overview from the north [J.A.]

Republic Polytechnic Campus | 2007
シンガポール理工系専門学校キャンパス

The design of the Republic Polytechnic's new campus is the result of a winning scheme for an invited international competition held in the summer of 2002. The overall organization provides innovative solutions to a high density campus and unique pedagogical program centered on "Problem Based Learning", the first in Singapore. These solutions incorporate considerations for individual inquiry and collaborative learning and to their place making. Once occupied by an old British prison camp, the site of the new Republic Polytechnic is

Aerial view of campus

1. Agora
2. Library
3. Lawn
4. Study Cluster
5. Faculty Center
6. Republic Polytechnic Center

Longitudinal section (scale:1/3000)

located on a sloping terrain and adjacent to a National Park and dense forest.

As the Fifth Polytechnic in Singapore, the Republic Polytechnic was originally made up of five schools and has now expanded to eleven. The campus plan concentrates the main educational programs within a central nucleus (termed the Learning Hub) comprised of eleven 40m x 40m multi-storey "Pods" with vertically stacked floors that are tied together at the first three floors through a large elliptical space, the "Agora", for collective learning with open terraced floors that follow the site terrain. The supporting "Satellite" facilities— Culture Center, Sports Complex and Housing Block— are located on the periphery.

These collective spaces consist of a large library, reading spaces, food courts, and specialized teaching facilities including wet labs, lecture theaters and workshops. Two large

Compositional form

Mega form

Group form

3 paradigms of Collective Form

[D.P.]   Agora of De Meerpaal in Dronten (designed by Frank van Klingeren)

and six small courtyards cut into the roof of the Agora, providing amenity, natural light, and views. The roof of the Agora is designed as a large landscaped Lawn that is sloping together with the site terrain. The "Lawn" connects to the third floor level of the Pod buildings where more collective learning spaces are allocated, including lecture theaters and food courts. The Culture center hosts a wide variety of events and functions open to the general public.

2002年夏、国際設計競技の結果、我々はシンガポール理工系専門学校（リパブリック・ポリテクニック）の設計者に選定された。シンガポール北部のウッドランドに位置する20haの敷地に、1万3000人の学生と4000人のスタッフが利用する24万㎡のキャンパスが、シンガポールで5番目のポリテクニックとしてつくられた。リパブリック・ポリテクニックの「プロブレム・ベースド・ラーニング（PBL）」という、学生の自主性を重視した教育方針に基づいて、柔軟性と機能性に富んだキャンパス計画が提案された。さらに起伏のある既存の地形を活かしながら、隣接するナショナルパークとつなげられた、〈公

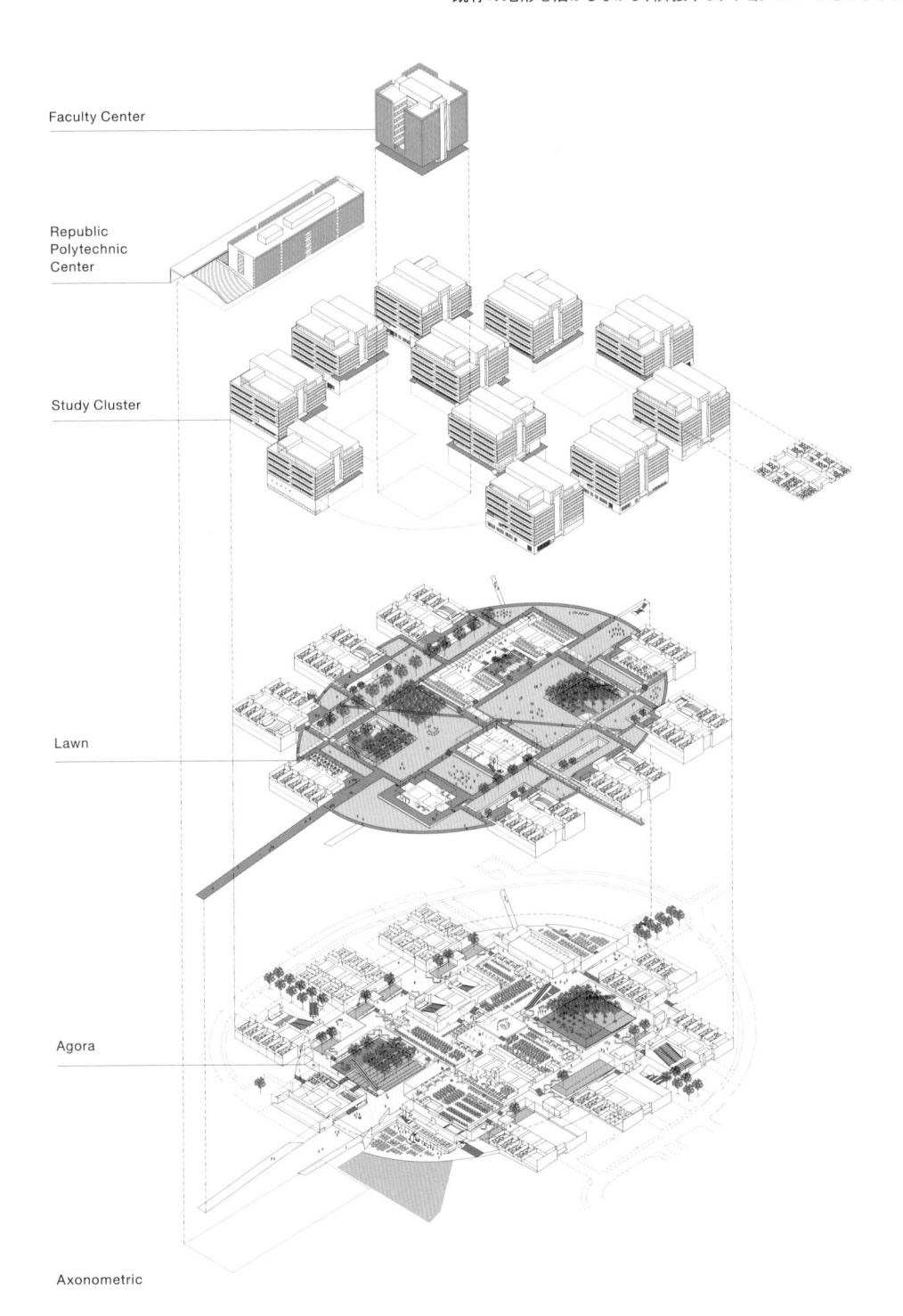

Faculty Center

Republic Polytechnic Center

Study Cluster

Lawn

Agora

Axonometric

園の中のキャンパス〉をつくりだしている。

東西の小高い丘にはさまれた谷状の土地に学生の活動の中心となるラーニングハブを配置し、それを取り囲むように管理棟、カルチャーセンター、スポーツコンプレックス、エネルギーセンター、住宅・保育園棟などの「サテライト」施設が配置されている。「アゴラ」と「ローン」と名付けられた二つの楕円形の空間がすべてのポッドをつなぎ、キャンパス全体を統合している。アゴラは既存の地形に対応して8.4mの高低差をもつ段状に連続する空間であり、図書館や食堂、大講義室、特別実験室など学生のための様々な共有プログラムを提供している。八つのコートヤードと外周部から光が射し込むアゴラには、学生や教師の様々な交流を喚起するような多様な空間がつくられている。アゴラ上部に重ねられたローンは、芝と樹木で覆われた屋外空間であり、傾斜した地形に建つ各「ポッド」の3階レベルをつないでいる。フードコートや講堂などの一般利用者向けの機能は、このローンレベルに配置されている。キャンパス全体を覆う歩廊のネットワークがローン上に広がり、それらがローンを親しみやすいスケールの緑の空間にしている。そこは単

View of the Lawn

The central part of the Agora [J.A.]

なる歩行空間ではなく、授業やイベントに利用され、木陰に学生たちが集うアクティビティーの高い空間である。アゴラとローンが互いにつながり、魅力的で立体的なランドスケープをつくりだしている。

The reading area of the library

[J.A.]

Various scenery in the Agora

[J.A.]

Republic Polytechnic Expansion & Singapore Institute of Technology | 2015
シンガポール理工系専門学校拡張工事&シンガポール工科大学キャンパス

Located on the western edge of Republic Polytechnic Campus, Singapore Institute of Technology (SIT) provides publicly-funded degree programs from industry-acclaimed overseas universities tailored for polytechnic graduates. A Pre-employment Training Building was also planned next to the SIT building as an extension to the Republic Polytechnic Campus.

既存キャンパス内西側に、シンガポール国外の大学のカリキュラムをポリテクニック卒業生に提供するシンガポール工科大学（SIT）を新築。併せてリパブリック・ポリテクニック（RP）卒業生のための職業訓練棟を増築した。

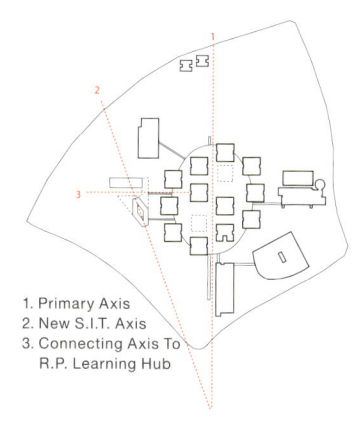

1. Primary Axis
2. New S.I.T. Axis
3. Connecting Axis To R.P. Learning Hub

Campus axes

- Existing Campus
- New Campus

Figure and ground

Exterior view -2015

Aerial view of campus (new building in red)

Tokyo Denki University Tokyo Senju Campus | 2012
東京電機大学　東京千住キャンパス

Celebrating its 100th year anniversary in 2007, Tokyo Denki University relocated its main campus from Kanda— where it was originally founded— to the new Tokyo Senju Campus. The new campus' urban design aims to establish a unique identity through the incorporation of plazas and create a new "agora"— an open, multi-functional civic atmosphere.

Three plazas along the surrounding streets define the campus border, while connecting the surrounding neighborhood to

Aerial view of campus [T.K.]

View from the north [T.K.]

the university. A central Campus Plaza and two bridges spanning above it provide pedestrian links and integrate the campus as a whole. The Plaza is used for daily activities and special events, such as performances and festivals.

The concept of an "agora" was pursued and realized via these plazas and streets which connect public spaces on the lower floors. The civic nature is also enhanced by the sequential organization of public programs, including the loggia in front of the station, cafe, galleries along the street, auditorium, library, cafeteria at Campus Plaza, lounge and the gymnasium. The "agora" is open for students and neighborhood residents alike. It is hoped that wide-ranging activities in these public spaces will generate a lively atmosphere and energize the cityscape.

Three original towers were designed above the "agora"— a Research Tower, Classroom Tower, and Laboratory Tower.

View from the west

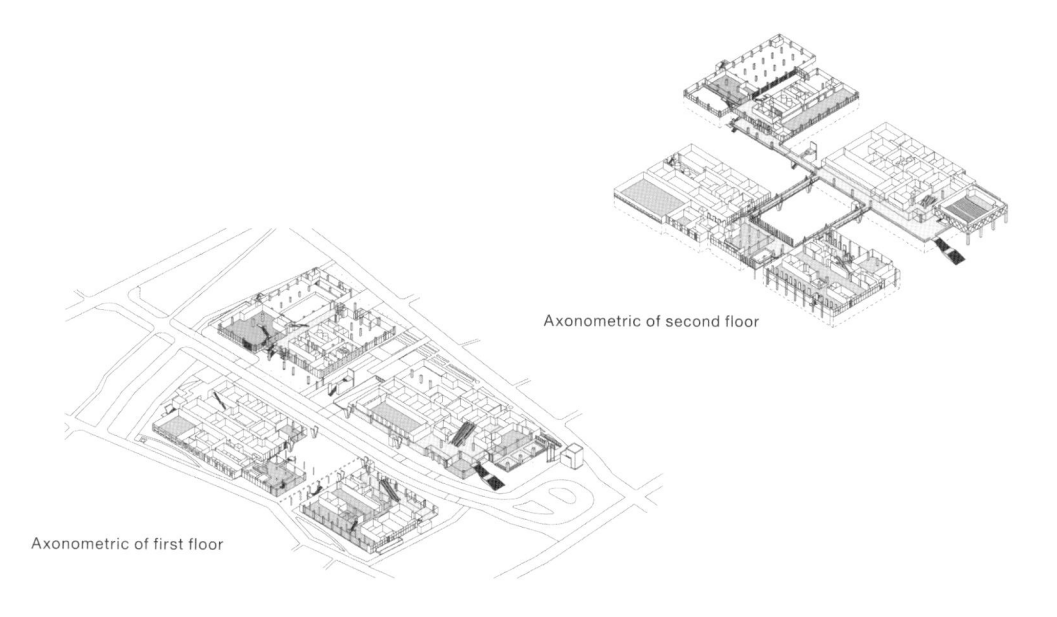

Axonometric of second floor

Axonometric of first floor

The second phase, planned two years after the completion of Phase I, will house classrooms and research labs in the high-rise portion, while extending the "agora" concept on the lower floors via workshops, lounges, an atrium, and a public sports gym.

東京電機大学は、創立100周年を機に創立地神田から北千住に移転し、新しく東京千住キャンパスとして開設された。まず、アーバンデザインにおいて〈プラザ〉と〈アゴラ〉というパブリック性の高い空間により、アイデンティティーのある風景の実現を目指した。道沿いの三つの〈プラザ〉はキャンパスとしての領域を形成する公共空間であると同時に、地域と大学の間に新しい結び付きをつくりだす場となる。中心部にある〈キャンパスプラザ〉は囲まれたスクエアな空間によってキャンパスの一体性を象徴しており、さらにその上部を渡る2本のブリッジにより回遊性が生まれ、キャンパス全体のつなが

Entrance lounge of Building 2　　　　　[T.K.]

Reading area of Building 2　　　　　[T.K.]

Laboratory

りを高めている。〈プラザ〉は日常的なアクティビティーだけでなく、パフォーマンスや祭りなど非日常的なイベントの舞台となる。

その〈プラザ〉と道によって低層部の共用機能につながりをもたせ、駅前広場のロッジアとカフェ、道沿いのギャラリー、ホール、図書館、キャンパスプラザにある食堂、ラウンジ、体育館、それらを連続させることによって〈アゴラ〉というコンセプトを実現した。〈アゴラ〉は学生だけでなく地域の人々にも開かれた交流の場となり、その中に展開する多様なアクティビティーが、表情豊かな街並みの風景をつくりだす。〈アゴラ〉の上部に建つ三つのタワーの主要機能は、研究室棟、教室棟、実験室棟からなる。

第2期がその第1期完成の後2年目に始まり、タワー部を教室、研究室とし、低層部のアゴラには中央のアトリウム周りに、ものつくり教室、ラウンジのほか、地域に開かれたスポーツ施設などが計画されている。

Roof garden

Street view

Agora

Campus plaza

Perspective (Phase II in front left)

International College for Post-Graduate Buddhist Studies
2010

国際仏教学大学院大学

This college was established for graduate level Buddhist studies and research, offering up to a 5-year PhD degree. A total of 20 students attend the college—a small student body that yields an atmosphere of a research center, rather than a college. The new campus site was formerly a residence of the last Tokugawa Shogun, Yoshinobu Tokugawa, and the large ginko tree and greenery reflect the rich atmosphere of his thriving. Taking advantage of this existing greenery and sloping topography, the project consists of six low-rise

Exterior view from the south

[T.K.]

Site model

buildings, all with small footprints, and connected by courtyards and exterior spaces visible from the interiors. The strategy creates a sense of standing in the woods, a quiet and serene atmosphere appropriate for research and learning.

For researchers spend long hours on surveys and analyses, transitory spaces serving an important function, different from research rooms. The simple act of strolling may inspire a different outlook on a stagnant idea. Each main space of the campus is distinctly designed so that the students experience these transitory spaces as they walk through different parts of the campus. As the campus greenery also changes by season, the spatial sequence inspire unexpected ideas throughout the year.

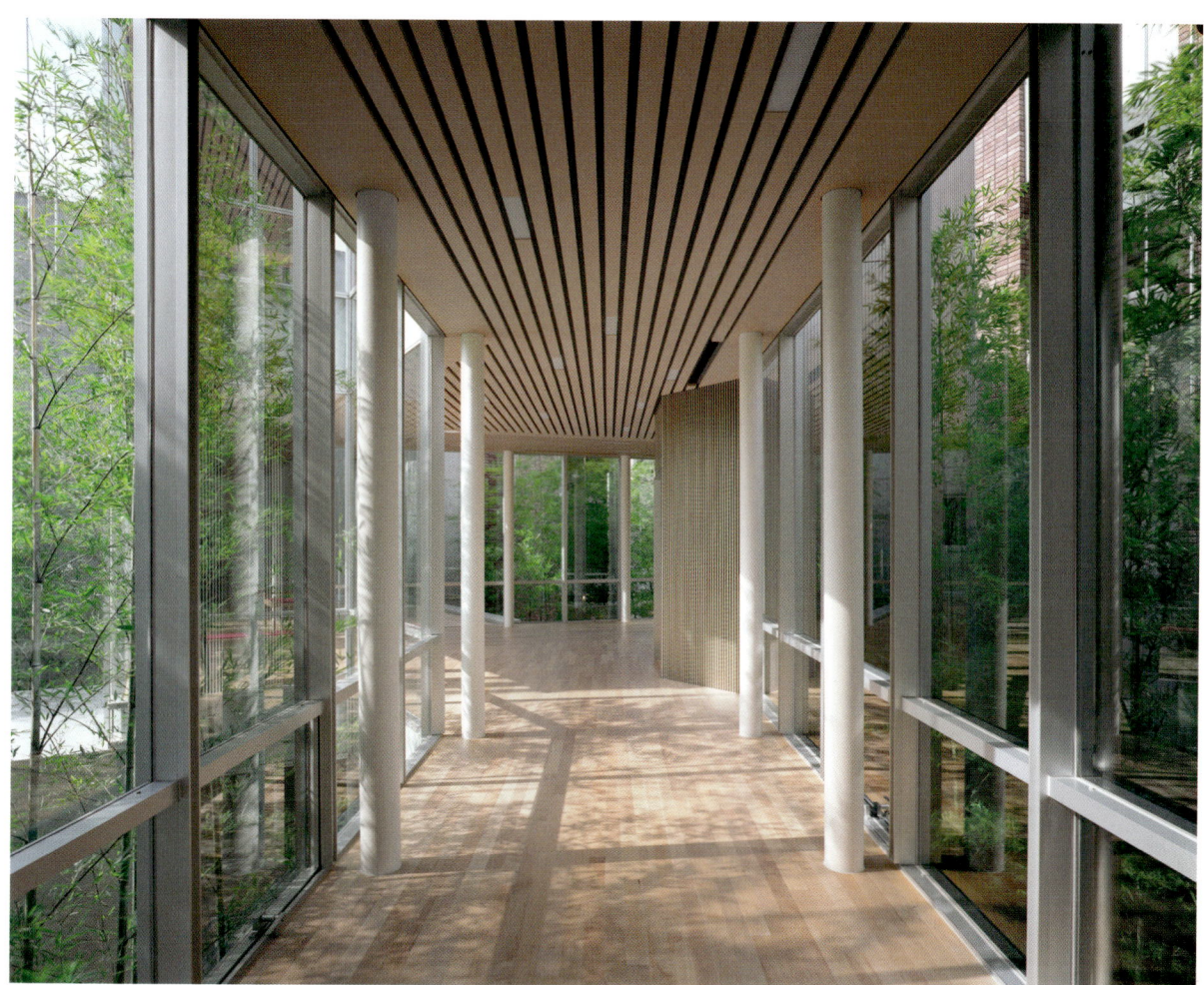

Entrance corridor

Entrance corridor surrounded by bamboo trees

Model of entrance corridor

この大学は仏教学の研究者を志す学生を対象とした、大学院のみの大学である。総学生数は博士課程までの5学年で20名ほどの規模であり、大学というよりは研究所のような構成となっている。この新キャンパスの敷地は15代将軍徳川慶喜の終焉の地であり、屋敷ゆかりの大銀杏をはじめ様々な木々が生い茂る緑豊かな環境の場所である。既存の緑と起伏に富んだ地形を活かしつつ、建築を小規模な六つの棟で計画して、高さも低層に抑えている。このような分棟状の配置は建築の周りに庭や外部空間を生み、室内からは木立ちの中にいるような風景を望むことができる。そうして建築に内包された庭の緑と外周部の林により、静かで落ち着きのある研究・教育の場を創出している。

Kasuga Hall [T.K.]

Stair to Kasuga Hall [T.K.]

長い時間を調査や思索に費やす研究者にとって、移動の空間は研究スペースとはまた別の重要な意味を担っていよう。逍遥は思索にとっても停滞した思考を転換する契機となるのではないか。そのための足掛かりに空間のしつらえを切り換え、移動とともに異質な場へと導く。そして季節で趣を変える木立ちを楽しみながら逍遥する時、思考は予期せぬ道へと踏み出していくであろう。

Reading area

Terrace overlooking a courtyard

The Bihar Museum | 2015
ビハール博物館

The Bihar Museum in Patna is the winning scheme of an open international design competition in 2011. The generous 5.3 hectare plot along Patna's Bailey Road allowed for a variety of planning approaches, while demanding sensitivity to its low-scale surroundings and prominent tree growth. In response, the building was conceived of as a "campus"— an interconnected landscape of buildings and exterior spaces with a modest but dynamic profile, allowing for planning flexibility in harmony with the existing site conditions.

Aerial view from the east

Each program zone (entrance/event, exhibition, administration, and educational) is given a distinct presence and form within the complex. These program zones are linked together via a series of interior and exterior courtyards and corridors, ensuring that interior spaces retain a strong connection to the surrounding landscape while remaining sheltered and comfortable throughout the year.

This constant presence of the natural environment within the museum "campus" will create a rich, unique experience with each visit, one that changes with time and season. It is hoped that this will encourage repeat visitors, and— together with world-class exhibits— ensure a lasting educational impact for the children of Bihar and other visitors from across the world.

The museum's exterior is characterized by extensive use of weathering steel, a durable material that creates a dignified

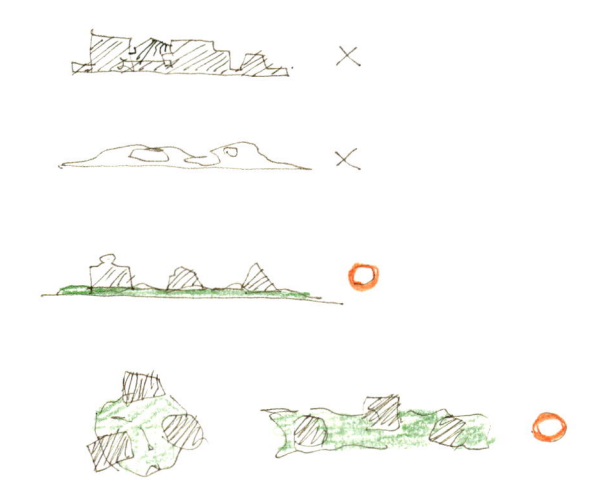

Maki's first visit to India -1959

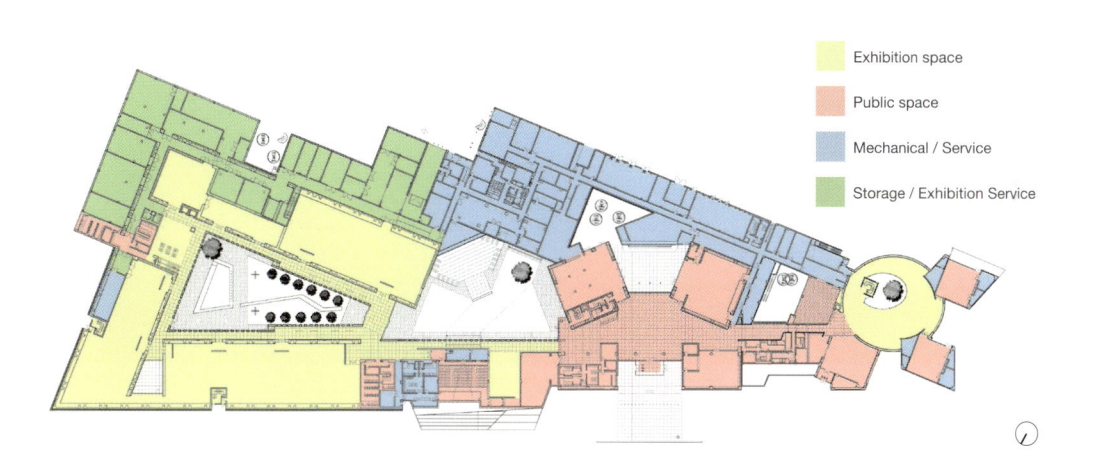

Ground floor plan (scale:1/2500)

Model photo of north elevation

contrast to the surrounding greenery. The weathering steel symbolizes India's historical achievements in metallurgy as well as its current prominence in the international steel industry.

パトナ市のビハール博物館は2011年にオープン形式で行われた国際設計競技の優勝案である。パトナ市のベイリー通りに沿った5.3haという広大な敷地は、変化に富んだ敷地計画のアプローチを可能にし、一方でその低層規模の周辺部や豊かに成長した樹木に対する配慮が求められていた。こうした条件に対して我々はビハール博物館を〈キャンパス〉、控えめでありながら力強い表情を維持し、既存の敷地状況にふさわしく柔軟に計画できるような、内部空間と外部空間が相互に連結したランドスケープとして考えたのである。

View of Children's Museum

Gallery elevation from the northwest

Aerial view from the south

それぞれのゾーン（エントランスと催事、展示室、管理部門、そして児童と教育）は建物群の中で明確な存在感と独自の形態が与えられた。これらのゾーンはいくつもの内外の中庭と回廊によってつなぎ合わされ、内部空間に周囲のランドスケープとの強い連続感を確保しながら、年間を通じて快適な環境を保持している。

博物館の〈キャンパス〉の内部に、このように自然環境が常にあることは、訪れるたびに時と季節により異なる豊かでほかでは味わうことのない体験をつくりだす。このことが来館者の再訪を促し、そして国際水準の常設および企画展示とともにこのビハール博物館がビハールの子供達や世界各地から来る来館者に長く教育的な影響力を保つことが望まれている。

博物館の外装は広範囲に用いられたコールテン鋼によって性格づけられている。これは耐久性のある材料で、そのコンテクストを補完し、周囲の緑樹に威厳のあるコントラストを生み出す。コールテン鋼は冶金の分野におけるインドの伝統的な業績であるだけでなく、国際的にも鉄鋼業界では目下重要な存在となっていることを象徴している。

View from Lounge

View from Gallery roof

Passive Town Kurobe | 2016
パッシブタウン黒部モデル

The Kurobe Housing Project is an effort by YKK, a Japanese manufacturing company famous for its zippers and curtain wall systems, to realize a sustainable "passive town". The 3.7-hectare master plan proposes to organize six collective housing sectors around a communal zone. Maki project site is located along the eastern road and consists of two "Street Buildings" (including housing and a commercial mall) and four "Residence Buildings" (including housing units only)—whose internal organization is centered around a common

Site model from the west

space. This community altogether consists of 44 apartment units.

The project aims to provide a comfortable living environment with minimal energy consumption by improving thermal performance of insulation and openings, minimizing air filtration, and taking advantage of natural resources, such as sunlight and wind. Living room terraces, balconies, sun rooms, and verandas are designed to take advantage of sunlight and wind while also offering hints about the flow of time and changing seasons. The buildings are designed to blend in with a new grove of trees and are hoped to propose a new community model that co-habitates with nature.

Perspective of the common space

Wind analysis

YKKは黒部のハウジング計画において、持続可能な社会にふさわしいパッシブタウンの実現を目指している。マスタープランでは3.7haの開発地の中央に共用のセンターコモンを配し、その周りに6街区の集合住宅地が計画されている。我々の計画するこの街区は東前面道路沿いに位置し、商業施設の入るモールと住居の一体となった街路棟2棟と、内側のコモンスペースを取り囲む住居棟4棟からなり、総戸数44戸の計画である。

地域の気候風土を活かしたパッシブデザインによる省エネルギーの住まいとして、建物の断熱・気密・開口部などの性能を高め、日照や風などの自然のポテンシャルを積極的に活用することで、最小限の設備エネルギーによって住まい環境の快適性を得ることができる。自然との接触率の高い、リビングテラス、バルコニー、サンルーム、縁側などのデザインにより、自然の光や風だけでなく、時間や季節とともに移ろう自然を享受し得る住まいとなっている。住居群は雑木林のランドスケープに溶け込み、豊かな自然と共存する新しいコミュニティーを形成している。

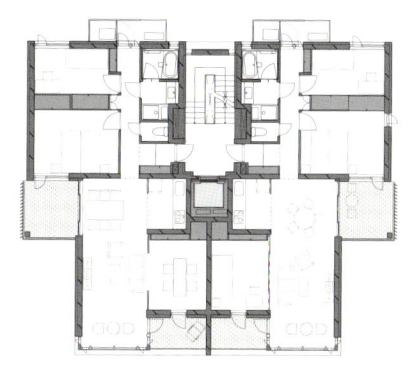

Unit plan

Cusco Samana Hotel & Residences
クスコ・サマナ・ホテル&レジデンス

This site (elevation 3,000 meters) is located 40 kilometers northwest of Cusco, Peru near the famous Moray ruins. The Andes Mountains offer a spectacular alpine backdrop, and the evening sky is filled with stars against a pitch black sky. It is a unique setting, combining the vibrant nature of the Andean highlands and the mystique of Incan culture.

Conceived as an oasis from everyday life, the master plan includes a medium-term stay hotel, a villa complex, a

Aerial view of hotel complex

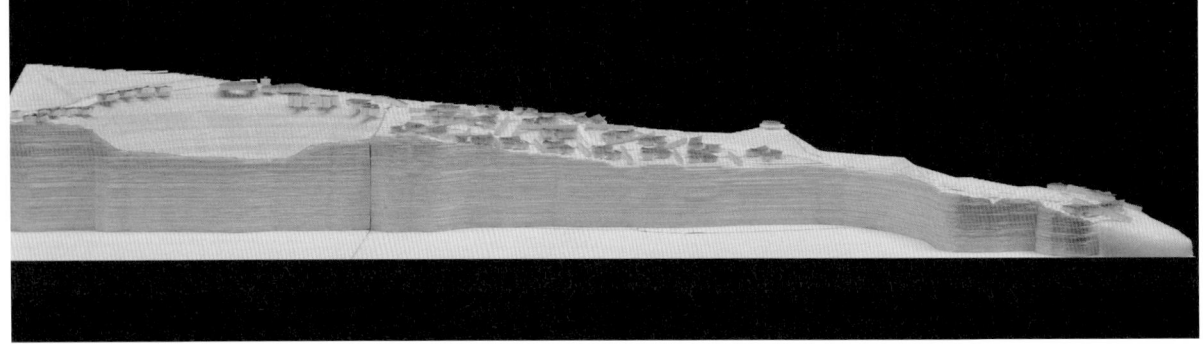

Site model

敷地はクスコから北西40km、丸い段状のすり鉢で知られるモライ遺跡の近くにある。標高は3000mを超えるペルーの高地であり、山脈を背景に豊かな自然の起伏が眺望され、夜は満点の星が漆黒の空を覆い尽くす。ここはアンデス高地の自然とインカの神秘性を併せ持つ場所であり、非日常の時を楽しむ、滞在型のホテルと別荘群、レストラン（設計：KMDW）のコンプレックスによる計画である。それぞれの建築を分棟化、低層化してスケールを抑え、地形になじませるとともに、屋根や石の基壇を用い、モダンでありながら地域性も感じさせる集落のような風景を目指している。敷地の中には、巨大なすり鉢状の窪みや小山があり、この特徴的な地形を活かし、窪みに沿ってホテルのセントラルファシリティとスパ、スィートおよびスタンダードの各客室な

restaurant (designed by KMDW) and spa facilities. To minimize scale and harmonize with the unique terrain, the architecture is divided into discreet, low-rise volumes; stone foundations and a variety of roof forms give the complex a modern but regionally sensitive character, akin to local villages. The hotel central facilities, spa, and suites are located in the center of the site, arrayed around the rim of a deep recess. The villas are organized radially around the center of an adjacent knoll, while the restaurant is integrated into a hillside overlooking the site to the north.

The hotel's central facility consists of the main lobby, galleries, and restaurants, and is characterized by a circular courtyard and water feature echoing the surrounding natural recess. The galleries and restaurants face across this open, water-filled center.

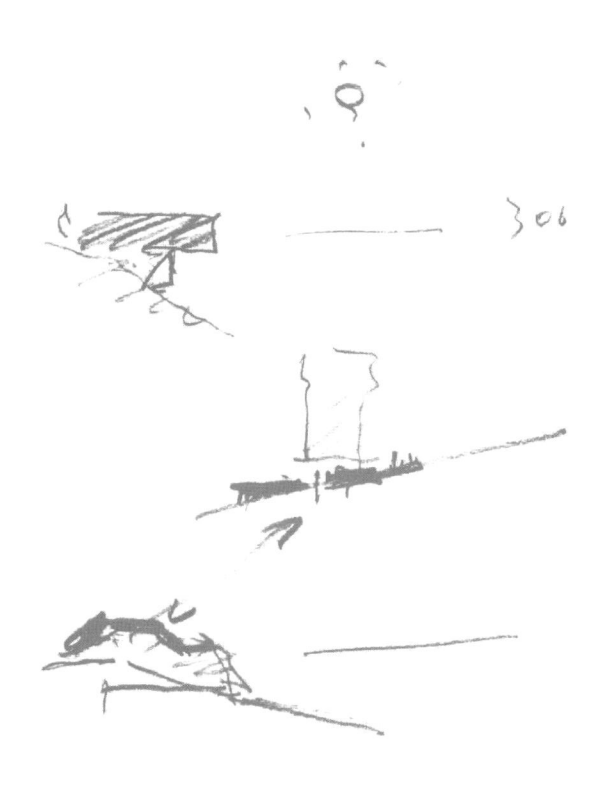

Conceptual image

Perspective

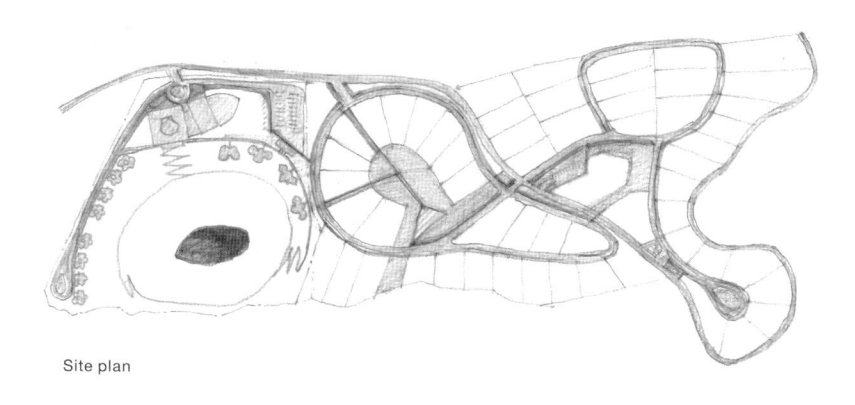

Site plan

どの建築群を弓形に配置している。一方、別荘はモアイのように段状につくった丘を中心に放射状に群立させ、脇の小山にはレストランが計画されている。ホテルのセントラルファシリティでは中央の水を張った中庭を介してロビー、ギャラリー、レストランなどが向き合い、自然のヴォイドであるすり鉢の窪みに対し、建築の中心もヴォイドとして、空間相互の関係性をつくっている。

◎ **Form & Counter Form**

◎ フォーム&カウンターフォーム

Makuhari Messe & North Hall | 1989, 1997

幕張メッセ & 北ホール

The Nippon Convention Center, commonly known as Makuhari Messe, was the winning scheme for an invited national competition held among seven firms in the summer of 1986. The 552-hectare site sits in a strategic location halfway between Narita International Airport and Central Tokyo. Nippon Convention Center was the first comprehensive

Aerial view of the complex (Makuhari Messe at back, North Hall in front)

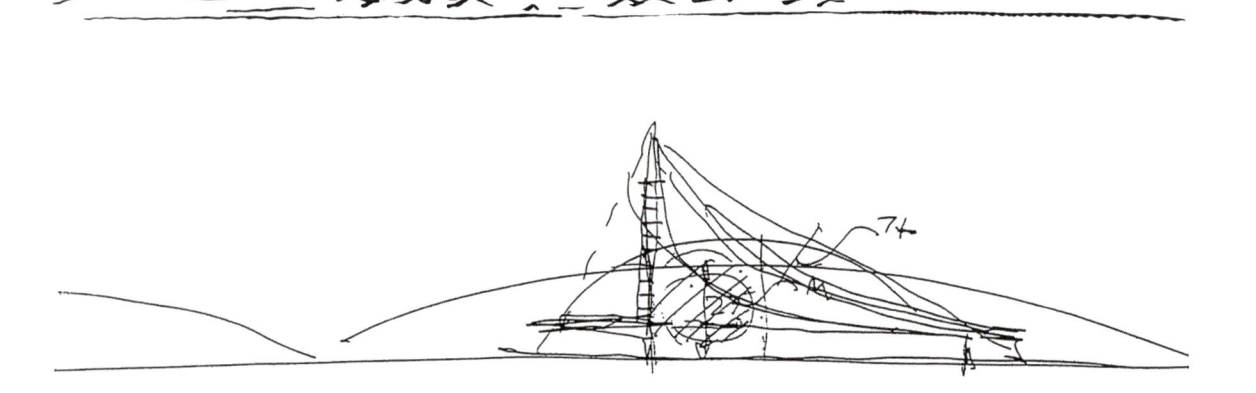

convention complex of its kind in Japan.

The planning began with the allocation studies of the required program into independent buildings of various geometric and architectonic forms. The volumes of the Event Hall, International Conference Center, and Exhibition Hall, entered through a grouping of red mushroom shaped canopies, are juxtaposed with the giant arch of the Exhibition Hall. These buildings, with their pedestrian arcades, exterior stairs, and sculptural elements, provide a sense of human scale for visitors approaching the massive complex. Altogether, the volumes of the foreground buildings and the giant arch of the exhibition hall in the rear create a metaphorical silhouette that abstracts a natural landscape of hills and mountains, giving birth to a new city image.

Interior view of North Hall

North Hall

A few years after the construction of the initial Makuhari Messe, it became evident from the increasing scale of its use that construction of additional exhibition halls would be necessary. The necessity to span long-distances provided an opportunity to create an enormous, expressive roof form, which has become a key design element for both Makuhari Messe Phases I and II. While the arched roof of Phase I suggests the image of mountains, for Phase II, the silhouette was inverted to create a curving roof, which represents a large wave. The roofs of Phase II use a hybrid suspension structure consisting of a series of curved steel trusses suspended from vertical steel poles at 12-meter intervals.

The exhibition hall in use

幕張メッセという名で知られる日本コンベンションセンターは、1986年の夏に国内で7社を指名した招待コンペでの最優秀案である。552haの敷地は、成田国際空港と東京の都心を結ぶ線上のちょうど中間という極めて戦略的な位置にある。日本コンベンションセンターは、コンベンションに必要とされる施設を完全に満足させた建築群としては日本で最初の施設である。

この計画は、要求されたプログラムにそれぞれ独立した様々な幾何学的、建築学的形態を与えて配置することから始まった。イベント・ホール、国際会議場、そして展示ホールのヴォリュームにアクセスするには、マッシュルーム状の赤い屋根の集合体を通り抜けることになるのだが、そうした様々な形態が展示ホールの巨大なアーチと対置される。こうした建築群が、歩行路のアーケードや外部階段、彫刻的エレメントなどとともに、巨大な施設を訪れた人々にヒューマンスケールを感じさせる役割を果たしている。前景にいくつかの建物があり背景に展示ホールという巨大なアー

Pedestrian bridge added in 2009 [S.O.]

View from Event hall to North Hall -1997 [T.K.]

チがあるという全体の構成は、丘や山並みの連なりといった自然の景観を連想させるようなシルエットを形成し、新たな都市イメージを生み出している。

北ホール

最初の幕張メッセ建設後数年が経ち、展示規模が増大していることから展示ホールの増設が望まれるようになった。第1期と同様に大スパンを飛ばす架構が必要であるために、巨大な屋根をどのように表現するかがもっとも重要なデザイン要素となった。第1期のアーチ状の屋根が山並みを表現していたのに対し、第2期の屋根はそのイメージを逆転させ空に向かって開かれた曲面とすることで、大きな波を表現している。第2期の屋根には、12mピッチで並べた垂直の鋼管から吊り下げられた曲線のスチール・トラスを連続させた、ハイブリッド吊構造が用いられている。

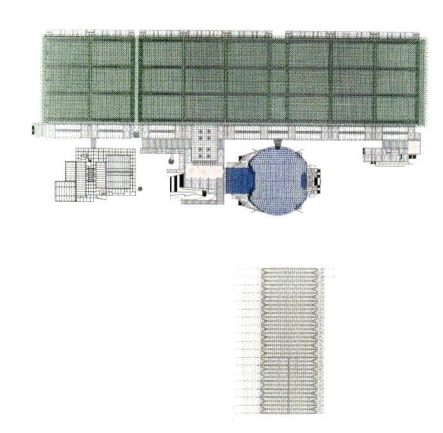

Roof structure plan

Conceptual model of North Hall [T.K.]

Hokusai, Kajikazawa in Kai Province
(from *Thirty-six views of Mount Fuji*)

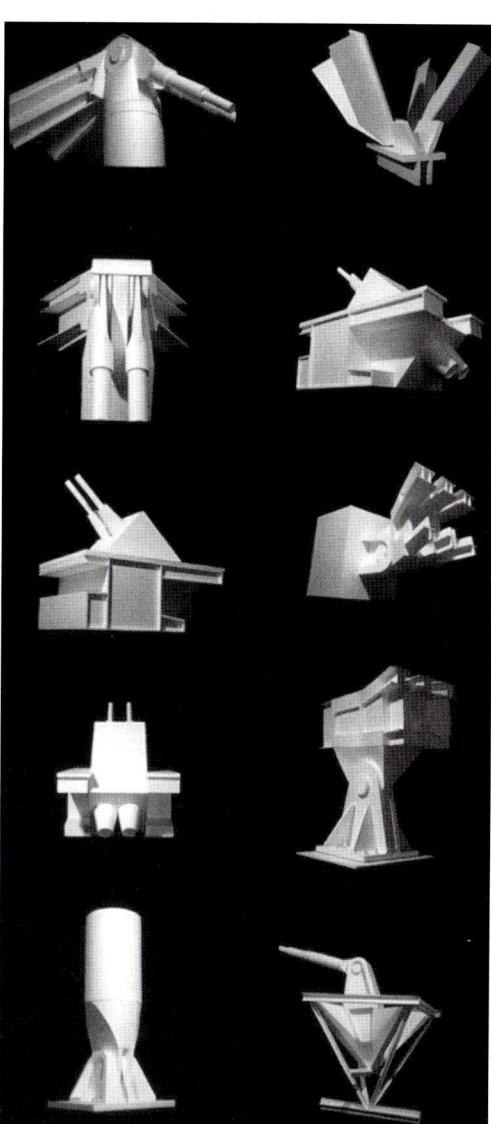

Study models of joint detail

Photograph during construction

Taipei Main Station Area Redevelopment | 2016
台北駅再開発計画

This project is a winning scheme of an invited international competition. The City of Taipei and its Transportation Department have long been planning to build a new Airport Express Terminal to the west of Taipei Main Station. They, furthermore, plan to develop a landmark office, retail, and hotel complex above and around the new terminals. This project area for the Taipei Main Station occupies a strategic location at the center of Taipei that is dotted by a number of important historical buildings and places. It forms a part of

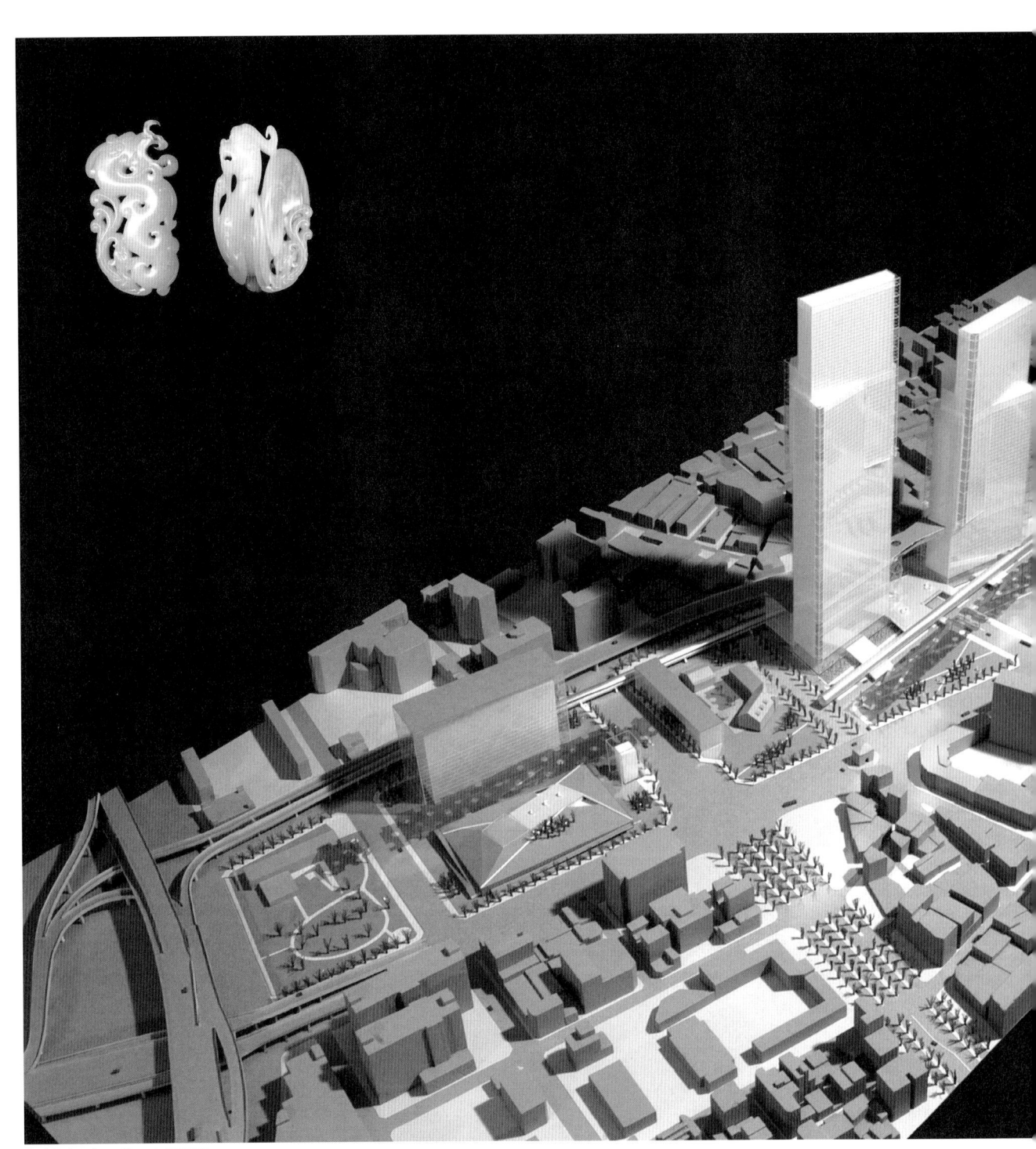

Aerial view from the southwest

city spine that stretches from the Danshuei River to Huashan and beyond to the Shin-Yi sub-city center district.

The Gate Towers will be a symbolic visual presence for the development, even from a great distance. The towers are slab structures that combine the two street geometries in such a way as to represent the mixed uses they house: retail, office and hotel. The buildings not only echo the grid of the surrounding neighborhood streets, but also each other through subtle differentiations in height and volume. The interconnected relationship between the two towers represents the Long – Feng metaphor. Separate, but intertwined, they respond to each other across space, making two forms a unity. The towers, also, have two axes aligned with same aspects of city spine.

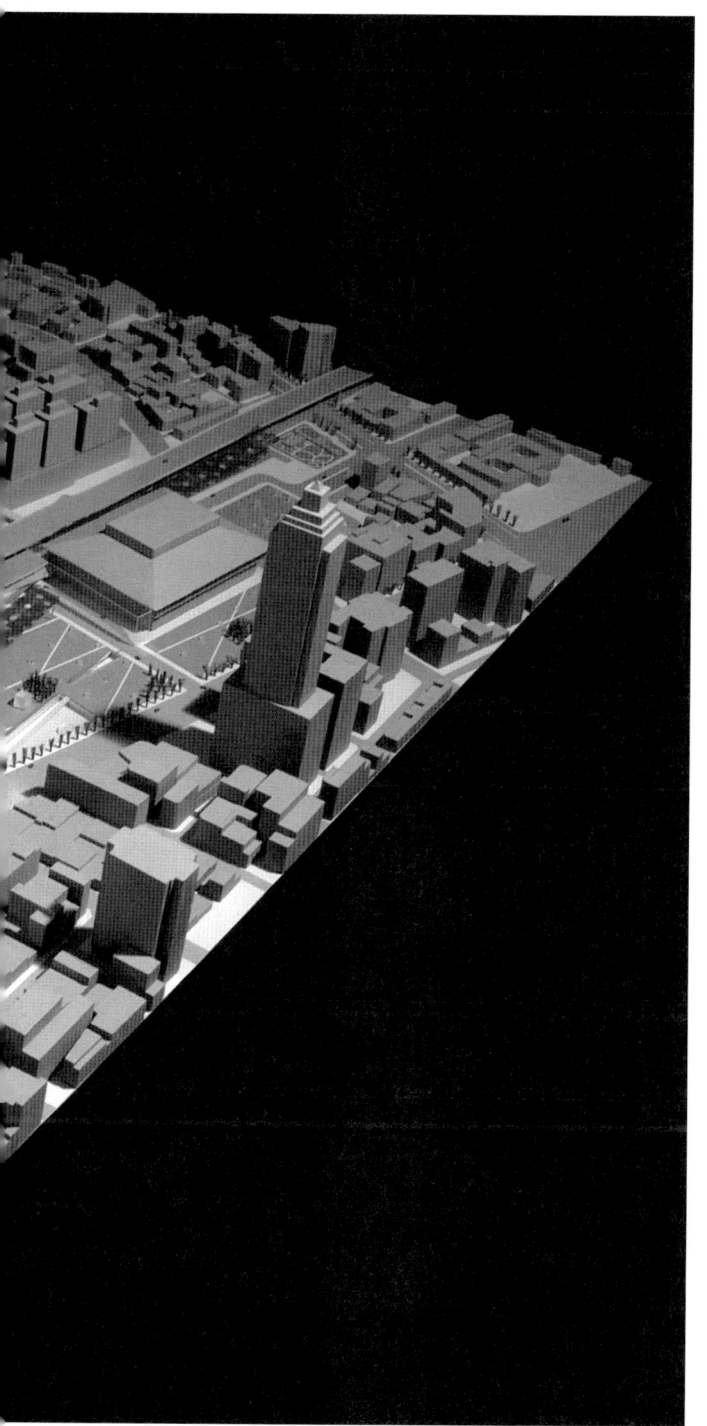

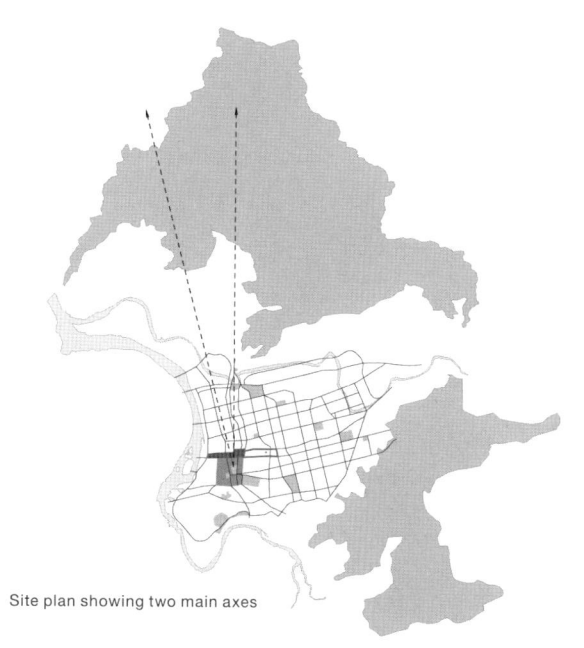

Site plan showing two main axes

Aerial view from the east

このプロジェクトは招待国際コンペにおいて選ばれた最優秀案である。台北市と同市交通局は、かねてより、新しいエアポートエクスプレスターミナルを台北中央駅の西側に建設することを計画していた。同時に、新ターミナル上部とその周辺には、ランドマークとなるようなオフィス、商業、ホテルを含んだ複合施設の開発計画が進められている。この台北中央駅地域は、多くの歴史的建造物などが点在し、淡水川から始まり華山地区、信義副都心へと続く台北市主要部の一部分をなす重要な地域である。

2棟のゲートタワーは、遠方からも見えるような再開発計画の視覚的シンボルとなる。タワーの形態は、2本の都市軸の統合と、商業、オフィス、ホテルというプログラムの複合を立体的に表現している。またこの2棟は、龍と鳳凰をモチーフとして、離れて建ちながら相互に関係し合う形態をもって、一体の空間を生み出している。また、白いセラミック印刷が施されたガラスの表層は、二つの都市軸と対応して異なる角度をもち、眺める場所や天気、時間によって、変化するシルエットをつくりだす。

Section diagram

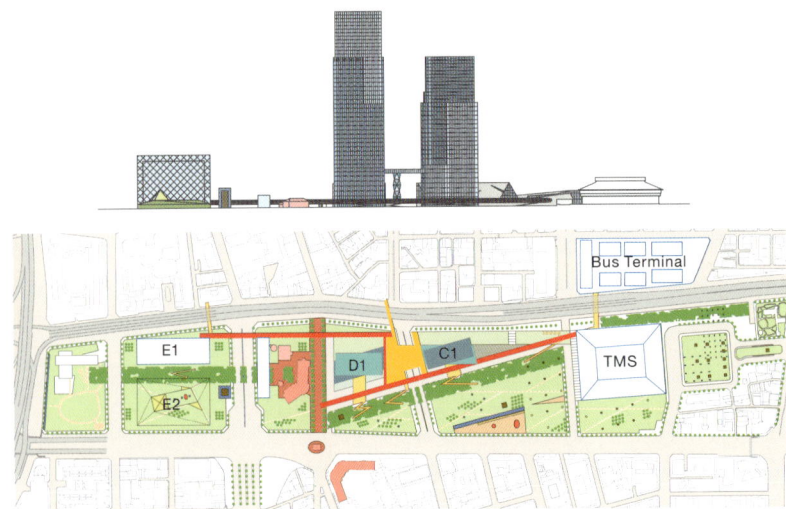

Diagram

Station atrium

◎ **Participation with Collective Forms**

◎ 集合体への参加

TV Asahi | 2003
テレビ朝日

TV Asahi, one of five major private broadcasting companies in Japan, is planned within a large private urban renewal project in central Tokyo named Roppongi Hills. TV Asahi was one of the largest landholders within the development area when the project was originally conceived in 1986.

The shape of the building responds to the

Evening view from the north

Aerial view of the Roppongi district [M.B.]

Site plan

curves of the two adjacent major streets and the natural contours of the site, creating a rounded space that envelops visitors with a feeling of warmth.

The building is surrounded by a series of open spaces, which have provided a new pedestrian oriented urbanity for the immediate neighborhood. At the southeastern corner of the site, there is a large luminescent glass wall with six Arabic numbers constantly changing from 9 to 1— a project designed by artist Tatsuo Miyajima called 'Counter Void'. This artwork has a strong presence at the corner plaza and signals the entrance to TV Asahi. To the north of the corner plaza, an elevated platform— the 'Entrance Square'— offers a peaceful environment defined by a cascading water

Southeast elevation [T.K.]

Cascade [T.K.]

terrace at its eastern edge.

As TV Asahi operates 24 hours a day, special attention was given to the building's appearance at night. The glass-walled atrium is the icon of the project; a point of interface between the public and private domains.

六本木ヒルズの一角に、日本の5大民放局の一つであるテレビ朝日の新本社を設計した。テレビ朝日は主要な地権者として再開発組合、関係行政機関等とともに、初期の構想から17年間にわたってこの地域の市街地再開発に携わってきた。

建物の形態はこのカーブする2本の道路と敷地の自然地形に即しながら、丸く膨らみのある形によって人を優しく包み込む空間をつくりだすとともに、建物を俯瞰すると木魚とか魚の頭のような形となっている。

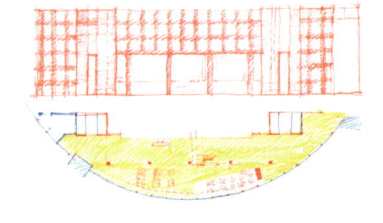

Atrium [T.K.]

建物の周りを取り囲む様々な外部空間は、周縁に向かって新しい都市景観を展開している。敷地南東のコーナーにあるガラスの大きな光る壁には、六つのデジタルの数字が規則的に9から1に変化する宮島達男によるアートが常に点滅し、この作品「カウンター・ボイド」はテレビ朝日への導入部の表象にもなっている。ゲートプラザの北側の高い位置にあるエントランス広場は、その東端の部分にカスケードによる水のテラスを設け、静かな憩いの場を提供している。24時間稼動のテレビ朝日として夜の建物の表情が特に意識された。

ガラスのアトリウムはこの新しいテレビ朝日を象徴する空間で、パブリックとプライベートの領域の境界をつなぐ場となる。透明なガラススクリーンのアトリウムからの眺めは庭園の緑と背景の都市風景が重層しながら展開する。

Reception lobby with mural by Sol LeWitt

Art work by Tatsuo Miyajima

View along Keyaki-zaka

Square 3, Novartis Campus | 2009
スクエア 3 ノバルティス キャンパス

In 2005, Maki and Associates were commissioned to design a new office building for the Swiss pharmaceutical company, Novartis at its headquarters campus in Basel. The project was tasked to respond to the Novartis' new working environment guidelines known as "The New Multi-Space Concept", which calls for an open office environment, encouraging mobility, adaptability, and interaction between employees with unique character and identity to replace private cellular offices. To enhance the transparency of the

North elevation

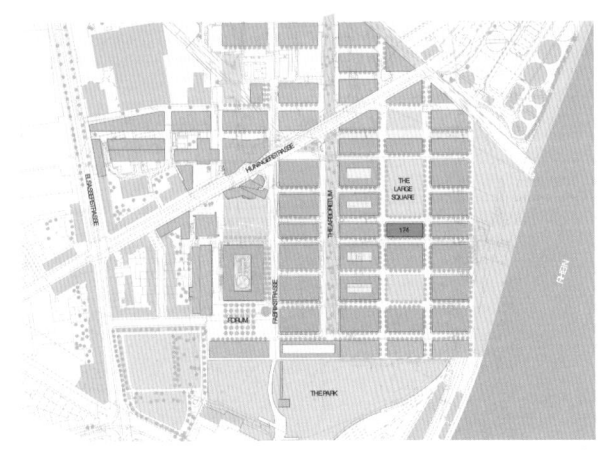

Campus plan (Maki building in dark grey)

working environment, the service cores have been located at alternating ends of the building to give the working space a clear diagonal view across the entire floor. This planning strategy also enlivens the given square floor plate to provide a fluid and dynamic spatial configuration.

The radial symmetry concept has been applied to the ceiling as well, consisting of sloping aluminum panels configured in a diagonal pattern that reinforces the clear view and guides the eye towards the open corners of the building. Sufficient natural lighting led by inclined ceiling panels and indirect lighting from the work stations help attain a clean ceiling design, further enhancing the continuity of the work space. To create an interconnected and dynamic working environment, the entire building consists of one continuous open space. Each floor plate is connected by a double height space and circular staircase at the ends of the building, allowing staff to move freely between different floor levels.

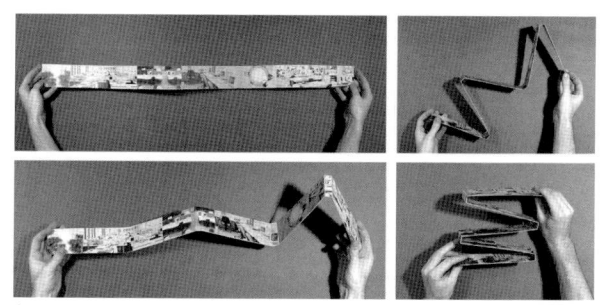

Conceptual model

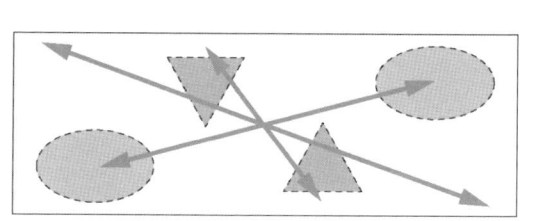

Radial symmetry diagram

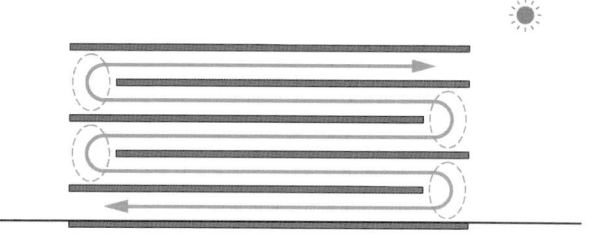

Continuous open space diagram

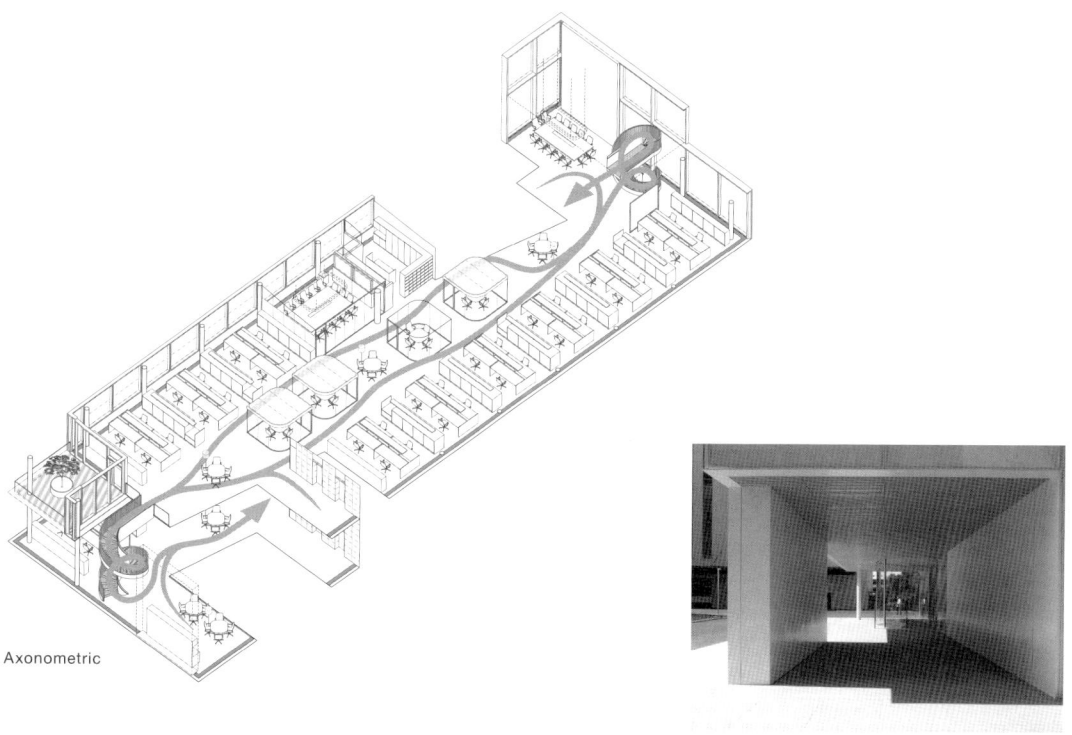

Axonometric

Entrance

Furthermore, social spaces— the break area, outdoor terrace, and conference zone— have been located within the double height space to allow interaction and to foster a community among the various working groups within the building.

2005年、世界的に有名な製薬会社であるノバルティスグループの新しいオフィスビルの設計を依頼された。オフィスの空間構成は、ノバルティスの掲げる「マルチスペースコンセプト」と呼ばれる新しい業務空間についてのコンセプトから着想を得ている。そこでは、建物内の研究員や職員の積極的な交流を促すような開放的で、透過性と可変性に富んだオフィス環境が求められていた。

この要求に基づき、各階が2層の吹抜け空間を介してひと筆書きで連続す

Open meeting room upon entry

Upper floor office

るオフィス空間が設計された。建物の両端に1層ずつずれながら配置された吹抜け空間には、テラス、会議スペースなど、異なる階の利用者が休息し交流する場が提供されている。吹抜けの彫刻的ならせん階段によって、コアを利用しなくとも自由に各階を移動することができる。このひとつながりのオフィス空間は、各部局の編成の変化に伴う必要面積の変化にも柔軟に対応することができる。

また、階段やエレベーターを含むコアを矩形の平面の対角線上に配置することにより、階全体を見通す斜め方向の視線を誘導し、透明性の高い流動的なオフィス空間を生み出している。

この点対称の構成は天井のデザインにも反映され、アルミパネルの緩やかな傾斜とパンチングのパターンが、コーナー部の開放的なテラスや吹抜け空間へと導くように設計された。外壁に向かって傾斜した天井に沿って射し込む自然光と、ワークステーションに備え付けられた間接照明によって、明るいオフィス空間が実現されている。

Double-height break area

Open office space

Open office space

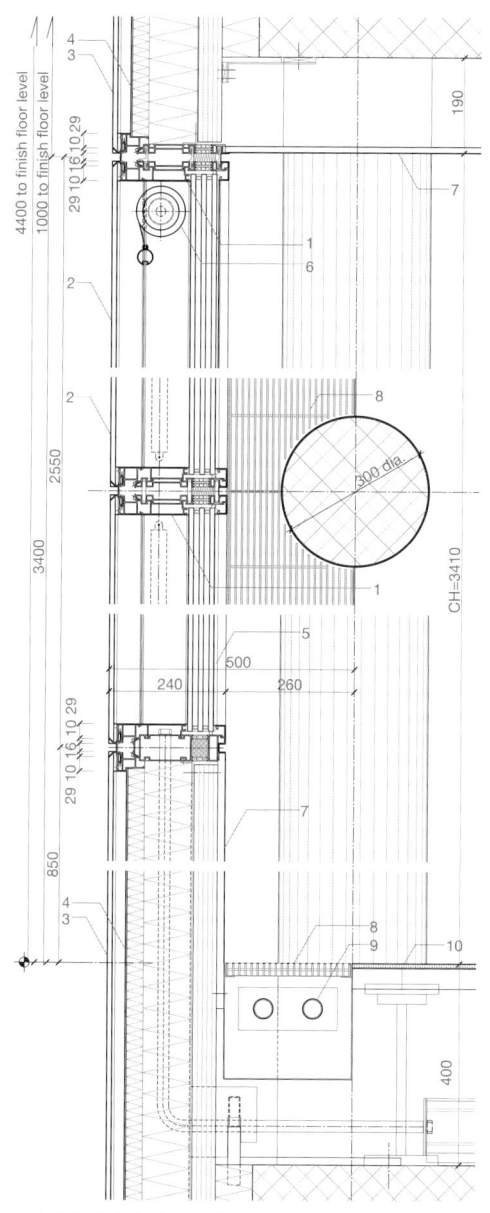

1 Extruded aluminum unitized sash frame
  pvdf coated
2 10mm thk. low iron glass
  with 60% white ceramic frit
  (1.5mm dots, 1950 above finish floor)
  with low-e coating
3 10mmthk. low iron glass
4 Pvdf coated aluminum panel
5 Insulated glass unit
  (6mm+A14mm+6mm+A14mm+6mm)
6 Motorized roller shade screen
7 Painted gypsum board
8 Aluminum grill
9 Radiant heating tube
10 Tile carpet over raised floor system

Typical facade detail (scale:1/15)

Facade corner detail

4 World Trade Center | 2015
4 ワールド・トレード・センター

4 World Trade Center belongs to a collective group of buildings in the World Trade Center Redevelopment that is guided by the master plan by Studio Daniel Libeskind. Of the towers planned for the site, this building follows Towers 1, 2, and 3 in height, reaching 977 ft and comprised of 72 floors. The group of buildings surrounding the National September 11 Memorial is intended to form a spiraling effect through stepping building heights, with 4WTC positioned at the end of the rotational pivot.

The design takes on a two-fold approach — creating a "minimalist" tower that would assume an understated, reverent position opposite the memorial while also developing a more active podium intended to foster interaction with the immediate urban environment at pedestrian level, bringing energy and vitality as part of the overall downtown redevelopment effort.

The office lobby facing Greenwich Street features three entrances— one each on Cortlandt, Liberty, and Greenwich Streets. The lobby is symmetrical in its composition and offers panoramic views of the World Trade Center (WTC) site. The inner core wall of the lobby is clad in polished black granite to mirror the memorial and aligned in its geometry with the footprint of the South Tower, now a reflecting pool.

The building's facade is clad in floor-to-ceiling windows utilizing composite glass with reflective low emissive coatings intended to achieve a matte metallic quality. This gives the tower an abstract quality— minimal, light, cool, and ephemeral, changing with the light of day. Seen from a distance, the tower possesses a unique angular profile that is chiseled at its crown, assuming a position amid the spiral composition proscribed under the master plan for the site.

Elevation form Liberty Street [TE.]

View from 7 World Trade Center [SPI]

4WTC at twilight [C.R.]

Site model

4 ワールド・トレード・センターは、ダニエル・リベスキンドのマスタープランに基づくワールド・トレード・センター（WTC）再開発計画の一部分である。メモリアルを中心に囲む4棟のタワーは、1WTCを頂点として空へと上昇していくスパイラルを描いている。その端点に位置する我々の4WTCは高さ297.79m、地上72階建ての建物である。

この計画で、我々は二つのコンセプトを提案している。メモリアルに相対する敷地にふさわしい、静謐で抽象的なイメージをもつタワーをつくること、そして一方で、ダウンタウン再開発の一部と位置づけ、歩行者レベルに活気のある都市空間を提供する基壇をつくりだすことを試みている。

コートランド、リバティー、グレニッチ通りにそれぞれ入口をもつ高さ14mのオフィスロビーからは、WTC全体を見渡すことができる。黒い花崗岩で仕上げられたロビーの壁は、公園と正対するように配置され、そこにはメモリアルパークの風景が写しだされる。またエレベーターホールは、メモリアルパークの並木を連想させるよ

4WTC blending into the sky　　　　　　　　　　　　　　　　　　　　　　　　　　　　　　　[M.W.]

Skyline of New York　　　　　　　　　　　　　　　　　　　　　　　　　　　　　　　　　　[M.W.]

Church Street　　　　　　　　　　　　　　　　　　　　　　　　　　　　　　　　　　　　　[SPI]

うな、6層のクリアー塗装を施した高光沢の木パネルで仕上げられている。

建物は、反射率の高いコーティングを施した複層ガラスのファサードで覆われ、金属質で光沢のある外観をつくりだしている。それは建物にミニマルで軽く繊細な、そして光とともに変化する抽象的なイメージを与える。遠くから望む4WTCは独特な鋭角の輪郭を示して、マスタープランが掲げるスパイラル状に上昇する建築群の表現を明確にすることであろう。

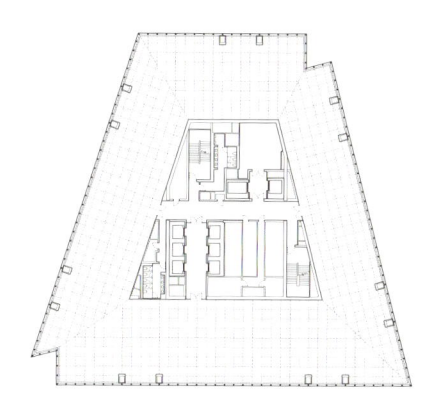

Upper floor plan : 57th - 72nd floor

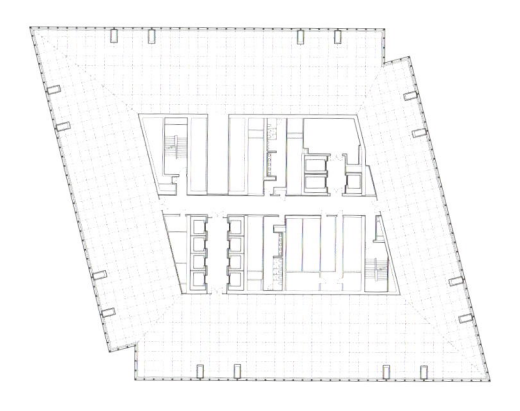

Lower floor plan : 15th - 54th floor

Aerial view from World Financial Center [SPI]

Office interior

View from National 9-11 Memorial Park

Sky | Trees | Water

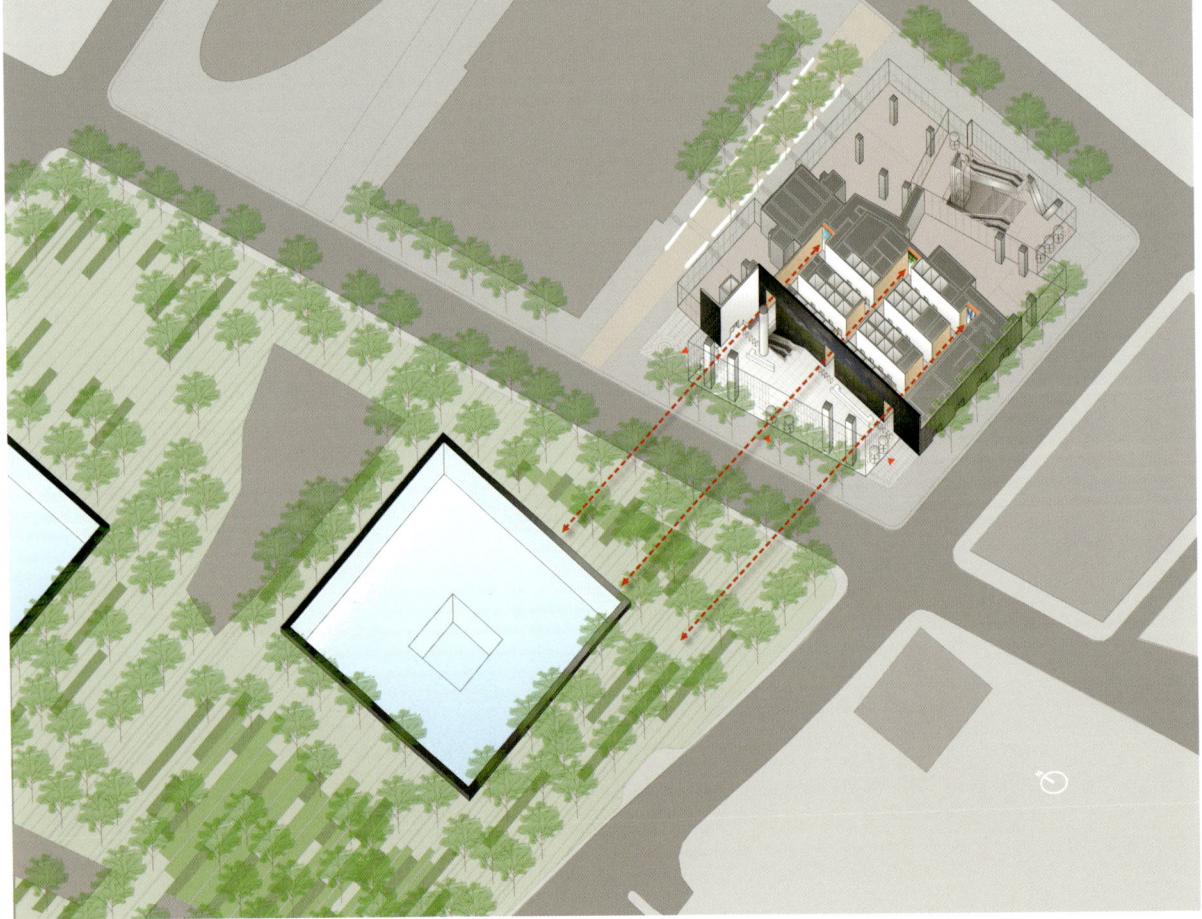

Concept diagram of the three Office Lobby corridors

Office Lobby [A.C.]

Transit Hall

View from National 9-11 Memorial Park

4WTC opening ceremony - November 13, 2014

View from National 9-11 Memorial Park

North view of Midtown Manhattan

Curtain wall mock-up

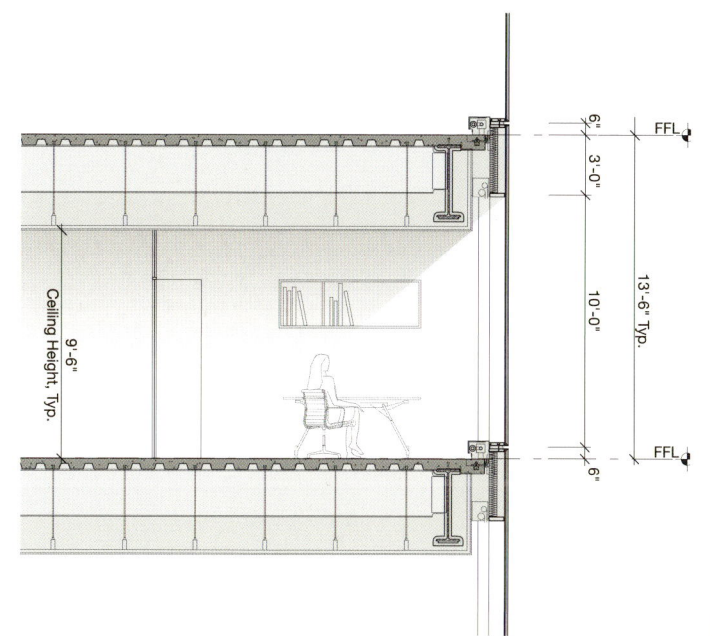

Typical Section (scale: 1/8"=1'-0")

Terrace on 57th floor

◎Circular Collective Form

◎円の集合体

Nalanda University Competition
| 2013
ナランダ大学　コンペ案

Nalanda University was a major center of Buddhist Studies between the fifth and twelfth century in northeast India. With over 2,000 teachers and 10,000 students, Nalanda attracted scholars from places as distant as China, Korea, Japan, and Turkey. Near the end of the twelfth century, its campus was destroyed by Islamic invaders.

Site model

Perspective

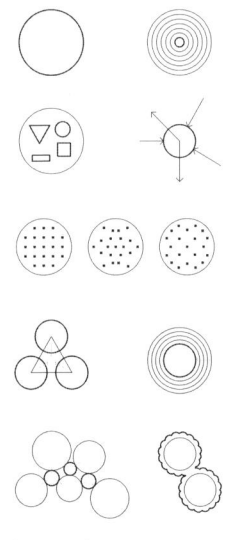

Concept diagrams

Re-established in 2010, Nalanda launched an international competition to select the architect for its new campus. We proposed a highly sustainable "development network" rather than a formalized "Master Plan" — a framework in harmony with natural life rhythms, filled with gaps to be filled in over time.

The traditional Indian village form is circular. Aggregations of circular forms are particularly well adapted to the control of program connections and separations. Their size easily adjusts to site conditions and to a diversity of scale and building types. Reminiscent of traditional villages, the circle form fosters intricate groupings, distinct but overlapping communal spaces, and a complex network of public and private zones— a new type of collective form, without pre-ordained order or hierarchy.

ナランダ大学は5世紀から12世紀にかけて仏教研究の中心であった大学で、現在のインド北東ビハール州に位置している。2000人の教員と1万人の学生が集う全寮制の大学として、中国、韓国、日本、チベット、モンゴル、トルコ、スリランカや東南アジア全域といった遠方からも研究者が集まっている。12世紀の終わりにナランダはイスラム教徒の侵入者によって破壊された。

2010年に再建されたナランダ大学はラージギル(もともとのキャンパスの南)に大きな敷地を確保し、今後の大学の成長を見据えた第1期建設のために国際コンペを開催した。我々の提案は、建築形態を決定する〈マスタープラン〉というよりも高度にサステイナブルな〈成長ネットワーク〉であり、自然の生命体のリズムと調和し、時の経過に応じて変化する要望を受けとめられるような余白をたくさんもたせた枠組みを提案している。

伝統的なインドの集落は丸い平面形をしている。もともとヒエラルキーをもたない構成として、円形の集合体は特にプログラムの結合/分離をコントロールしやすい形態であり、それぞれのサイズをプログラムや敷地に応じて調整することで様々なスケールやビルディング・タイプを収容することができる。こうした理由で新しいナランダ大学キャンパスを構成する原理として円形モチーフを採用したのだが、それは伝統的集落を連想させるだけではなく、常に開かれた形態であることを示唆するためでもある。円を主体とした構成は、複雑なグルーピングやそれぞれ独自性をもちながら互いに重なり合うような共用空間、そしてパブリックとプライベートなゾーンの複雑なネットワークを可能にしてくれる。この構成は、あらかじめ想定した秩序やヒエラルキーとは無縁の新しいタイプの群造形だといえるだろう。

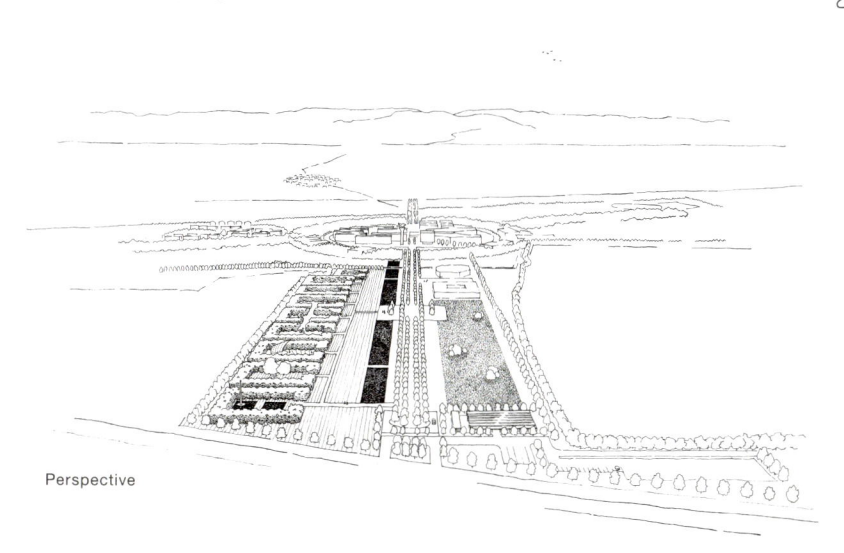

Concept diagrams

Perspective

5 | Scenery

情景

Architecture undoubtedly creates scenery at the moment of its completion. Then visitors approach the building, and various other scenes develop— sometimes as expected by the designers, and sometimes unexpected. As architects, we cannot ignore this automatic socialization inherent to architecture.

Certainly, architects put a great deal of thought and energy into the process of design production. For example, when we design a space, we imagine visitors and ourselves in the as-yet unrealized space, and gradually compose its form, proportion, dimensions, and materiality. However, no matter how precise or certain the calculations, space— when realized— announces its independence as a form of architecture. It could be said that a wall between the created space and architect inevitably rises.

At times, architecture awaits us with a warm welcome; at other times, it asks us why things have happened the way they did.

Scenery reflects architecture's social capacity. Scenery shows how people interact with the places and spaces provided by architecture. When scenery yields images completely unexpected by architects or clients, it is especially joyous.

建築は、完成した時に疑いもなく一つの風景をつくりだす。やがて人々が建物に参加することによって、様々な情景が展開し始める。時に我々が予期していたかたちで、またあるときは全く異なった姿で。我々はこうした建築が本来的にもつ社会的自動性を無視することはできない。

確かに我々はすべての思考とエネルギーを生産の過程で注ぎ込む。たとえば一つの空間の設計を例にとってみよう。まだ現実に立ち現れない空間に自分自身を、あるいは様々な人々をもぐりこませながら、形態を、プロポーションを、寸法を、そして材質性について思いを巡らし、次第に構築していく。しかし、いかに緻密な計算と確信をもってつくりあげても、空間は立ち上がった瞬間、建築そのものの自立を宣言する。そこにはもはやどうしようもない壁が、製作者と出来上がったものの間に存在し始めるといってもよい。

建築は時に我々を暖かく迎えてくれるし、時にどうしてこうなってしまったかと訴えかけてくる。

情景はその建築の社会性を写し出す。情景とはその建築が提供する場所・空間に、どのように人々が関わり合うかを示す。その情景が写し出すものは、時に建築家も施主も全く予期しなかったものがあった時、それは建築家に格別の歓びを与えるものである。

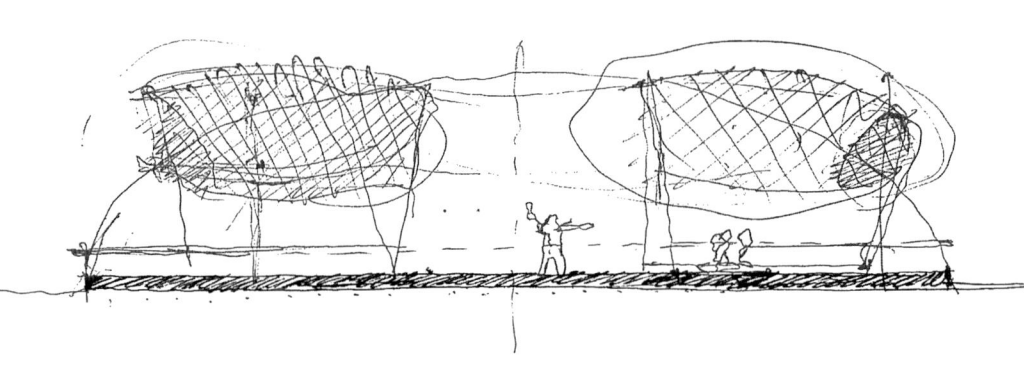

Katoh Gakuen Elementary School -1972

Katoh Gakuen Elementary School -1972 [O.M.]

Courtyard, International College for Post-graduate Buddhist Studies -2010

Children

Human beings have a unique tendency to feel and act as a result of what they see when they are in a space. For example, children's behavior is universal, regardless of cultural background or generation.

子供

人間は空間の中で見ることによって、何かを感じ、そして振る舞うという特性をもっている。たとえば子供の振る舞いは文化、時代を問わずユニヴァーサルである。

Plaza, Tokyo Denki University Tokyo Senju Campus -2012

Haus der Hoffnung -2012

Park, Kaze-no-Oka Crematorium -2012

Haus der Hoffnung -2012

Chahar Bagh Boulevard, Isfahan, Iran -1959

Yerba Buena Center for the Arts -1993

Esplanade, SPIRAL -1985

Tokyo Denki University Tokyo Senju Campus -2012

Solitude

Nietzsche once wrote that solitude was his dearest home. Throughout this past half century, I have encountered great public spaces for solitude in various parts of the world. From this, I have concluded that great public spaces can be enjoyed in solitude, and enjoyed even more with a crowd.

孤独

ニーチェは「孤独は私の故郷である」といった。
私はこの半世紀の間、世界の様々なところで素晴らしい独りのためのパブリックスペースに出会ってきた。そしてそこから得た結論の一つは、素晴らしいパブリックスペースとは独りでも、また多くの群集が集まった時にでも素晴らしいスペースであるということであった。

Cafe, Hillside Terrace -2011

Hillside Plaza -2015

Republic Polytechnic Campus -2007

Mihara Performing Arts Center -2007

4 World Trade Center -2013

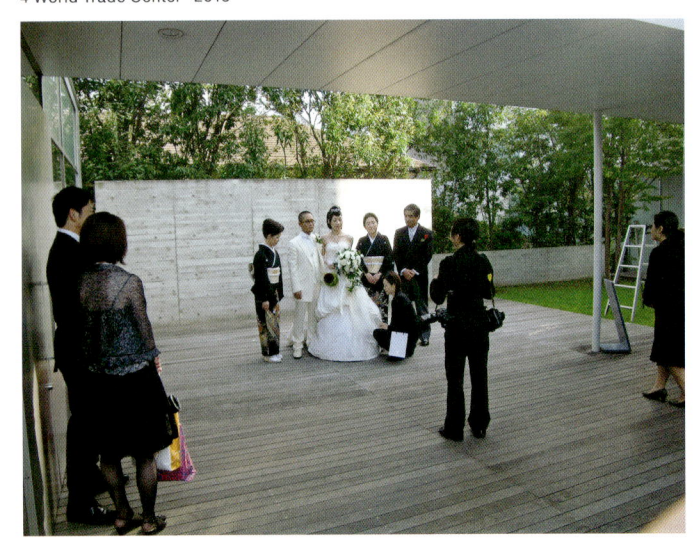

Hillside West -2009

Mihara Performing Arts Center -2008

Hillside Terrace -2004

Yerba Buena Center for the Arts -1993 [P.P.]

Terrace, Square 3, Novartis Campus -2009

Mihara Performing Arts Center -2007

Roof garden, SPIRAL -1995

[SP.]

Delight

In *The Ten Books on Architecture*, Vitruvius wrote that architecture is "firmitas, utilitas, and venustas". The last Latin word "venustas", translated as "beauty", has also been recently reinterpreted as "delight"—a universal value that human beings expect in architecture. In fact, while beauty is dependent on generation, region, and culture, delight is a universal expression shared by humans and animals. It is expected that architecture will generate a variety of joyful emotions through its expression and form.

Katoh Gakuen Elementary School -1972

Washington University in St. Louis
Sam Fox School of Design and Visual Arts -2006

歓び

ヴィトルヴィウスは建築十書の中で、建築は「用・強・美」であるという有名な言葉を残している。最後の「美」と訳されたラテン語の「venustas」は、建築に対して人間が期待するより普遍的な価値、すなわち美ではなく「歓び」ではなかったかと、最近いわれ始めている。つまり美は時代、地域、文化などによって異なってくるのだが、歓びは人間もまた動物も共有の感情表現であるからだ。

当然、建築の表現・形態によって様々な歓びを生み出すことが期待される。

Floating Pavilion -1996

[J.S.]

Republic Polytechnic Campus -2007

6 — Collective Form of Open Spaces

オープン・スペースの集合体

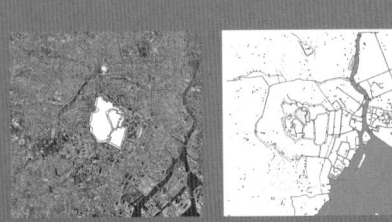

Washington Square, New York, USA

Yoyogi Park, Tokyo, Japan

Meisho Edo Hyakkei (*One Hundred Famous Views of Edo*). Hiroshige Utagawa (1856-1858).

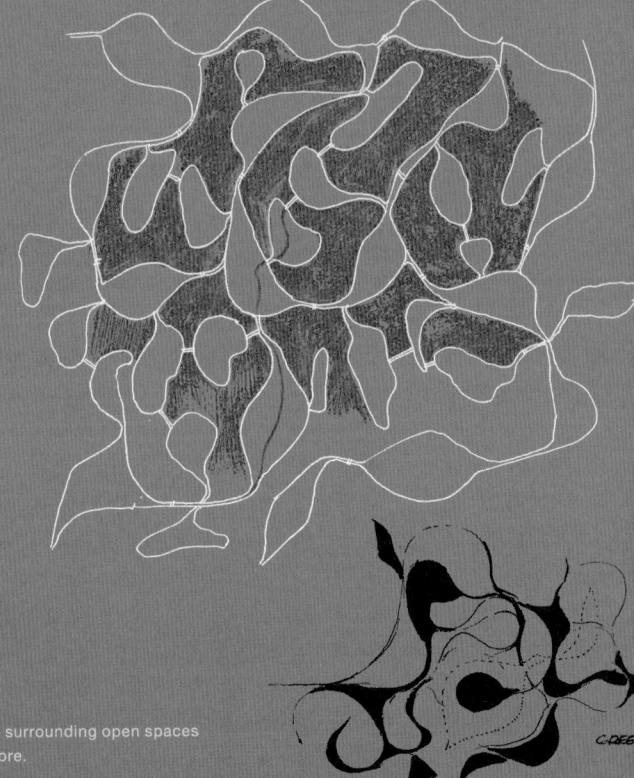

Minamihara, Chiba, Japan

The Imperial Palace and the surrounding open spaces together serve as Tokyo's core.

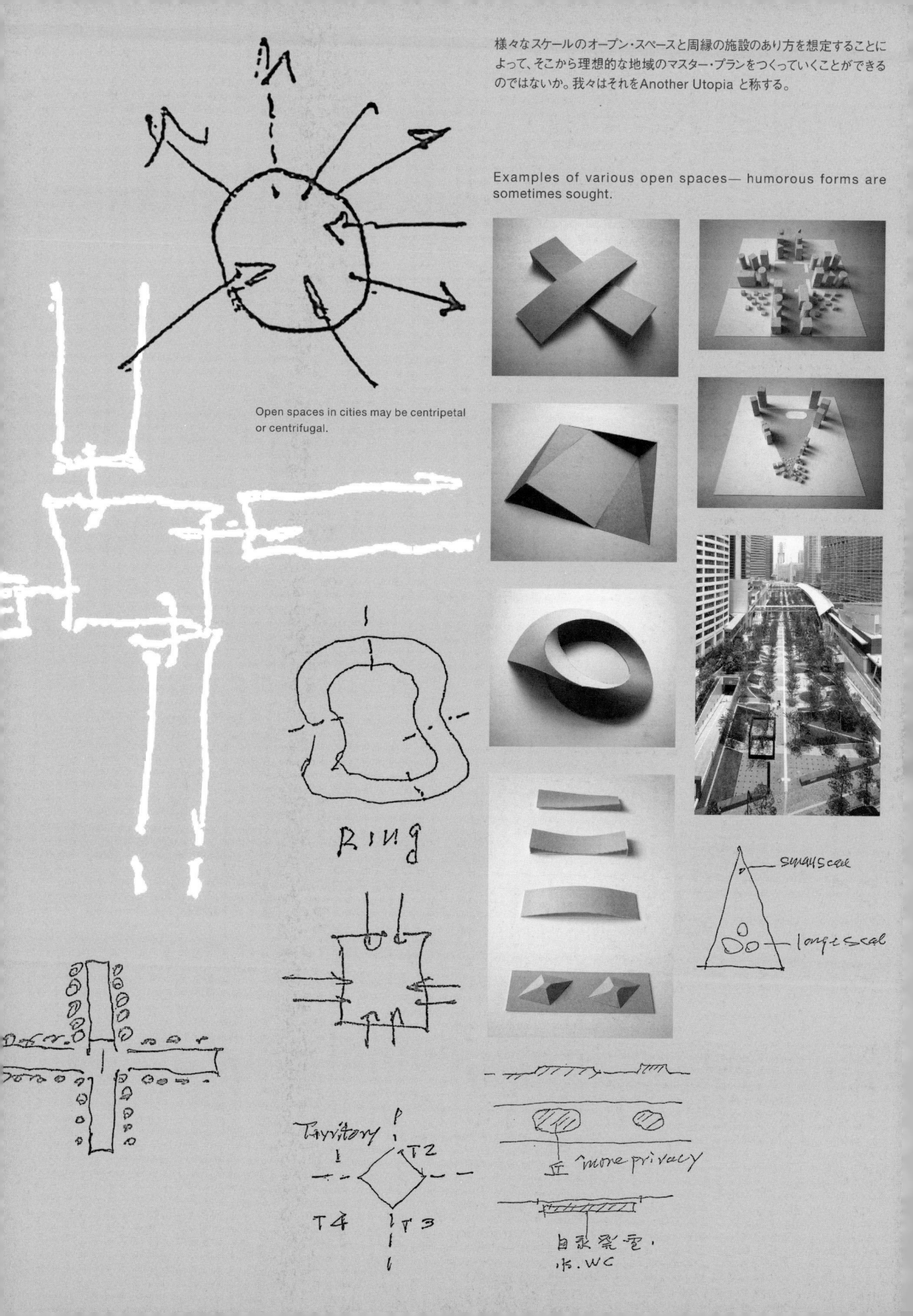

様々なスケールのオープン・スペースと周縁の施設のあり方を想定することによって、そこから理想的な地域のマスター・プランをつくっていくことができるのではないか。我々はそれをAnother Utopia と称する。

Examples of various open spaces— humorous forms are sometimes sought.

Open spaces in cities may be centripetal or centrifugal.

Fumihiko Maki
Curriculum Vitae

Birth
1928, Tokyo

Academics
1952	Bachelor of Architecture, University of Tokyo
1953	Master of Architecture, Cranbrook Academy of Art
1954	Master of Architecture, Graduate School of Design, Harvard University
1958-60	Graham Foundation Fellow
1956-61	Associate Professor, Washington University
1962-65	Associate Professor, GSD Harvard University
1965-85	Visiting Critic, universities in United States and Europe
1979-89	Professor, Department of Architecture, University of Tokyo

Professional Affiliations
Registered Architect, Japan
Registered Architect, Germany
Member, Japan Institute of Architects
Honorary Fellow, American Academy of Arts & Sciences
Honorary Fellow, American Institute of Architects
Honorary Fellow, Royal Institute of British Architects
Honorary Fellow, Bund Deutscher Architekten
Honorary Fellow, French Academy of Architecture
Officier de L'Ordre des Arts et des Lettres, France
Other affiliations include institutions in Scotland, Australia, Mexico, Czech, and Taiwan

International Awards
1987	Reynolds Memorial Award for SPIRAL
1988	Chicago Architecture Award
1988	Wolf Prize, Israel
1990	Thomas Jefferson Medal in Architecture, Charlottesville, Virginia
1993	The Pritzker Architecture Prize
1993	UIA (Union of International Architects) Gold Medal
1993	Prince of Wales Prize in Urban Design, Harvard University for Hillside Terrace
1999	Arnold Brunner Memorial Prize in Architecture, American Academy of Arts and Sciences
1999	Praemium Imperiale, The Japan Art Association
2011	AIA (The American Institute of Architects) Gold Medal

Domestic Awards
1963	Japan Institute of Architecture Prize for Toyoda Memorial Hall
1969	Mainichi Art Prize for Rissho University Campus
1980	Japan Art Prize for Hillside Terrace
1985	Japan Institute of Architecture Prize for Fujisawa Municipal Gymnasium
1992	The Asahi Prize
1998	Togo Murano Award, Murano Memorial Foundation for Kaze-no-Oka Crematorium
2001	The Grand Prize of Japan Institute of Architecture
2012	The Japan Art Academy Award
2013	Person of Cultural Merit (Japan Ministry of Education, Culture, Sports, Science & Technology)

Essay Publications
1960	Metabolism 1960 (Bijutsu Shuppan-sha)
1964	Investigations in Collective Form (Washington University in St. Louis)
1980	Miegakure suru Toshi (Kajima Publishing)
2008	Nurturing Dreams (MIT Press)

Project Publications
1980-99	Contemporary Japanese Architects: Fumihiko Maki 1~4 (Kajima Publishing)
1996	Fumihiko Maki: Buildings and Projects (Princeton Architectural Press)
2003	The Architecture of Fumihiko Maki (Jennifer Taylor, Birkhäuser)
2008	Fumihiko Maki (Phaidon Press) In Progress: Fumihiko Maki Overseas (Shinkenchiku-sha)
2012	Power of Space: Fumihiko Maki's Recent Works 2007-2015, a+u special issue (Shinkenchiku-sha)
2013	Fumihiko Maki: 1960-2013 (ArchiCreation)

槇 文彦 プロフィール

経歴
- 1928　東京生まれ
- 1952　東京大学工学部建築学科卒業
- 1953　クランブルックアカデミーオブアーツ修士修了
- 1954　ハーバード大学デザイン学部大学院修士修了
- 1956-61　セントルイス・ワシントン大学建築学部准教授
- 1962-65　ハーバード大学デザイン学部准教授
- 1979-89　東京大学工学部建築学科教授
- 1965　（株）槇総合計画事務所設立、代表として現在に至る

所属
- 日本建築家協会名誉会員
- アメリカ芸術・科学アカデミー名誉会員
- アメリカ建築家協会（AIA）名誉会員
- 英国王立建築家協会（RIBA）名誉会員
- ドイツ連邦建築家協会名誉会員
- フランス建築アカデミー名誉会員
- その他スコットランド、オーストラリア、メキシコ、チェコ、台湾の建築家協会の名誉会員

受賞
国際賞
- 1987　AIAレイノルズ賞
- 1988　ウルフ賞
- 1990　トーマス・ジェファーソン建築賞
- 1993　プリツカー賞
  - UIA（国際建築家連盟）ゴールドメダル
  - プリンス オブ ウェールズ都市デザイン賞
- 1998　フランス芸術・文化功労勲章
- 1999　アーノルド ブルンナー記念建築賞
  - 高松宮殿下記念世界文化賞
- 2011　AIA ゴールドメダル

国内賞
- 1963　日本建築学会賞
- 1967　毎日芸術賞
- 1973　文部大臣芸術選奨
- 1980　日本芸術大賞
- 1985　日本建築学会賞
- 1989　紫綬褒章
- 1992　朝日賞
- 1998　村野藤吾賞
- 2001　日本建築学会大賞
- 2012　恩賜賞・日本芸術院賞
- 2013　文化功労者

主なる著書
- 1980　見えがくれする都市　鹿島出版会
- 1992　記憶の形象　筑摩書房
- 2006　ヒルサイドテラス+ウエストの世界　鹿島出版会
- 2008　夢を育んで― 都市・建築のエッセイ集（英）MITプレス
- 2013　漂うモダニズム　左右社
- 2015　応答漂うモダニズム　左右社

主なる作品集
- 1980-99　現代の建築家シリーズ
  - 槇 文彦 1-4巻　鹿島出版会
- 1987　槇 文彦の建築（英）
  - セルジ・サラ著エレクタモニトゥアー社
- 1996　槇 文彦の建築とプロジェクト（英）
  - プリンストン アーキテクチャー プレス
- 2002　槇 文彦の建築（英）
  - ジェニファー・テイラー著バークハウザー社
- 2008　槇 文彦の建築（英）
  - ファイドン プレス
  - In Progress 槇 文彦
  - 最新海外プロジェクト　新建築社
- 2012　Power of Space：槇 文彦の近作2007-2015 a+u 臨時増刊
  - 新建築社
- 2013　槇 文彦の建築(1960-2013)
  - 建築創作

Project Chronology
1960-2020
プロジェクト年表

1960	Nagoya University Toyoda Memorial Hall Nagoya, Aichi	
1960	Washington University in St. Louis Steinberg Hall St. Louis, USA	
1960	Shinjuku Terminal Redevelopment Project Shinjuku, Tokyo	
1961	Competition for Diamond Heights Housing Development San Francisco, USA	
1963	Chiba University Inohana Memorial Hall Chiba, Chiba	
1964	K project	
1965	Movement Systems in the City Boston, USA	
1967, 1968	Rissho University Kumagaya Campus Kumagaya, Saitama	
1967	Rinkai Center Building Osaka, Osaka	
1968	Golgi Structure	
1969	Hillside Terrace Phase I Shibuya, Tokyo	
1969	Mogusa Community Center Hino, Tokyo	
1970	Senri Civic Center Building Senri, Osaka	
1970	Senboku Archaeological Museum Senboku, Osaka	
1970	Park House Shirogane Shinagawa, Tokyo	
1971	Kanazawa Ward Offices Yokohama, Kanagawa	
1972	St. Mary's International School Setagaya, Tokyo	
1972	Osaka Prefectural Sports Center Takaishi, Osaka	
1972	Katoh Gakuen Elementary School Numazu, Shizuoka	
1972	PREVI Low-Cost Housing Lima, Peru	
1972	Hiroo Homes & Towers Minato, Tokyo	
1973	Brasilia Japan Embassy Brasilia, Brazil	
1972-1986	Marine Park Yokohama Yokohama, Kanagawa	
1973	Hillside Terrace Phase II Shibuya, Tokyo	
1974	Noba Kindergarten Yokohama, Kanagawa	
1974	Toyota Kuragaike Memorial Hall Toyota, Aichi	
1974	Tsukuba University Central Building Tsukuba, Ibaraki	
1975	National Aquarium, Okinawa Kunigami, Okinawa	
1976	Austrian Embassy in Japan Minato, Tokyo	
1977	Kota Kinabalu Sports Center Sabah, Malaysia	
1977	Kojimachi Nishikawa Building Chiyoda, Tokyo	
1977	Hillside Terrace Phase III Shibuya, Tokyo	
1978, 1981	Namiki Elementary School Yokohama, Kanagawa	
1978	Sea Side Town in Kanazawa Yokohama, Kanagawa	
1978	Iwasaki Museum Ibusuki, Kagoshim	
1978	Maki Residence Shinagawa, Tokyo	
1979	Lounge in Jun Ashida Building Shibuya, Tokyo	
1979	Royal Danish Embassy Shibuya, Tokyo	
1979	Windsor House Shinagawa, Tokyo	
1980	Residence in Takanawa Minato, Tokyo	
1980	Kawawa Lower Secondary School Yokohama, Kanagawa	
1981	Kyoto Craft Center (ABL) Higashiyama, Kyoto	
1981	Toranomon NN Building Minato, Tokyo	
1981	Mitubishi Bank Hiroo Branch Minato, Tokyo	
1981	Keio University Library, Mita Campus Minato, Tokyo	
1982	Keio University Library Renovation, Mita Campus Minato, Tokyo	
1982	YKK Guest House Kurobe, Toyama	
1983	Residence in Shirokanedai Minato, Tokyo	
1983	Dentsu Kansai Branch Kita, Osaka	
1984	Fujisawa Municipal Gymnasium Fujisawa, Kanagawa	
1984	Cedar Stone Villa Shibuya, Tokyo	
1984	Garden Plaza Hiroo Minato, Tokyo	
1984	Minami Osawa Housing Project, Tama New Town Hachiouji, Tokyo	
1985	West Plaza at Yokohama Central Station Yokohama, Kanagawa	
1985	International Pavilions for Tsukuba Expo '85 Tsukuba, Ibaraki	
1985	Keio University Hiyoshi Library Yokohama, Kanagawa	
1985	Keio University Graduate School, Mita Campus Minato, Tokyo	
1985	SPIRAL Minato, Tokyo	
1986	National Museum of Modern Art, Kyoto Sakyo, Kyoto	
1987	Iwasaki Art Museum Annex Ibusuki, Kagoshima	
1987	Hillside Terrace Phase V Shibuya, Tokyo	
1988	Tsuda Hall Shibuya, Tokyo	
1989	Competition for Zeebrugge Ferry Terminal Zeebrugge, Belgium	
1989	Dai-Tokyo Fire & Marine Insurance Shinjuku Building Shibuya, Tokyo	
1989	TEPIA Minato, Tokyo	
1989	Nippon Convention Center (Makuhari Messe) Makuhari, Chiba	
1989	Toyama Shimin Plaza Toyama, Toyama	
1990	Tokyo Metropolitan Gymnasium Shibuya, Tokyo	
1990	Competition for Palazzo del Cinema Lido, Italy	
1990	Competition for Stuttgart Museum Contemporary Art Stuttgart, Germany	
1990	Children's House Oswiecim, Poland	
1990	Keio University Shonan Fujisawa Campus Fujisawa, Kanagawa	
1991	Competition for Kyoto Symphony Hall Kyoto	
1991	Competition for Frankfurt am Main Center Frankfurt, Germany	
1992	Competition for Salzburg Congress Center Salzburg, Austria	
1992	Hillside Terrace Phase VI Shibuya, Tokyo	
1993	Nakatsu Obata Memorial Library Nakatsu, Oita	
1993	Sandoz Tsukuba Research Institute Tsukuba, Ibaraki	
1993	YKK R&D Center Sumida, Tokyo	
1993	Yerba Buena Center for the Arts San Francisco, USA	
1994	Graduate School Research Center, Keio University Shonan Fujisawa Campus Fujisawa, Kanagawa	
1994	Kirishima International Concert Hall Makizono, Kagoshima	
1995	Isar Büropark Munich, Germany	
1995	Tokyo Church of Christ Shibuya, Tokyo	
1996	Fukuoka University Helios Plaza Jonan, Fukuoka	

1996	Kanagawa University Auditorium Yokohama, Kanagawa	
1996	Floating Pavilion Groningen, Netherlands	
1997	Kaze-no-Oka Crematorium Nakatsu, Oita	
1997	Shinohara Community Center Yokohama, Kanagawa	
1997	Natori Performing Arts Center Natori, Miyagi	
1997	Nippon Convention Center (Makuhari Messe), Phase II Makuhari, Chiba	
1998	Competition for Tottori Prefectural Museum of Art Tottori	
1998	Hillside West Shibuya, Tokyo	
1999	Competition for Vuosaari Tower Vuosaari, Finland	
1999	Toyama International Conference Center Toyama, Toyama	
2000	Fukushima Gender Equality Center Nihonmatsu, Fukushima	
2001	Maki Solitaire Dusseldorf, Germany	
2002	Noma House Shibuya, Tokyo	
2002	Fukui Prefectural Library and Archives Fukui, Fukui	
2002	TRIAD Hotaka, Nagano	
2002	Rolex Toyocho Building Koto, Tokyo	
2002	Competition for Bavaria Gelande Hamburg St. Pauli Hamburg, Germany	
2003	Competition for Hong Kong Ocean Terminal Extension Hong Kong, China	
2003	Yokohama I-Land Tower Yokohama, Kanagawa	
2003	TV Asahi Minato, Tokyo	
2003	Toki Messe/Niigata Convention Center Niigata, Niigata	
2004	The National Institute for the Japanese Language Tachikawa, Tokyo	
2004	Tokyo University Law School Learning Center Bunkyo, Tokyo	
2005	Former Fuji Bank Visual Media / Culture Center Yokohama, Kanagawa	
-	Nakatsu Arts Center Nakatsu, Oita	
2006	Washington University in St. Louis Sam Fox School of Design and Visual Arts St. Louis, USA	
2006	Shimane Museum of Ancient Izumo Izumo, Shimane	
2007	Republic Polytechnic Campus Woodlands, Singapore	
2007	Mihara Performing Arts Center Mihara, Hiroshima	
2008	The Delegation of the Ismaili Imamat Ottawa, Canada	
2007	Nagoya University Toyoda Memorial Hall Renovation Nagoya, Aichi	
2009	Massachusetts Institute of Technology, The Media Lab Complex Cambridge, Massachusetts	
2009	University of Pennsylvania Annenberg Public Policy Center Philadelphia, USA	
2009	Square 3, Novartis Campus Basel, Switzerland	
2009	Rolex Nakatsu Building Osaka, Osaka	
2009	Makuhari MesseⅢ, Pedestrian Bridge Chiba, Chiba	
2009	Jewish Community of Japan Shibuya, Tokyo	
2009	Kanagawa University, Shonan Hiratsuka Campus Building11 Hiratsuka, Kanagawa	
2010	International College for Post-graduate Buddhist Studies Bunkyo, Tokyo	
2012	Tokyo Denki University Tokyo Senju Campus Phase I Adachi, Tokyo	
2012	Machida City Hall Machida, Tokyo	
2012	Shimizu Performing Arts Center Shizuoka, Shizuoka	
2012	Haus der Hoffnung Natori, Miyagi	
2013	Chateaucreux District Development (Phase I) Saint-Etienne, France	
2013	Competition for Nalanda University Bihar, India	
2013	51 Astor Place New York, USA	
2013	345 East Village Promenade East Hanover, USA	
2014	Chiba University Inohana Memorial Hall Renovation Chiba, Chiba	
2014	Aga Khan Museum Toronto, Canada	
2015	4 World Trade Center New York, USA	
2015	Skyline Orchard Boulevard Orchard, Singapore	
2015	Republic Polytechnic Expansion & Singapore Institute of Technology Woodlands, Singapore	
2015	Nagano City Hall & Nagano Performing Arts Center Nagano, Nagano	
2015	The Bihar Museum Patna, Bihar, India	
2015	Singapore Mediacorp Buona Vista One-North, Singapore	
2016	Taipei Main Station Area Redevelopment Taipei, Taiwan	
2016	Shenzhen Sea World Cultural Arts Center Shenzhen, China	
2016	Passive Town Kurobe Kurobe, Toyama	
2017	Tsuda College Sendagaya Campus Shibuya, Tokyo	
2017	The Japanese Sword Museum Sumida, Tokyo	
2017	King's Cross R1 London, UK	
2018	Tokyo Denki University Tokyo Senju Campus Phase II Adachi, Tokyo	
-	Cusco Samana Hotel & Residence Cusco, Peru	
-	Miraisozojuku Fujisawa, Kanagawa	
-	King's Cross R2 London, UK	
-	United Nations Consolidation Building New York, USA	
-	Beirut Block 20-02 Beirut, Lebanon	
-	Palau Ocean Research Institute Palau	

Project Data
プロジェクトデータ

Project Name
プロジェクト名
1. Location
   所在地
2. Site area
   敷地面積
3. Building area
   建築面積
4. Total floor area
   延床面積
5. Structural system
   主要構造
6. Collaborating Architect/
   Architect of Record
   協力事務所
7. Structural engineer
   構造設計
8. Mechanical/electrical engineer
   設備設計
9. Other consultants
   その他コンサルタント
10. Contractor
    施工者
11. Completion date
    完成年

Nagoya University Toyoda Memorial Hall
名古屋大学豊田講堂
1. Nagoya, Aichi
2. 375,851 m²
3. 2,935 m²
4. 6,268 m²
5. SRC; 2 stories+1 basement
7. Aoki Structural Engineers (1960),
8. Makino Structural Engineers (2007)
10. Takenaka Corporation (1960), Sogo Consultants (2007)
11. Takenaka Corporation 1960; renovation completed in 2007

Washington University in St. Louis Steinberg Hall
セントルイス・ワシントン大学 スタインバーグ・ホール
1. St. Louis, Missouri USA
4. 36,646 sf
6. Local Architect: Russell, Mullgardt, Schwarz & Van Hoefen
7. Structural: Eason Thompson Associates
11. 1960

Katoh Gakuen Elementary School
加藤学園初等学校
1. Numazu, Shizuoka
2. 6,782 m²
3. 2,185 m²
4. 3,148 m²
5. SRC, Steel frame; 2 stories+1 basement
7. Kimura Structural Engineers
8. P.T. Morimura & Associates
9. Color Scheme: Ray Komai Furniture: Endo Planning
10. Tekken Kensetsu Construction Company
11. 1972

Brasilia Japan Embassy
在ブラジル日本大使館
1. Brasilia, Brazil
2. 25,000 m²
4. 4,087 m²
5. RC, Steel frame; 2 stories
7. Aoki Structural Engineers
8. P.T. Morimura & Associates
11. 1972

Iwasaki Museum
岩崎美術館
1. Ibusuki, Kagoshima
2. 9,805 m²
3. 1,114 m²
4. 1,347 m²
5. RC; 1 story +1 basement
7. Kimura Structural Engineers
8. Sogo Consultants
10. Hazama Corporation
11. 1978

Rissho University Kumagaya Campus
立正大学 熊谷キャンパス
1. Kumagaya, Saitama
2. 360,000 m²
4. 20,148 m²
5. SRC, Steel frame; 5 stories+1 basement
7. Ohsawa Laboratory, Aoki Structural Engineers
8. Sakurai Consultants
9. Sculpture: Masayuki Nagare
10. Joint venture of Takenaka and Matsui Corporations
11. 1967 (Phase I), 1968 (Phase II)

National Aquarium, Okinawa
沖縄国際海洋博 水族館
1. Kunigami, Okinawa
2. 28,100 m²
3. 6,058 m²
4. 7,700 m²
5. SRC, Steel, Precast concrete frame; 3 stories+1 basement
7. Kimura Structural Engineers
8. P.T. Morimura and Associates
10. Joint venture of Kajima Corporation and others
11. 1975

Austrian Embassy in Japan
在日オーストリア大使館
1. Minato, Tokyo
2. 3,200 m²
3. 900 m²
4. 2,030 m²
5. RC, Steel frame; 2 stories+1 basement
7. Aoki Structural Engineers
8. Sogo Consultants
9. Furniture: Emerich Simoncic
10. Takenaka Corporation
11. 1976

Toyota Kuragaike Memorial Hall
トヨタ鞍池記念館
1. Toyota, Aichi
2. 35,000 m²
3. 3,042 m²
4. 4,320 m²
5. RC; 1 stories+1 basement
7. Kimura Structural Engineers
8. Sogo Consultants
10. Takenaka Corporation
11. 1974

United Nations Consolidation Building
新国連ビル
1. New York, New York USA
2. 2,680 m²
3. 2,385 m²
4. 86,400 m²
6. Architect of Record: FX Fowle Architects Competition in collaboration with Polshek Partnership Architects
7. Leslie E. Robertson Associates
8. WSP

9. Civil: Langan Engineering &
   Environmental Services
   Geotech: Muser Rutledge Consulting
   Engineers
   Vertical Transportation: Van Deusen &
   Associates
   Curtain Wall: R.A. Heintges & Associates
11. Competition First Prize, 2003; On Hold

Chiba University Inohana Memorial Hall
千葉大学ゐのはな記念講堂
1. Chiba, Chiba
2. 26,149 m²
3. 1,350 m²
4. 2,372 m²
5. RC; 3 stories+1 basement
7. Takenaka Corporation (1963), Hanawa Structural Engineers (2014)
8. Takenaka Corporation (1963), Sogo Consultants (2014)
10. Takenaka Corporationa
11. 1963, renovation completed in 2014

Yokohama I-Land Tower
横浜アイランドタワー
1. Yokohama, Kanagawa
2. 3,840 m²
3. 2,280 m²
4. 44,120 m²
5. Steel, SRC, RC; 27 stories+3 basements
7. Kimura Structural Engineers
8. Sogo Consultants
10. Joint venture of Takenaka and Shimizu, Toda Corporation
11. 2003

PREVI Low-Cost Housing in Lima, Peru
ペルー低所得層集合住宅
1. Lima, Peru
2. 80-150 m² per housing unit
4. 60-120 m² per housing unit
5. SRC block structure; 1-2 stories
6. Competition in collaboration with Kikutake Architects and Kisho Kurokawa Architect & Associates
   Design Development in collaboration with Kikutake Architects
11. 1972

Floating Pavilion
浮かぶ劇場
1. Groningen, Netherlands
3. 163 m²
4. 163 m²
5. Steel structure on RC barge
7. Structural Design Group
9. Performance Director: Dora van der Groen
   Planning: Department of City Planning and Economic Affairs, Groningen
10. Construction Management: Department of City Planning and Economic Affairs, Groningen
11. 1996

SPIRAL
スパイラル
1. Minato, Tokyo
2. 1,723 m²
3. 1,462 m²
4. 10,560 m²
5. SRC; 9 stories+ 2 basements
7. Kimura Structural Engineers
8. Sogo Consultants
9. Furniture: Maki and Associates+ Kazuko Fujie Atelier
   Signage: Masayoshi Nakajo
   Sculpture: Aiko Miyawaki
   Carpets: Kei Miyazaki
10. Takenaka Corporation
11. 1985

National Museum of Modern Art, Kyoto
京都国立近代美術館
1. Sakyo, Kyoto
2. 5,001 m²
3. 2,142 m²
4. 9,983 m²
5. RC, Steel frame; 4 stories+1 basement
7. Kimura Structural Engineers
8. P.T. Morimura and Associates
9. Furniture: Kazuko Fujie Atelier
   Carpets: Kei Miyazaki
   Signage: Kijuro Yahagi
   Chandeliers: Hidetoshi Ohno
10. Takenaka Corporation
11. 1986

Tokyo Metropolitan Gymnasium
東京体育館
1. Shibuya, Tokyo
2. 45,800 m²
3. 24,100 m²
4. 43,971 m²
5. RC, SRC, Steel (roof); 3 stories+ 2 basements
7. Kimura Structural Engineers
8. Sogo Consultants
9. Landscape: Equipe Espace
   Furniture: Kazuko Fujie Atelier
   Acoustics: NHK Technical Research Center + Yamaha Acoustic Research Center
10. Joint venture of Shimizu Corporation, Tokyu Construction and others
11. 1990

Yerba Buena Center for the Arts
イエルバ・ブエナ芸術センター
1. San Francisco, California USA
2. 4,994 m²
3. 3,456 m²
4. 5,338 m²
5. Steel moment frame; 2 stories
6. Collaborating architects: Robinson Mills+ Williams
7. Structural Design Engineers
8. SJ Engineers, FW Associates

9. Theatrical and lighting: S. Leonard Auerbach & Associates
   Graphics: Laura Hogan Design
   Bench: Kazuko Fujie Atelier
10. Turner Construction Company
    Construction Manager: Sumitomo Construction America, Contractor
11. 1993

Tokyo Church of Christ
東京キリストの教会
1. Shibuya, Tokyo
2. 1,244 m²
3. 947 m²
4. 2,242 m²
5. SRC, Steel (roof); 3 stories+1 basement
7. Kimura Structural Engineers
8. Sogo Consultants
10. Takenaka Corporation
11. 1995

Jewish Community of Japan
日本ユダヤ教団
1. Shibuya, Tokyo
2. 1,076 m²
3. 644 m²
4. 1,915 m²
5. RC, Steel; 2 stories+1 basement
7. Kojima Structural Design Office
8. P.T. Morimura and Associates
10. Toda corporation
11. 2009

Rolex Toyocho Building
ロレックス東陽町ビル
1. Koto, Tokyo
2. 1,697 m²
3. 1,503 m²
4. 11,042 m²
5. SRC, Steel; 7 stories+1 basement
7. Hanawa Structural Engineers
8. P.T. Morimura and Associates
10. Takenaka corporation
11. 2002

Rolex Nakatsu Building
ロレックス中津ビル
1. Osaka, Osaka
2. 784 m²
3. 667 m²
4. 4,863 m²
5. Steel; 7 stories+1 basement
7. Structural Design Office OAK
8. P.T. Morimura and Associates
10. Takenaka corporation
11. 2009

Skyline Orchard Boulevard
スカイライン・オーチャード・ブールバード
1. Orchard, Singapore
2. 3,326 m²
3. 425 m²
4. 19,055 m²
5. RC; 33 stories

6. Architect of Record: DP Architects
7. Beca Carter Hollings & Ferner (S.E.Asia)
8. Beca Carter Hollings & Ferner (S.E.Asia)
9. Quantity Surveyors: Rider Levett Bucknall
   Landscape: Ohtori Consultants
   Environmental, Design institute, DP Green
10. Kajima Overseas Asia
11. 2015

Nagano City Hall and Nagano Performing Arts Center
長野市第一庁舎・長野市芸術館
1. Nagano, Nagano
2. 13,004 m²
3. 5,784 m²
4. 28,463 m²
5. RC, Steel; 8 stories+ 2 basement
7. Umezawa Structural Engineers, lab.
8. Sogo Consultants
10. Joint venture of Maeda Corporation, Kitano Construction and others
11. 2015

Singapore Mediacorp
シンガポール・メディアコープ
1. Buona Vista One-North, Singapore
2. 15,000 m²
3. 13,400 m²
4. 118,400 m²
5. RC, SRC; 12 Stories+ 3 Basements
6. Architect of Record; DP Architects
7. Structure & Civil: Web Structures
8. Parsons Brinckerhoff
9. Environmental, Sustainability: DP Architects, AECOM
   Quantity Surveyor: Rider Levett Bucknall
   Fire Engineer: Arup Singapore
   Façade: Building Façade Group – HCCH Consulting
   Special Lighting: Lighting Planners Associates
   Traffic: CPG Consultants
   Security: Certis Cisco Consulting Services
   Work Place: M Mosers
   Project Manager: Jurong Consultants
10. Joint venture of Kajima Overseas Asia and Tiong Seng Contractors
11. 2015

Shenzhen Sea World Cultural Arts Center
深圳海上世界文化艺术中心
1. Shenzhen, China
2. 26,160 m²
3. 10,420 m²
4. 69,780 m²
5. RC, Steel, SRC; 4 Stories+2 Basements
6. Advisor: Fu Kecheng, Luo Bing
   Collaborating Architect; Kobayashi Maki Design Workshop
   Architect of Record; Capol International & Associates Group
7. Ove Arup & Partners International

8. P. T. Morimura & Associates
9. Client: China Merchants Real Estate (Shenzhen)
   Landscape: Studio On Site
   Lighting: Lightdesign
   Acoustic: Nagata Acoustics
11. 2016

YKK Guest House
前沢ガーデンハウス
1. Kurobe, Toyama
2. 56,124 m²
3. 754 m²
4. 1,695 m²
5. RC; 3 stories+1 basement
7. Hanawa Structural Engineers
8. Sogo Consultants
9. Furniture: Endo Planning +Kazuko Fujie Atelier
10. Shimizu Corporation
11. 1982

Fujisawa Municipal Gymnasium
藤沢市秋葉台文化体育館
1. Fujisawa, Kanagawa
2. 64,105 m²
3. 6,738 m²
4. 11,100 m²
5. RC, SRC, Steel (roof); 3 stories+1 basement
7. Kimura Structural Engineers
8. P.T. Morimura and Associates
9. Landscape: Parks Bureau, City of Fujisawa
   Signage: Maki and Associates+Akihiro Nagao
10. Hazama Corporation
11. 1984

Kirishima International Concert Hall
霧島国際音楽ホール
1. Makizono-cho, Kagoshima
2. 44,800 m²
3. 3,190 m²
4. 4,904 m²
5. RC, Steel frame (amphitheater); 2 stories+1 basement
7. Structural Design Group
8. Sogo Consultants
9. Acoustics: Yoichi Ando
   Lighting/Stage: Nagata Acoustics
   Landscape: Equipe Espace
10. Takenaka Corporation
11. 1994

Kaze-no-Oka Crematorium
風の丘葬斎場
1. Nakatsu, Oita
2. 33,317 m²
3. 2,515 m²
4. 2,260 m²
5. RC, Steel frame; 2 stories
7. Hanawa Structural Engineers
8. Sogo Consultants

9. Landscape: Toda Corporation
10. Tobishima Corporation
11. 1997

TRIAD
TRIAD
1. Hotaka, Nagano
2. 71,377 m²
4. Laboratory: 712 m²
   Gallery: 354 m²
   Guard House: 33 m²
5. RC, Steel frame; 1-2 stories
7. Delta Structural Consultants
8. Sogo Consultants
10. Noguchi Corporation
11. 2002

Mihara Performing Arts Center
三原市芸術文化センター
1. Mihara, Hiroshima
2. 39,533 m²
3. 4,054 m²
4. 7,421 m²
5. SRC, Steel frame; 2 stories+1 basement
7. Hanawa Structural Engineers
8. P.T. Morimura and Associaes
9. Acoustics: Nagata Acoustics
   Theater: Theater Workshop
   Landscape: Studio on site
10. Joint venture of Kumagai, Seim, and Sanyo Construction Corporations
11. 2007

Shimane Museum of Ancient Izumo
島根県古代出雲歴史博物館
1. Izumo, Shimane
2. 56,491 m²
3. 9,446 m²
4. 11,854 m²
5. SRC, Steel frame; 3 stories+1 basement
7. Hanawa Structural Engineers
8. Sogo Consultants
9. Landscape: Studio on site
   Furniture, Carpet: Kazuko Fujie Atelier
10. Joint venture of Obayashi, Nakasuji, and Iwanari Corporations
11. 2006

Haus der Hoffnung
希望の家　名取市文化会館多目的ホール
1. Natori, Miyagi
2. 27,550 m²
3. 428 m²
4. 234 m²
5. Wooden Structure; 1 Story
7. Mikio Koshihara, KAP
8. Sogo Consultants
10. Sato Kogyo
11. 2012

Aga Khan Museum
アガ・カーン ミュージアム
1. Toronto, Ontario Canada
2. 67,800 m²

3. 4,049 m²
4. 10,511 m²
5. RC, Steel frame; 2 stories+1 basement
6. Architect of Record: Moriyama & Teshima Architects
7. Halcrow Yolles
8. Mechanical: The Mitchell Partnership
   Electrical: Crossey Engineering
9. Landscape: Moriyama & Teshima Planners
   Cost: Curran Mccabe Ravindran Ross
   Lighting: Suzanne Powadiuk Design
   Acoustics: Aercoustics Engineering
   Food Service: Design.net
   Curtain Wall: Halcrow Yolles
   Accessibility: Associated Planning Consultants
   AV: Engineering Harmonics
   Civil: Delcan Corporation
   Code: Leber Rubes
   Hardware: Assa Abloy
   Planning: Lloyd Phillips & Associates
   Microclimate: Gradient Microclimate Engineering
   Theater: Theatre Consultants Collaborative
   Elevator: Soberman Engineering
   Specification: Spec Teknix
10. Carillion Canada
11. 2014

The Japanese Sword Museum
新刀剣博物館
1. Sumida, Tokyo
2. 2,186 m²
3. 1,076 m²
4. 2,579 m²
5. RC; 3 stories
7. Umezawa Structural Engineers, lab.
8. P.T. Morimura and Associates
9. Signage: Kijuro Yahagi
10. Toda Corporation
11. 2017

Keio Univeristy Mita Campus
慶應義塾図書館・新館
1. Minato, Tokyo
2. 48,400 m²
3. 1,621 m²
4. 15,188 m²
5. SRC; 7 Stories+5 basements
7. Kimura Structural Engineers
8. Sogo Consultants
10. Joint venture of Ando, Shimizu, Toda Corporation
11. 1981

Washington University in St. Louis Sam Fox School of Design & Visual Arts
セントルイス・ワシントン大学
サム・フォックス視覚芸術学部
1. St. Louis, Missouri USA
2. 113,334 sf
3. Kemper Art Museum: 32,511 sf
   Walker Hall: 12,588 sf
4. Kemper Art Museum: 67,203 sf
   Walker Hall: 33,538 sf
5. RC flat slab,
   Steel frame and roof, CMU walls; 3 stories
6. Architect of Record: Shah Kawasaki Architects
7. Jacobs Facilities
8. William Tao & Associates
9. Lighting: Horton Lees Brogden Lighting Design
   Signage, Graphics: Mgmt Design
   Landscape: Austin Tao & Associates
   Civil Engineers: Kuhlmann Design Group
   Code: Code Consultants
10. McCarthy Construction
11. 2006

University of Pennsylvania Annenberg Public Policy Center
ペンシルバニア大学
アネンバーグ・パブリックポリシーセンター
1. Philadelphia, Pennsylvania USA
2. 1,860 m²
3. 940 m²
4. 4,562 m²
5. Steel frame; 4 stories+1 basement
6. Architect of Record: Ballinger Architecture
7. Ballinger Engineering
8. Ballinger Engineering
9. Civil: Pennoni Associates
   Landscape: Lager Raabe Skafte Landscape Architects
   Lighting: The Lighting Practice
   Acoustics: Shen Milsom Wilke
10. Hunter Roberts Construction Group
11. 2009

Massachusetts Institute of Technology The Media Lab Complex
マサチューセッツ工科大学
メディア研究所
1. Cambridge, Massachusetts USA
3. 27,100 sf
4. 163,000 sf
5. Steel frame; 7 stories+1 basement
6. Architect of Record: Leers Weinzapfel Associates
7. Weidlinger Associates
8. Cosentini Associates
9. Structural design assistance: Structural Design Group
   Laboratory: RFD
   Civil: Green International
   Code: ARUP
   Access: Kessler McGuinnes and Associates
   Curtain Wall: Cupples International & YKK AP, R.A. Heintges & Associates
   Lighting: Lam Partners
   Elevator: Robert L. Seymour & Associates
   Landscape: Strata Design Associates
   Environmental: Viridian Energy & Enviromental
   Wind and Smoke Studies: Rowan Williams Davies & Irwin
   Hardware: Campbell|McCabe
   Geotech: Mcphail Associates
   Acoustic: Cavanaugh Tocci Associates
   Kitchen: Food & Wine Research
   Waterproofing: Thompson & Lichtner
   Specification: Steven R. McHugh
   General Contractor: Bond Brothers
   Construction Management: George B.H. Macomber Company
11. 2009

Tsuda College Sendagaya Campus
津田塾大学千駄ヶ谷キャンパス
1. Shibuya, Tokyo
2. 7,339 m²
3. 1,799 m²
4. 6,833 m²
5. RC, Steel frame; 5 stories+1 basement
7. Mitsubishi Jisho Sekkei
8. Mitsubishi Jisho Sekkei
9. Landscape; Equipe Espace
10. Toda Corporation
11. 2016

Hillside Terrace, Phases I-III
ヒルサイドテラス1期（A、B棟）
ヒルサイドテラス2期（C棟）
ヒルサイドテラス3期（D、E棟）
1. Shibuya, Tokyo
2. 7,320 m²
3. 2,682 m²
4. 9,263 m²
5. RC; 3 stories+1 basement
7. Yamaki Structural Engineers (I+II), Aoki Structural Engineers (III)
8. Sakurai Consultants (I+II), Sogo Consultants (III)
9. Furniture: Maki and Associates+Endo Planning
   Signage: Kei Kuritsu, ASPI, Makoto Motokura
10. Takenaka Corporation
11. 1969 (I), 1973 (II), 1977 (III)

Hillside Terrace, Phase V
ヒルサイドテラス5期（ヒルサイドプラザ）
1. Shibuya, Tokyo
2. 679 m²
3. 90 m²
4. 621 m²
5. RC; 1 story + 2 basements
7. Hanawa Structural Engineers
8. Sogo Consultants
10. Takenaka Corporation
11. 1987

Hillside Terrace, Phase VI
ヒルサイドテラス6期（F、G、H棟）
1. Shibuya, Tokyo
2. 3,302 m²

3. 2,233 m²
  4. 8,362 m²
  5. RC; 6 stories+ 2 basements
  7. Aoki Structural Engineers
  8. Sogo Consultants
  9. Bench: Kazuko Fujie Atelier
 10. Takenaka Corporation
 11. 1992

Keio University Shonan Fujisawa Campus
慶應義塾 湘南藤沢キャンパス
  1. Fujisawa, Kanagawa
  2. 313,009 m²
  3. 17,226 m²
  4. 42,882 m²
  5. RC, Steel (gymnasium roof); 4 stories+1 basement
  7. Kimura Structural Engineers, Structural Design Group, and Hanawa Structural Engineers
  8. P.T. Morimura and Associates
  9. Acoustics: Nagata Acoustics
     Landscape: Maki and Associates+ Equipe Espace
     Furniture: Maki and Associates+ Endo Planning
     Signage: Maki and Associates+ Akihiro Nagao
 10. Joint venture of Tokyu, Shimizu, Kajima, Taisei, Ando, Obayashi, Zenitaka, Nippon Kokudo Kaihatsu, Takenaka, Fujita, Mitsui, Toda Corporations
 11. 1994

Graduate School Research Center Keio University Shonan Fujisawa Campus
慶應義塾 湘南藤沢キャンパス 大学院研究所
  1. Fujisawa, Kanagawa
  2. 313,009 m²
  3. 1,299 m²
  4. 3,670 m²
  5. RC; 4 stories
  7. Kimura Structural Engineers
  8. P.T. Morimura and Associates
  9. Furniture: Endo Planning
     Signage: Edge Design Office
     Landscape: Equipe Espace
 10. Tokyu Construction
 11. 1994

Miraisozojuku
未来創造塾
  1. Fujisawa, Kanagawa
  2. 18,690 m²
  3. 3,344 m²
  4. 9,852 m²
  5. RC; 4 stories+1 basement
  7. Hanawa Structural Engineers
  8. P.T. Morimura and Associates
  9. Landscape: Equipe Espace

Isar Büropark
イザール・ビューロパーク
  1. Hallbergmoos, Germany
  2. 38,274 m²
  3. 14,357 m²
  4. 68,366 m²
  5. RC, Steel (roof); 5 stories+2 basements
  6. Project in collaboration with Schmidt-Schicketanz & Partner
  7. Schmidt-Stump & Frühauf
  9. Landscape: Sasaki Environment Design + Cordes & Partner
     Facade Engineer: Fuchs Ing.-Büro
 10. Philipp Holzmann-Held & Francke Bau AG
 11. 1995

Republic Polytechnic Campus
シンガポール国立科学技術専門学校
  1. Woodlands, Singapore
  2. 200,000 m²
  3. 72,409 m²
  4. 248,864 m²
  5. RC; 11 stories+1 basement
  6. Architect of Record: DP Architects
  7. Meinhardt (Singapore), Hanawa Structural Engineers
  8. Beca Carter Hollings & Ferner (S.E. Asia)
  9. Landscape: Ohtori Consultants Environmental Design
     Façade: Meinhardt Facade Technology
     Acoustics: Nagata Acoustics, Acviron Acoustics Consultants
     Transportation: MVA
     Security: CCD Australia
     Quantity Surveyor: Davis Langdon & Seah
     Project Management: PM Link
 10. Joint venture of China Construction (South Pacific) Development and Taisei Corporation
 11. 2007

Republic Polytechnic Expansion and Singapore Institute of Technology
シンガポール理工系専門学校拡張工事 & シンガポール工科大学キャンパス
  1. Woodlands, Singapore
  2. 10,002 m²
  3. 5,410 m²
  4. 24,639 m²
  5. RC, Steel; 6stories (RP), 9stories (SIT)
  6. DP Architects
  7. Meinhardt (Singapore)
  8. Beca Carter Hollings & Ferner (S. E.Asia)
  9. Landscape: Ohtori Consultants Environmental Design
     Landscape: DP Green
     Facade: Meinhardt Facade Technology
     Acoustics: Acviron Acoustic Consultants
     Project Management: Langdon & Seah Project Management

 10. Lian Soon Construction
 11. 2015

International College for Post-graduate Buddhist Studies
国際仏教学大学院大学
  1. Bunkyo, Tokyo
  2. 9,103 m²
  3. 2,149 m²
  4. 6,365 m²
  5. RC, steel; 3 stories+1 basement
  7. Takenaka Corporation
  8. Takenaka Corporation
  9. Landscape: Studio On Site
 10. Takenaka Corporation
 11. 2010

Tokyo Denki University Tokyo Senju Campus Phase I
東京電機大学 東京千住キャンパス
  1. Adachi, Toyama
  2. 19,960 m²
  3. 11,136 m²
  4. 72,758 m²
  5. [Buliding 1] Steel, SRC, RC + Seismic Isolation Structure; 14 stories+1 basement
     [Buliding 2] Steel, SRC, RC; 10 stories+1 basement
     [Buliding 3] Steel, RC; 5 stories
     [Building 4] Steel, SRC, RC; 10 stories
     [Bridge] RC, Precast Concrete
  7. Nikken Sekkei
  8. Nikken Sekkei
  9. Landscape: Studio On Site
     Lighting: SLDA
 10. Obayashi Corporation, Kajima Corporation
 11. 2012

Tokyo Denki University Tokyo Senju Campus Phase II
東京電機大学 東京千住キャンパス第2期計画
  1. Adachi, Toyama
  2. 19,960 m²
  3. 3,970 m²
  4. 33,051 m²
  5. Steel, RC, SRC; 12 stories+1 basement
  7. Nikken Sekkei
  8. Nikken Sekkei
 10. Obayashi Corporation
 11. 2017

The Bihar Museum
ビハール博物館
  1. Patna, Bihar, India
  2. 56,250 m²
  3. 19,000 m²
  4. 25,000 m²
  5. RC; [Gallery, Entrance, Children's Museum] 2 Stories [Administration] 4 Stories
  6. Architect of Record; Opolis
  7. Mahendra Raj Consultants

8. Design Bureau
   9. Landscape design; Ohtori Consultants, Forethought
      Lighting: AWA Consultants
  10. Larsen & Toubro
  11. 2015

Passive Town Kurobe
パッシブタウン黒部モデル
   1. Kurobe, Toyama
   2. 5,521 m²
   3. 1,502 m²
   4. 4,755 m²
   5. RC; 4 stories+1 basement
   7. Hanawa Structural Engineers
   8. Sogo Consultants
  10. Toda Corporation
  11. 2016

Cusco Samana Hotel & Residences
クスコ・サマナ・ホテル&レジデンス
   1. Cusco, Peru
   2. 155,261 m²
   3. Hotel: 5,668 m², Residence: 10,469 m², Restaurant: 570 m²
   4. Hotel: 9,143 m², Residence: 11,599 m², Restaurant: 961 m²
   5. Hotel: RC, Steel, Wood, Residence: RC, Restaurant: RC
   6. Collaborating Architect; Kobayashi Maki Design Workshop
      Architect of Record; Garcia + Torres arquitectos
   7. Hanawa Structural Engineers, Akira Suzuki / ASA
      Carlos Alberto Zavala Toledo
   8. Deustua Ingenieros Consultores
   9. Landscape; Studio On Site
  11. 2018

Makuhari Messe
幕張メッセ・日本コンベンションセンター
   1. Makuhari New Town, Chiba
   2. 173,191 m²
   3. 105,144 m²
   4. 131,043 m²
   5. RC + Steel; 4 stories+1 basement
   7. Kimura Structural Engineers+ Structural Design Group
   8. Sogo Consultants
   9. Landscape: Equipe Espace
      Signage: GK Sekkei
      Special exhibition interior: Kazuko Fujie Atelier
      Carpets: Kei Miyazaki
      Acoustics: NHK Engineering Service
      Lighting/Stage: Theatrical Engineering Research Center
  10. Joint venture of Shimizu, Kajima, Takenaka, Toshima, Mitsui Corporations (Exhibition Hall); Obayashi, Asahi Corporations (Event Hall); Taisei, Shin-Nippon Corporations (Conference Center)
  11. 1989

Makuhari Messe, Phase II North Hall
幕張メッセⅡ期・北ホール
   1. Makuhari New Town, Chiba
   2. 43,960 m²
   3. 30,572 m²
   4. 33,413 m²
   5. SRC + Steel (roof structure); 2 stories
   7. Structural Design Group
   8. Sogo Consultants
   9. Landscape: Esquipe Espace
  10. Joint venture of Shimizu, Obayashi, and Mitsui Corporations
  11. 1997

Taipei Main Station Area Redevelopment
台北駅再開発計画
   1. Taipei, Taiwan
   2. 470,000 m² [C1 site] 13,078 m² [D1 site] 18,515 m²
   3.
   4. [C1 site] 8,100 m² [D1 site] 11,400 m² [C1 tower] 207,000 m² [D1 tower] 306,000 m² [Station] 40,000 m²
   5. Steel, SRC, [C1 tower] 56 stories [D1 tower] 76 stories+ 4 basements
   6. Prime Civil Engineer: J. J. Pan and Partners, Architects and Partners
      Architect of Record: CECI Engineering Consultants
   7. Structural Design Group (Basic Design I)
      Evergreen Consulting Engineering, Envision Engineering Consultants (Basic Design II & Detail Design)
   8. Mechanical
      Basic Design: Sogo Consulting Engineering
      CECI Engineering Consultants
   9. Landscape: Studio On Site (Basic Design)
      Lighting: Lighting Planners Associates (Basic Design), Chrom33 Architectural Lighting Design
      Acoustics: Nagata Acoustics (Basic Design)
      Station design: Yasushi Ikeda and Akiko Kokubun / IKDS
  11. 2016

TV Asahi
テレビ朝日
   1. Minato, Tokyo
   2. 16,368 m²
   3. 9,469 m²
   4. 73,700 m²
   5. RC, SRC, Steel frame; 8 stories+3 basements
   7. Structural Design Group
   8. Sogo Consultants
   9. Landscape: Studio on site
      Lighting: Lighting Planners Associates
      Furniture, Carpet: Kazuko Fujie Atelier
  10. Takenaka Corporation
  11. 2003

Square 3, Novartis Campus
スクエア 3 ノバルティス　キャンパス
   1. Basel, Switzerland
   2. 924 m²
   3. 6,150 m²
   5. RC, Steel frame; 5 stories+2 basements
   6. General Planner/Local Architect: Zwimpfer Partner Architekten
   7. Civil/Structural: ZPF Ingenieure
   8. Mechanical: Todt Gmür + Partner
      Electrical: Sytek
      Plumbing: Locher, Schwittay Gebäudetechnik
   9. Facade: PPEngineering
      Lighting: Licht Kunst Licht
      Signage, Graphics: Stauffenegger + Stutz
  11. 2009

4 World Trade Center
4 ワールド・トレード・センター
   1. New York, New York USA
   2. 4,998 m²
   3. 4,877 m²
   4. 213,700 m²
   5. RC, Steel; 72 stories
   6. Architect of Record:
      Tower: AAI Architects
      Retail: Beyer Blinder Belle Architects & Planners
   7. Leslie E. Robertson Associates
   8. Tower: Jaros Baum & Bolles Consulting Engineers
      Retail: AKF Engineers
   9. Vertical Transportation:
      Tower: Jaros Baum & Bolles Consulting Engineers, Edgett Williams Consulting Group
      Retail: Van Deusen and Associates
      Code: Code Consultants Professional Engineers
      Curtain Wall: R.A. Heintges & Associates, Israel Berger & Associates
      Lighting: Fisher Marantz Stone
      Signage: Pentagram Design
      Acoustic: Cerami & Associates
      Security: Ducibella Venter & Santore, Weidlinger Associates
      Pedestrian Traffic: Trans Solutions
      Facade Maintenance: Entek Engineering
      Sustainable Design: S.D. Keppler & Associates
      Civil: Philip Habib & Associates
  10. Tower: Tishman Construction Corporation
      Retail: Joint venture of Tishman and Turner
  11. 2015

Maki and Associates Staff List
槇総合計画事務所所員リスト

Staff
所員

Iwao Shida	志田　巖	1965-
Tomoyoshi Fukunaga	福永　知義	1967-
Yukitoshi Wakatsuki	若月　幸敏	1973-
Hirochika Kashima	鹿島　大睦	1984-
Gary Kamemoto	亀本　ゲイリー	1984-
Yoshiki Kondo	近藤　良樹	1992-
Atsushi Tokushige	徳重　敦史	1992-
Shigeki Honda	本田　茂樹	1993-
Masahiro Chiba	千葉　昌広	1993-
Tatsutomo Hasegawa	長谷川　龍友	1995-
Kota Kawasaki	川崎　向太	1996-
Masayuki Midorikawa	緑川　雅之	1997-
Michel van Ackere		1997-
Kei Ito	伊藤　圭	1998-
Isao Ikeda	池田　偉佐雄	1999-
Masaru Sasaki	佐々木　将	2003-
Kazuo Sato	佐藤　和夫	2004-
Hisashi Nakai	中井　久詞	2006-
Takeshi Sora	空　剛士	2006-
Yoichi Honjo	本城　洋一	2006-
Yasuko Okuyama	奥山　靖子	2007-
Masahiro Ikawa	井川　雅裕	2008-
Yoshihiko Taira	平良　慶彦	2008-
Yukie Miyashita	宮下　雪絵	2008-
Tsuyoshi Tanaka	田中　剛	2008-
Yukiko Kuwahara	桑原　由起子	2008-
Dai Tomioka	冨岡　大	2008-
Yasutaka Fujie	藤江　保高	2009-
Kiwon Kim	金　起原	2011-
Hirofumi Ueda	植田　博文	2012-
Yuya Miyamoto	宮本　裕也	2012-
Haruka Kitta	橘田　はる香	2012-
Issei Horikoshi	堀越　一世	2012-
Masatoshi Ono	小野　雅俊	2012-
Michiyo Mori	森　路世	2013-
Ikuko Wada	和田　郁子	2013-
Shun-Min "Tony" Ko	髙　俊民	2013-
Hiroyuki Matsuda	松田　浩幸	2014-
Keita Tsuji	辻　啓太	2014-
Azusa Ino	猪野　梓	2014-
Noriko Arai	新井　典子	2014-
Tomoaki Todome	留目　知明	2015-

Former Staff
元所員

Name	Kanji	Years	Name	Kanji	Years
Hiroshi Saeki	佐伯　博司	1965-2000	Norio Yokota	横田　典雄	1989-1998
Yayoi Ono	小野　弥生	1965-2003	Naoki Kadowaki	門脇　直樹	1990-1995
Tamotsu Ozaki	尾崎　保	1965-1970	Masao Ichikawa	市川　雅雄	1990-1994
Seiichi Endo	遠藤　精一	1965-1968	Mark Mulligan		1990-1996
Koichi Naito	内藤　幸一	1965-1968	Minoru Kudaka	久高　実	1990-1994
Kenji Fukuzawa	福澤　健次	1965-1972	Paul Harney		1991-1993
Akira Murai	村井　啓	1965-1968	Tohru Ohnuma	大沼　徹	1991-2005
Masahiro Ono	小野　正弘	1965-1973	Masaaki Kurihara	栗原　正明	1991-2000
Koichi Nagashima	長島　孝一	1966-1969, 1972-1977	Hiromi Kouda	髙田　広美	1991-2002
Morikazu Shibuya	渋谷　盛和	1966-1983	Yasuo Nakata	仲田　康雄	1991-2004
Yasuo Watanabe	渡邉　泰男	1966-1971	Fabian Berthold		1992-1995
Akira Ozawa	小沢　明	1967-1975, 1977-1980	Takayuki Fumoto	麓　貴之	1992-1996
David Swan		1966-1969	Kohsuke Arai	荒井　浩介	1993-2003
Reiko Haba	波部　玲子	1968-1970	Osamu Sassa	佐々　修	1994-1997, 2006-2013
Ben Nakamura	中村　勉	1969-1977	Tomoya Sugiura	杉浦　友哉	1994-2012
Kazunori Ozaki	尾崎　和則	1970-1992	Geoffrey Moussas		1995-1997
Makoto Takashina	高品　信	1970-1974	Satoru Yamashiro	山代　悟	1995-2002
Seiji Okamoto	岡本　聖司	1970-1984	Jun Imaizumi	今泉　純	1995-2005
Goro Saigo	西郷　五郎	1970-1976	Jun Takahashi	高橋　潤	1996-2006
Seiji Yukutomi	行冨　誠一	1970-1975	Brendon Levitt		1998-2000, 2004-2005
Conrad Brunner		1971-1971	Ryuji Takaichi	髙市　竜二	1999-2006
Katsuhiko Nishida	西田　勝彦	1971-1990	Kiwa Matsushita	松下　希和	2000-2006
Makoto Motokura	元倉　眞琴	1971-1976	Daisuke Yano	矢野　大輔	2002-2006
Hiroshi Watanabe	渡辺　洋	1971-1977	Jun Ito	伊藤　潤	2002-2007
Hideaki Hoshina	保科　秀明	1972-1977	Makoto Otake	大竹　慎	2002-2008
Kazuo Teramoto	寺本　和雄	1972-1978	Yasushi Nishimura	西村　恭史	2004-2011
Yoko Kobayashi	小林　洋子	1972-1977	Benjamin Albertson		2005-2010
Akira Kuryu	栗生　明	1973-1979	Yuki Yamada	山田　勇希	2005-2014
Eiji Watanabe	渡辺　英二	1973-1992	Alvaro Bonfiglio		2006-2012
Fumiko Tanaka	田中　文子	1974-1976	Nana Shirai	白井　菜々	2006-2013
Tsuneaki Nakano	中野　恒明	1974-1984	Ellen Kristina Krause		2007-2008
Toshihide Mori	森　俊偉	1974-1990	Takeshi Mitsuda	光田　武史	2007-2013
Keisuke Yamamoto	山本　圭介	1974-1989	Souichiro Marubayashi	丸林　荘一郎	2007-2008
Heather Cass		1974-1975	Yoshiya Kamitamari	上玉利　佳哉	2008-2009
Hidetoshi Ohno	大野　秀敏	1976-1983	Takuya Takahashi	髙橋　卓也	2008-2012
Tokihiko Takatani	高谷　時彦	1976-1989	Jennifer Joyce Tan Arandez		2009-2011
Naruya Kamihara	上原　成也	1976-1993	Ronald Lim		2011-2012
Yutaka Hirota	廣田　豊	1977-1987	Souichiro Ajima	安島　総一郎	2011-2014
Norio Takata	高田　典夫	1978-1990	Michael Sypkens		2011-2013
Yuzo Yamanaka	山中　雄象	1978-2001	Kelly Lwu		2013-2015
Hiroshi Miyazaki	宮崎　浩	1979-1989			
Kiyohide Sawaoka	澤岡　清秀	1980-1992			
Jun Aoki	青木　淳	1980-1991			
Fumito Sato	佐藤　文人	1981-2003			
Kei Mizui	水井　敬	1982-2001			
Toshio Hachiya	蜂谷　俊雄	1983-2003			
Reiko Tomuro	戸室　令子	1983-1996			
Kenichi Nakamura	中村　研一	1984-1991, 1993-1998			
Akira Uenishi	上西　明	1984-1997			
Jun Watanabe	渡辺　純	1985-1990			
Koichi Tanaka	田中　耕一	1986-1994			
Noriko Kawamura	川村　紀子	1986-1996			
Yasushi Ikeda	池田　靖史	1987-1995			
Tetsuya Mori	森　哲哉	1987-1995			
Yoshitaka Wada	和田　吉貴	1987-1997			
Shuji Oki	沖　周治	1987-1997			
Steve Dayton		1987-1989			
Masaaki Yoshizaki	吉崎　存亮	1987-2003			
Takao Masuda	増田　多加男	1987-2005			
Shigekazu Miyamoto	宮本　繁和	1988-1993			
Akiko Kokubun	國分　昭子	1988-1997			
Lawrence Matott		1988-1990			

Fumihiko Maki, Maki and Associates 2015
Time, Figure, Space
—Toward the Construction of Place

Exhibition

Venue:
Daikanyama Hillside Terrace
  Building A Hillside Gallery
  Hillside Plaza
  Building F Hillside Forum

Period:
October 17 - November 29, 2015

Organizer:
Maki and Associates

Special sponsors:
Takenaka Corporation
Kajima Corporation

Sponsors:
Asahi Facilities Inc.
Obayashi Corporation
Kandenko Co., Ltd.
Sanko Metal Industrial Co.
Shimizu Corporation
Shinryo Corporation
Taisei Corporation
Toda Corporation
Rolex (Japan) Limited
Harmonic Drive Systems Inc.
Maeda Corporation
YKK Corporation

Cooperation:
Asakura Real Estate
Art Front Gallery
Wacoal Art Center

Fumihiko Maki, Maki and Associates 2015
時・姿・空間―場所の構築を目指して

展覧会

会場:
代官山ヒルサイドテラス
  A棟ヒルサイドギャラリー
  ヒルサイドプラザ
  F棟ヒルサイドフォーラム

会期:
2015年10月17日～11月29日

主催:
株式会社槇総合計画事務所

特別協賛:
株式会社竹中工務店
鹿島建設株式会社

協賛:
株式会社アサヒ ファシリティズ
株式会社大林組
株式会社関電工
三晃金属工業株式会社
清水建設株式会社
新菱冷熱工業株式会社
大成建設株式会社
戸田建設株式会社
日本ロレックス株式会社
株式会社ハーモニック・ドライブ・システムズ
前田建設工業株式会社
YKK株式会社
（50音順）

協力:
朝倉不動産株式会社
株式会社アートフロントギャラリー
株式会社ワコールアートセンター

Photo Credit
写真クレジット

T.K.	Toshiharu Kitajima	北嶋俊治	出典	
JA.	Shinkenchiku-sha	新建築社写真部	p.55 bottom right	Collection of Department of Architecture,
O.M.	Osamu Murai	村井 修	p.55 右下	The University of Tokyo School of Engineering
S.M.	Satoru Mishima	三島 叡		東京大学大学院工学系研究科建築学専攻所蔵
M.Y.	Makoto Yoshida	吉田 誠		
C.Y.	Chiaki Yasukawa	安川千秋	p.83 bottom right	Souichi Yagisawa, Masanobu Yoshimoto,
T.I.	Takeji Iwamiya	岩宮武二	p.83 右下	Akira Yoshimura
S.O	Sigeo Ogawa	小川重雄		"Land and buildings in Cities - Analysis of Tokyo・
S.K.	Shokokusha	彰国社写真部		cities" Tokyo Denki University Press
H.K.	Hiroshi Kobayashi	小林浩志		八木澤壮一, 吉本正信, 吉村彰「都心の土地と建物―東京・
N.P.	Nacasa & Partners	ナカサ アンド パートナーズ		街の解析」東京電機大学出版局, 1987
T.O.	Tomio Ohashi	大橋富夫		
K.M.	Kaneaki Monma	門馬金昭	p.85 bottom left	"Nikkei Architecture" 16, December 1985 (First
hpb	Hiro Photo Building.	ヒロ・フォトビルディング		Published)
YU.	YUKAI	ゆかい		『日経アーキテクチュア』1985年12月16日号(初出)
KMDW	KMDW	小林・槇デザインワークショップ		
ASPI	ASPI	ASPI	p.87 3 images at	Courtesy of SPIRAL/Wacoal Art Center
F.K.	Fumiya Kawada	川田奎也	top left	©スパイラル／株式会社ワコールアートセンター
M.B.	MORI Building	森ビル	p.87 左上3つ	
K.I.	Katsuhiro Ichikawa	市川勝弘		
Y.W.	Yuya Wada	Yuya Wada	p.90	"Nikkei Architecture" 29, December 1986 (First
A.C.	Art Court Gallery	Art Court Gallery		Published)
T.M.	Toyota Motor	トヨタ自動車		『日経アーキテクチュア』1986年12月29日号(初出)
H.T.	HILLSIDE TERRACE	ヒルサイドテラス		
SP.	SPIRAL	スパイラル	p.155 top, p.156 top	"Nikkei Architecture" 9, July 2007 (First Published)
Y.Y.	Yasuyuki Yanagisawa	柳澤恭行	p.155 上, p.156 上	『日経アーキテクチュア』2007年7月9日号(初出)
A.G.	Anton Grassl/ESTO		p.241 bottom left	Katsushika Hokusai, Kajikazawa in Kai Province,
L.R.	Lukas Roth, Köln		p.241 左下	Thirty-six Views of Mt Fuji
B.L.	Berthold + Linkersdorff			葛飾北斎：富嶽三十六景 甲州石班沢
J.S.	John Stoel		p.280 top right	Utagawa Hiroshige, Fukagawa Hachiman yama-
P.P.	Paul Peck		p.280 右上	hiraki, Meisho Edo Hyakkei
R.B.	Richard Barnes			歌川広重：名所江戸百景 深川八まん山ひらき
J.T.	Jeffrey Totaro			
B.H.	Barry Halkin			
R.P.	Robert Pettus			
DP.	DP Architects			
SPI	SPI			
TE.	Tectonic			
M.P.	Matteo Piazza			
M.V.	Moez Visram, courtesy Imara (Wynford Drive) Limited.			
C.R.	Cooper Ray			
M.W.	Mark_W_NYC			
Cover	Cooper Ray Anton Grassl/ESTO Toshiharu Kitajima			

Publication

Essay:
Fumihiko Maki
Yuzuru Tominaga
David B. Stewart

Translation:
Hiroshi Watanabe (English)
Kenichi Nakamura (Japanese)

Editorial Collaboration:
Fumihiko Maki
Tomoyoshi Fukunaga
Yukitoshi Wakatsuki
Gary Kamemoto
Tatsutomo Hasegawa
Kota Kawasaki
Hisashi Nakai
Yasuko Okuyama

Design+Editorial cooperation:
Kijuro Yahagi

Fumihiko Maki,
Maki and Associates 2015
Time, Figure, Space
—Toward the Construction of Place

Author : Fumihiko Maki
Publisher : Fumio Tsubouchi
Printing and Binding :
Toppan Printing Co., Ltd.

© First Published in Japan,
10 October, 2015
by Kajima Institute
Publishing Co., Ltd.
2-5-14 Yaesu, Chuo-ku, Tokyo
104-0028 Japan
Tel. +81 3 6202 5200

All rights reserved.
No parts of this publication
may be reproduced,
stored in a retrieval system,
or transmitted in any form or by
any means (electronic,
mechanical, photocopying,
recording, or otherwise),
without the prior consent of
the publisher.
Printed in Japan.

URL:
http://www.kajima-publishing.co.jp
E-mail:
info@kajima-publishing.co.jp

作品集

執筆:
槇 文彦
富永 讓
デイヴィッド・B. スチュワート

翻訳:
渡辺 洋（英訳）
中村研一（和訳）

編集:
槇 文彦
福永知義
若月幸敏
亀本ゲイリー
長谷川龍友
川﨑向太
中井久詞
奥山靖子

デザイン＋編集協力:
矢萩喜從郎

槇 文彦＋槇総合計画事務所2015
時・姿・空間―場所の構築を目指して

発行：2015年10月10日　第1刷発行

編著者：槇 文彦
発行者：坪内文生
発行所：鹿島出版会
　　　　〒104-0028
　　　　東京都中央区八重洲2丁目5番14号
　　　　電話 03-6202-5200
　　　　振替 00160-2-180883
印刷・製本：凸版印刷

© Fumihiko Maki,
Maki and Associates, 2015
ISBN978-4-306-04626-9 C3052
Printed in Japan
落丁・乱丁本はお取替えいたします。
本書の無断複製（コピー）は
著作権法上での例外を除き禁じられております。
また、代行業者などに依頼して
スキャンやデジタル化することは、
たとえ個人や家庭内の利用を
目的とする場合でも著作権法違反です。

本書の内容に関するご意見・ご感想は
下記までお寄せください。
URL:
http://www.kajima-publishing.co.jp
E-mail:
info@kajima-publishing.co.jp